OMG! 365 Salmon Recipes

(OMG! 365 Salmon Recipes - Volume 1)

Kathi Hager

Content

38

365 Awesome Salmon Recipes

***

1. 1st Place Baked Salmon Recipe

Serving: 6 | Prep: | Cook: 15mins | Ready in:

Ingredients

- 6 4-oz salmon fillets, each 1 in. thick
- 1 Tablespoon olive oil
- Splash lemon juice(enough to moisten each fillet)
- Fresh rosemary to taste
- paprika to taste
- adobo seasoning to taste
- black pepper to taste
- salt to taste
- honey to taste
- 1/4 Cup chopped pecans
- Non-stick cooking spray

Direction

- Preheat oven to 450 degrees F. In oven, preheat baking dish drizzled with olive oil.
- Place fillets skin-side down on flat surface, rub with lemon juice.
- Sprinkle with seasonings in following order:
- Rosemary - paprika - adobo - black pepper - and salt.
- Lightly drizzle with honey; sprinkle with pecans and seal with generous coating of cooking spray.
- Place fillets skin-side down in preheated baking dish.
- Bake 10 - 15 minutes or until fillets flake easily with fork.
- Serves 6

- Exchanges: 3 meats, 1/2 fat

2. Alaska Salmon And Grilled Vegetable Lasagna Recipe

Serving: 8 | Prep: | Cook: 60mins | Ready in:

Ingredients

- 14-3/4 ounce Alaskan salmon drained and flaked
- 1 pound lasagna noodles cooked
- 52 ounces marinara sauce
- 1/2 teaspoon garlic minced
- 2 teaspoons fennel seed slightly crushed
- 2 tablespoons fresh basil chopped
- 1 eggplant sliced lengthwise
- 1 zucchini sliced
- 1 red bell pepper sliced
- 1/2 red onion sliced
- 1 pound mozzarella cheese grated
- olive oil
- 1/2 teaspoon salt
- 1 teaspoon freshly ground black pepper

Direction

- Preheat oven to 350.
- Add marinara sauce, garlic and fennel seed to a sauce pot then bring to a boil.
- Reduce to a simmer then add basil and cook 10 minutes.
- Heat a grill.
- Lightly brush both sides of vegetables with olive oil and season with salt and pepper.
- Place on grill and cook until tender then remove from grill and chop into medium dices.
- Place in a bowl and mix together.
- Spread a light layer of marinara sauce mixture into bottom of an oven proof casserole dish.
- Lay out a base of cooked noodles overlapping them slightly.

- Cover noodles with a layer of 1/2 the grilled vegetable mix spreading evenly over the noodles.
- Top the vegetables with 1/2 of the salmon and 1/3 of the cheese then add 1/3 of remaining sauce.
- Add the next layer of noodles and repeat the layering.
- Add a final layer of noodles topped with the remaining sauce followed by remaining cheese.
- Carefully press everything down then cover with plastic wrap then foil.
- Place in oven and cook 50 minutes then remove from oven and let stand 15 minutes.

3. Ancho Glazed Salmon With Sweet Potato Fries Recipe

Serving: 4 | Prep: | Cook: 12mins | Ready in:

Ingredients

- 2 medium sweet potatoes
- 1 Tbsp. sugar
- 1 tsp. salt
- 1 tsp. ground cumin
- 1 tsp. ground ancho chili pepper or chili powder
- olive oil cooking spray
- 4 5- to 6-oz. skinless salmon fillets
- 2 Tbsp. fresh cilantro sprigs

Direction

- 1. Preheat broiler. Scrub potatoes. Halve lengthwise; cut in 1.4-inch slices. Place on greased rack of unheated broiler pan. In bowl combine sugar, salt, cumin, and chili pepper. Coat potatoes with cooking spray; sprinkle both sides with half the spice mixture. Broil 4 inches from heat 10 minutes or until tender; turn once midway through cooking.
- 2. Meanwhile, rinse salmon; pat dry. Sprinkle with remaining spice. In skillet cook fish in 1

tablespoon hot olive oil over medium heat 8 to 12 minutes or until fish flakes when tested with fork; turn once midway through cooking. Add cilantro. Serves 4.

4. Angel Hair Pasta With Smoked Salmon In Tomato Sauce Dated 1966 Recipe

Serving: 4 | Prep: | Cook: 30mins | Ready in:

Ingredients

- 6 ounces thinly sliced smoked salmon
- 8 ounces angel hair pasta
- 1 large clove garlic, minced
- 3 tablespoons olive oil
- 2-1/4 cups seeded and chopped tomatoes divided
- 1/2 cup dry white wine
- 3 tablespoons drained large capers
- 1-1/2 teaspoon dill weed
- 1-1/2 teaspoon sweet basil
- 1/2 cup freshly grated parmesan cheese

Direction

- Cut smoked salmon with the grain into 1/2" wide strips and reserve.
- Cook pasta as package directs.
- Meanwhile in large skillet stir and cook garlic in hot oil over medium heat until garlic is golden.
- Add 2 cups tomatoes, wine, capers, dill weed and basil then stir and cook until mixture is hot.
- Drain pasta then place in large serving bowl and toss pasta with tomato mixture.
- Add salmon and cheese then toss gently and garnish with remaining tomatoes and parsley.

5. Angel Hair Pasta With Smoked Salmon And Dill Dated 1966 Recipe

Serving: 6 | Prep: | Cook: 30mins |Ready in:

Ingredients

- 6 ounces angel hair pasta
- 1/2 cup whipping cream
- 1/2 cup milk
- 1/4 cup chopped fresh dill
- 1/4 cup chopped green onions
- 1-1/2 tablespoons drained capers
- 1 teaspoon grated lemon peel
- 4 ounces thinly sliced smoked salmon cut into thin strips

Direction

- Cook pasta in large pot of boiling salted water until just tender but still firm to bite.
- Drain well then return to same pot.
- Combine cream, milk, dill, onions, capers and lemon peel in heavy small saucepan.
- Bring to boil over medium high heat.
- Add sauce to pasta then toss to coat.
- Add salmon and toss to combine then season with salt and pepper and serve.

6. Apple Cider Cured Smoked Salmon Recipe

Serving: 4 | Prep: | Cook: 25mins |Ready in:

Ingredients

- 1 cup brown sugar
- 1/4 cup salt
- 4 cups apple cider or juice
- 2 cinnamon sticks
- 1 teaspoon fennel seeds
- 1 teaspoon whole allspice
- 1 teaspoon black peppercorns
- 1 bay leaf
- 1 teaspoon red pepper flakes
- 6 sprigs thyme or 1/2 teaspoon dried thyme
- 1 large salmon fillets (about 1 pound each), skin and pin bones removed
- A small bundle of wood chips or chunks

Direction

- To make the brine: In a saucepan, combine the brown sugar, salt, and apple juice and bring to a boil. Add the remaining brine ingredients, remove from the heat, and cool. This brine can be made 2 to 3 days in advance and kept in the refrigerator.
- Submerge the salmon fillets in the liquid brine for at least 6 hours or overnight, refrigerated. Remove the salmon from the brine and place, uncovered, on a wire rack set in a sheet pan. Refrigerate the fillets for at least 6 hours, or overnight, to dry them out. (A dry fillet will take on smoke quicker than a moist fillet)
- To smoke the salmon: In an outdoor grill, make a small fire using mesquite charcoal or briquettes. Once the fire has burned down to a hot bed of coals, after about 1 hour, place the soaked wood on the coals. Position the grate 8 to 12 inches above the smoking wood and place the salmon fillets on the grate.
- Cover the grill and shut any open-air vents. After 5 minutes, check the heat of the grill; large fillets will be cooked and smoked through in approximately 30 minutes if the heat is low, about 300 to 350 degrees F, while a hotter fire will cook the fillets in 15 to 20 minutes. Serve the salmon hot off the grill.

7. Apricot Ginger Glazed Salmon Recipe

Serving: 4 | Prep: | Cook: 15mins |Ready in:

Ingredients

- 1 pound wild salmon fillet (copper river is the best!)
- salt and freshly ground black pepper
- 3 tablespoons apricot jam or preserves
- 3 teaspoons grated fresh ginger
- 2 teaspoons soy sauce
- 1/2 teaspoon crushed red pepper (optional)

Direction

- Preheat oven to 450°F.
- Cut fillets into equal servings. Pat salmon dry and season with salt and pepper; place skin side down on greased or parchment-lined (for easy clean up) rimmed baking sheet.
- In small bowl, stir together jam, ginger and soy sauce - and red pepper if you want to add some spicy-hot to it. Spread evenly over salmon.
- Roast 10 to 15 minutes, or until salmon flakes easily. The glaze may caramelize a bit.

8. Asiago Herb Encrusted Salmon Recipe

Serving: 8 | Prep: | Cook: 10mins | Ready in:

Ingredients

- 2/3 cup dry, unseasoned breadcrumbs
- 1/4 cup grated asiago cheese
- 2 sprigs fresh rosemary
- 1/2 tbsp garlic powder
- 1 tbsp dried basil
- 1/2 tsp black pepper
- 1 egg, beaten with
- 1/4 cup buttermilk
- 1 1/2 lb sockeye salmon, cut into 8 equal pieces
- 2 tsp olive oil

Direction

- Combine breadcrumbs through pepper in a shallow dish.

- Pour egg and buttermilk mixture into another shallow dish.
- Dip each salmon piece into buttermilk mixture, then coat completely in breadcrumb mix, pressing it onto the fish, and set onto a plate.
- Cover and refrigerate 30 minutes - 1 hour.
- Heat oil in a non-stick fry pan over medium heat.
- Add fish in one layer and cook 5 minutes per side.

9. Asian Marinated Salmon Recipe

Serving: 4 | Prep: | Cook: 60mins | Ready in:

Ingredients

- 4 6oz salmon filets (boneless, skinless)
- 3T soy sauce
- 1T rice vinegar
- 1T hoisin sauce
- 1T chili - garlic paste
- 1T minced ginger
- 1tsp sugar

Direction

- Mix all ingredients except for salmon in a non-reactive bowl.
- Place salmon in a large ziplock bag.
- Pour marinade over salmon.
- Marinate for 30 minutes.
- Place salmon and marinade in baking dish sprayed with non-stick spray.
- Bake in 350-degree oven for 20 minutes or until fish flakes easily with a fork.

10. Asian Salmon Burgers With Pickled Cucumber On Pumpernickel Recipe

Serving: 4 | Prep: | Cook: 10mins | Ready in:

Ingredients

- 1 large cucumber (about 1 pound)
- 1 tablespoon cider vinegar
- 1 1/2 teaspoons sugar
- 1/4 teaspoon dried hot red pepper flakes
- 1 large egg white
- 1 tablespoon soy sauce
- 1/2 teaspoon grated peeled fresh gingerroot
- a 3/4-pound piece salmon fillet, skin discarded and fish cut into
- 1/4-inch pieces
- 1/2 cup fine fresh bread crumbs
- 2 scallions, chopped fine
- 1 teaspoon mustard seed
- 1 teaspoon vegetable oil
- 4 small green-leaf lettuce leaves
- 8 slices firm pumpernickel (about 10 ounces)

Direction

- With a Japanese rotary slicer (see note this page) cut cucumber into 1 long spiral. (Alternatively, with a sharp knife cut cucumber into very thin slices.) In a bowl toss cucumber with vinegar, sugar, red pepper flakes, and salt to taste.
- In another bowl whisk together egg white, soy sauce, and gingerroot until combined well and stir in salmon, bread crumbs, scallions, mustard seeds, and salt to taste. In a food processor purée 1/3 cup salmon mixture and return to salmon mixture remaining in bowl. (Alternatively, chop 1/3 cup salmon mixture fine and mash to a paste with flat side of a knife.) Stir mixture to combine and form into four 3/4-inch-thick patties. Drain cucumber well.
- In a large non-stick skillet heat oil over moderately high heat until hot but not smoking and cook patties until golden, about 2

minutes on each side. Cook patties, covered, over moderate heat until just cooked through, about 5 minutes more. Arrange lettuce leaves on 4 pumpernickel slices and top with salmon burgers, pickled cucumber, and remaining 4 pumpernickel slices.

11. Asian Salmon Fillets Recipe

Serving: 2 | Prep: | Cook: 35mins | Ready in:

Ingredients

- 1/4 lb. slice of salmon per person
- butter
- garlic powder
- powdered ginger
- ground pepper
- orange juice
- soy sauce

Direction

- Grease a baking dish with butter
- Place the salmon skin-side down in it
- Sprinkle with the garlic powder, ginger, and freshly ground pepper.
- Sprinkle some soy sauce over the fish and then pour orange juice in, about 1/2 inch deep.
- Dot the top of the fish with butter.
- Cover and microwave on high if making two or three servings. For two servings I nuke this 3 1/2 minutes. If preparing for numerous people I'd cook on a lower power and adjust the time so the fish doesn't explode.

12. Asian Salmon Tacos Recipe

Serving: 4 | Prep: | Cook: 10mins | Ready in:

Ingredients

- 2 T. hoisin sauce

- 1 T. honey
- 1 tsp. hot chili-garlic sauce
- 1 T. sesame oil
- 8 oz. boneless, skinless salmon fillets
- 1 tsp. peanut oil
- 1 green pepper, sliced into thin strips
- 1 small eggplant, sliced into bite-sized pieces
- 1 c. matchstick-sliced kohlrabi
- 1 large ripe tomato, sliced into thin wedges
- Small flour tortillas
- soy sauce (optional)

Direction

- Combine the first four ingredients to form a paste and rub generously onto the salmon fillets. Broil for 3 minutes per side or until the fish flakes easily with a fork and the juices run clear. Flake the fish into bite-sized pieces and keep warm.
- Meanwhile, heat the peanut oil over high heat in a skillet and add the pepper strips and eggplant pieces. Stir-fry for 5 minutes or until crisp-tender
- Arrange the salmon pieces, hot vegetable mixture and kohlrabi and tomato in the flour tortillas to form soft tacos
- Drizzle soy sauce on the tacos if desired

13. BBQ Salmon With Broccolini Recipe

Serving: 4 | Prep: | Cook: 10mins | Ready in:

Ingredients

- 3 bunches broccolini
- 4 salmon fillets, approx 1/2lb each
- for the sauce:
- 10 anchovies in oil, finely chopped
- 1 sprig rosemary, leaves picked and chopped
- extra virgin olive oil
- juice and zest 1 lemon
- lemon halves, to serve

Direction

- Heat a BBQ over high heat.
- For the sauce: combine all ingredients adding enough olive oil to give it a good oozy sauce consistency. Season with pepper and set aside.
- Bring a large saucepan of salted water to the boil. Cook broccolini for 3-4mins or until just tender. Drain and toss through about half of the dressing. Keep warm.
- Meanwhile, rub the salmon with olive oil and season well. BBQ for 3-4 minutes on each side or until cooked to your liking. Which for my dad is extremely well done and dried out and for my mum is still nice and pink in the middle.
- Divide broccolini between the 4 plates. Top each with a piece of salmon and drizzle over remaining sauce.

14. BLT Baked Salmon For Two Recipe

Serving: 2 | Prep: | Cook: 25mins | Ready in:

Ingredients

- 12 oz salmon- 2 six ounce pieces
- 1/4 cup mayonnaise
- 2 tablespoons unsw. ketchup (no sugar/low carb/diabetic)
- 6 pieces sun-dried tomatoes soaked in 1/4 cup of warm vermouth
- 4 strips bacon, cooked, cut in 1" pieces
- 1/4 cup chopped onion
- olive oil
- 1 head of romaine sliced in half vertically and grilled on an indoor grill pan.

Direction

- Mix mayo and ketchup to make the top coating.

- Heat vermouth in small sauce pan just below simmer and add the tomatoes to plump for a few minutes.
- Spray casserole dish with non-stick spray. Lay salmon pieces in and cover with dressing.
- Cut up drained tomatoes and lay on top; sprinkle with chopped onion. Pour leftover vermouth in the casserole to help steam the salmon
- Bake at 400 for 20 min.
- Meanwhile, grill the romaine brushed with olive oil and sprinkled with kosher salt and cracked black pepper
- If the salmon looks a little anemic, put under broiler for just a few minutes to brown top.
- Serve on top of chopped grilled romaine.
- Top with broken cooked bacon pieces.
- Dinner for two, fast and easy.

15. Baked Lemon Pepper Salmon Recipe

Serving: 4 | Prep: | Cook: 35mins | Ready in:

Ingredients

- 1 large salmon fillet
- 2 lemons
- 1 Tbsp lemon zest (optional)
- 2 Tbsp unsalted butter
- 1 Tbsp lemon pepper
- sea salt
- fresh ground black pepper

Direction

- Place salmon fillet on sheet of aluminum foil, make sure foil is big enough to crinkle over salmon until almost meets in the middle. Take one lemon, slice in half down the middle. Squeeze juice of one half over the fillet and slice other half in 1/4 inch slices, set slices aside. Sprinkle lemon pepper evenly over the fillet, as well as much sea salt and pepper you prefer. I generally don't use much, probably

about 1/4 tsp, as the salmon itself has such good flavor. Take bits of the butter and place all over the salmon, then place slices neatly over the top of the salmon fillet. Fold aluminum foil over the salmon but do not seal shut. Bake 25-35 minutes at 375F, until the salmon flakes easily with a fork.
- If cooking on a BBQ, make sure you rake your coals to the outer edges of your BBQ and place the foil in the center of the grill, so that the heat is not directly under your fish.

16. Baked Salmon Recipe

Serving: 4 | Prep: | Cook: 17mins | Ready in:

Ingredients

- 4 pieces salmon
- 2 tbls parm cheese
- 1 small piece red pepper
- 1-2 cloves garlic
- 1 tbls mayo
- 1/4 cup cream cheese softened

Direction

- Cut red pepper into small pieces.
- Crush garlic.
- Mix 1 tablespoon parm cheese with mayo, garlic, cream cheese and red pepper.
- Place salmon on baking sheet and cover with sauce and sprinkle with left over parm cheese.
- Bake at 350 for 15- 20 min till cooked through.
- Serve and enjoy.

17. Baked Salmon Stuffed With Spinach Cream Cheese Recipe

Serving: 2 | Prep: | Cook: 12mins | Ready in:

Ingredients

- 2-3 oz. fresh spinach, chopped
- 1/4 cup cream cheese, room temperature
- Pinch of nutmeg
- salt and pepper
- 2 (6-8 oz.) salmon fillets about 1-inch thick, with skin on
- olive oil
- 3/4 cup fresh breadcrumbs from a crusty Italian-style bread
- 4 TB. melted butter
- 1/4 cup grated parmesan cheese

Direction

- Put spinach in a small saucepan with 1 TB. of water.
- Cook 1-2 minutes just to wilt the spinach. Rinse with cold water and squeeze dry.
- Combine spinach with cream cheese and nutmeg. Season with salt and pepper.
- Cut a 1/2-inch deep slit in the middle of each salmon fillet, with skin side down.
- From the bottom of the slit, cut the fillet horizontally about 1-inch in both directions to form a pocket for the stuffing.
- Fill with the cream cheese mixture.
- Preheat oven to 450 degrees F.
- Brush a baking sheet with olive oil.
- Sprinkle salmon with salt and pepper.
- Combine breadcrumbs, butter and Parmesan cheese.
- Top each fillet with the crumbs, covering each top and pressing to adhere.
- Place salmon on baking sheet.
- Bake 12 minutes or until fish is opaque. Serve with grilled vegetables, if desired.

18. Baked Salmon Stuffed With Spinach And Cream Cheese Recipe

Serving: 2 | Prep: | Cook: 12mins | Ready in:

Ingredients

- 1 cup fresh spinach, chopped
- ¼ cup cream cheese, room temperature
- Pinch of nutmeg
- salt and pepper
- 2 8 oz. 1" thick salmon fillets with skin on
- olive oil
- ¾ cup fresh breadcrumbs
- 4 TB. melted butter
- ¼ cup grated parmesan cheese

Direction

- Filling:
- Put spinach in a small saucepan with 1 tbsp. of water.
- Cook 1-2 minutes just to wilt the spinach.
- Rinse with cold water and squeeze dry.
- Combine spinach with cream cheese and nutmeg.
- Season with salt and pepper.
- Salmon:
- Cut a ½-inch deep slit in the middle of each salmon fillet, with skin side down.
- From the bottom of the slit, cut the fillet horizontally about 1-inch in both directions to form a pocket for the stuffing.
- Fill with the cream cheese mixture.
- Preheat oven to 450 degrees F.
- Brush a baking sheet with olive oil.
- Sprinkle salmon with salt and pepper.
- Combine breadcrumbs, butter and Parmesan cheese.
- Top each fillet with the crumbs, covering each top and pressing to adhere.
- Place salmon on baking sheet.
- Bake 12 minutes or until fish is opaque.

19. Baked Salmon Stuffed And Wrapped In Grape Vine Leaves Recipe

Serving: 6 | Prep: | Cook: 35mins | Ready in:

Ingredients

- 800g salmon in one piece (not tail end)
- 10-12 preserved grape vine leaves
- 1 small fennel bulb
- 3 tblspns roasted pine nuts (preroast for 10 mins at 180 deg C)
- 1/4 cup currants, reconstituted in verjuice
- 3 x 1/4 preserved lemons, skin only, sliced thinly
- 1/2 red (spanish) onion, small dice
- 1 tblspn chopped chervil
- 2 tblspns fennel leaves (from top of bulb used in baking)
- 50g butter
- 1/4 cup verjuice

Direction

- OVERNIGHT
- Reconstitute the currants in verjuice.
- Roast the pine nuts and allow to cool.
- COOKING DAY
- Preheat oven to 120 deg C.
- Slice the base of the fennel bulb and spread over a small baking tray (reserve the top for garnish).
- Cut the salmon into two equal pieces.
- Make a stuffing by mixing together the roasted pine nuts, currants, finely chopped onion, herbs and 25g of butter to hold it together.
- Rinse the grape leaves, pat dry and lay out on a fresh chopping board for the 'salmon sandwich'.
- Place one piece of salmon down and season well with salt and pepper.
- Place all stuffing on top.
- Place second piece of salmon on top of the stuffing mix and season well.
- Wrap the parcel in the vine leaves and tie with string, making sure the leaves are covering all the salmon.
- Place this parcel on top of the sliced fennel, add verjuice/white wine and the rest of the butter.
- Bake at 120 deg C for 50 minutes, turning once after 25-30 mins.
- Baste with pan juices once or twice through cooking.

- Notes:
- At the finish of cooking time, take salmon parcel from the oven and allow to rest for 10 mins upside down.
- Turn oven up to 200 deg C to finish cooking the fennel.
- Return the rested salmon parcel to the oven to 'flash' reheat before cutting off the string and carving into thick slices.
- Garnish with the fennel tops and a spray of chervil along with a verjuice beurre blanc.

20. Baked Salmon With Mustard Sauce Recipe

Serving: 4 | Prep: | Cook: 20mins | Ready in:

Ingredients

- 1 cup sour cream
- 1/3 cup chopped fresh dill
- 3 tablespoons finely chopped onion
- 2 tablespoons Dijon mustard
- 1 ½ pound center-cut salmon fillet with skin
- 2 teaspoons minced garlic

Direction

- Whisk sour cream, dill, onion and mustard in small bowl to blend. Season sauce to taste with salt and pepper. Let stand at room temperature 1 hour.
- Preheat oven to 400° F. Lightly oil baking sheet. Place salmon, skin side down, on prepared sheet.
- Sprinkle with garlic, salt and pepper; spread with 1/3 cup sauce. Bake salmon until just opaque in center, about 20 minutes. Serve with remaining sauce.

21. Baked Salmon With Tarragon Recipe

Serving: 4 | Prep: | Cook: 20mins | Ready in:

Ingredients

- 4 salmon fillets
- 1 small, finely chopped onion
- 2 slices of thin bacon, diced
- 3 ounces (90g or ¾ stick) butter
- Quarter teaspoon dried tarragon
- 2 tablespoons lemon juice
- Large sheet of buttered kitchen foil
- double cream or crème fraîche

Direction

- Pre-heat the oven to 400F (200C or Gas Mark 6). Fry the finely chopped onion in butter in a pan until soft and golden (but not burnt). Add the bacon and tarragon and cook for another two minutes; then stir in the lemon juice.
- Place a large piece of buttered kitchen foil in an ovenproof dish, place the salmon fillets on this and cover with the onion and bacon mixture. Fold over the foil and seal to make a parcel. Bake for 15-20 minutes.
- Serve with a teaspoonful of thick cream or crème fraiche and fresh vegetables

22. Barbecued Salmon Recipe

Serving: 2 | Prep: | Cook: 10mins | Ready in:

Ingredients

- 2 ½ pounds fresh salmon fillets
- salt and pepper to taste
- lemon juice to taste
- butter Baste
- 1 cup butter
- 2 cloves garlic minced
- ¼ cup soy sauce
- 2 T. Dijon mustard
- Dash worcestershire sauce
- Dash of ketchup

Direction

- Combine butter, garlic, soy sauce, mustard Worcestershire sauce and ketchup in small saucepan. Heat until well blended, stir frequently (Do not boil)
- Set aside to be used during final preparation
- Preparation
- Sprinkle salmon with salt, pepper and lemon juice
- Baste with butter baste
- Place on 2 layers of heavy duty foil
- Place foil over medium coals
- Grill until salmon begins to flake, baste frequently
- Baste again just before serving

23. Barbecued Salmon With Horseradish Crushed Potato Recipe

Serving: 4 | Prep: | Cook: 20mins | Ready in:

Ingredients

- 1-1/2 pounds potatoes peeled and halved
- 1 teaspoon salt
- 1 cup hot milk plus extra
- 2 teaspoons green horseradish spice
- 2 tablespoons butter
- 1/4 teaspoon sea salt
- 1/2 teaspoon freshly ground black pepper
- 4 thick salmon fillets
- vegetable oil for grilling
- 1 teaspoon lime or lemon juice
- 1 tablespoon light olive oil

Direction

- Place potato in a large saucepan then add salt and water to cover and bring to boiling.

- Cook potato 15 minutes then drain and shake over heat until dry.
- Crush with a masher or push through a sieve.
- Beat in milk, 1 teaspoon horseradish powder, salt and pepper.
- Cover with 3 tablespoons hot milk and butter then seal pan with tight fitting lid.
- Rinse salmon very lightly and pat dry with absorbent kitchen paper.
- Preheat barbecue or ribbed grill pan to medium hot then brush the rack or pan with vegetable oil.
- When oil is hot brush salmon lightly with vegetable oil and place on rack or pan.
- Cook 6 minutes turning once.
- Mix remaining horseradish with lime juice and oil until well combined.
- To serve spoon creamed potato onto 4 warm serving plates.
- Peel away skin of salmon steaks and arrange on top.
- Drizzle horseradish mixture around edge of each plate then serve while warm.

24. Barbeque Roasted Salmon Recipe

Serving: 6 | Prep: | Cook: 30mins | Ready in:

Ingredients

- 1/3 cup pineapple juice
- 1/4 cup fresh lemon juice
- 6 salmon fillets
- 1/4 cup brown sugar
- 1 tablespoon chili powder
- 1 tablespoon lemon zest
- 1 teaspoon ground cumin
- 1/2 teaspoon ground cinnamon
- 1/2 teaspoon salt

Direction

- Combine pineapple juice, lemon juice and salmon fillets in a bag and seal.

- Marinate in the refrigerator for an hour then remove salmon and discard juices.
- Combine next 6 ingredients and mix well then rub mixture on each fillet.
- Place fillets in a baking dish coated with cooking spray and bake at 400 for 15 minutes.
- Serve with fresh lemon slices.

25. Barbeque Salmon Steaks Recipe

Serving: 4 | Prep: | Cook: 20mins | Ready in:

Ingredients

- 4 salmon steaks
- 3 tablespoons melted butter
- 1 tablespoon fresh lemon juice
- 1 tablespoon white wine vinegar
- 1/4 teaspoon grated lemon peel
- 1/4 teaspoon garlic salt
- 1/4 teaspoon salt
- 1 teaspoon hot pepper sauce

Direction

- Combine all ingredients except salmon stirring thoroughly.
- Generously brush both sides of salmon steaks with mixture.
- Barbeque on a well-oiled grill over hot coals.
- Make a tent of foil or use barbeque cover and place over salmon.
- Barbeque for 8 minutes per side depending.
- Baste frequently turning once brushing with sauce.

26. Bbq Salmon With Roasted Corn Amp Black Bean Salsa Recipe

Serving: 4 | Prep: | Cook: 8mins | Ready in:

Ingredients

- 4 salmon Filets, 6 to 8 oz. each
- kosher salt & fresh ground pepper
- extra virgin olive oil for searing
- ½ cup honey-Citrus BBQ Sauce
- FOR THE salsa
- 1 cup canned black beans, drained & rinsed
- 1/4 cup chopped cilantro
- 1 cup roasted corn, removed from cob
- 1/2 cup lime juice
- 1/2 medium red onion, diced
- 1/4 cup olive oil
- 1/2 medium red bell pepper, diced
- 1/2 tablespoon ground cumin
- 1/2 medium poblano pepper, diced
- 1/2 tablespoon black pepper
- 1/2 cup seeded diced tomato
- 1 tablespoon salt
- SWEET AND SMOKEY BBQ SAUCE
- 1/3 cup apple cider vinegar
- 1 cup ketchup
- 3 tablespoons brown sugar
- 1 tablespoon yellow mustard
- 1 tablespoon molasses
- 2 tablespoon worcestershire sauce
- 1 teaspoon liquid smoke
- juice of 1 orange
- 1 teaspoon salt 1/2 tsp dried crushed red pepper
- 1 tsp hot sauce
- 1 tsp soy sauce

Direction

- SALSA DIRECTIONS
- Combine all ingredients in a large bowl up to and including the cilantro
- In a separate bowl, add the lime juice and spices, whisk in the olive oil a little at a time. Add to the salsa and toss gently to combine. Refrigerate for at least one hour.
- SALMON COOKING DIRECTIONS
- Preheat oven to 425 degrees.
- Pre-heat skillet over medium heat, (I like to use a good quality non-stick skillet for the first part of this process, but a cast iron skillet or grill pan will also work, or this can also be done on the grill.)

- Salt & pepper both sides of the salmon filets and drizzle some olive oil in the pan.
- Sear the filets no more than 3 minutes on each side.
- Carefully transfer the salmon to a foil or parchment lined sheet pan and brush generously with the barbecue sauce on the top and sides of each filet.
- Place the pan in a 425 degree oven for 5 minutes or until the barbecue sauce begins to caramelize.
- Serve over a mound of the roasted corn & black bean salsa and garnish with a few sprigs of fresh cilantro.
- SWEET & SMOKEY BBQ SAUCE DIRECTIONS
- Combine vinegar, liquid smoke, and brown sugar. Stir until sugar is dissolved.
- Add and combine the rest of ingredients well and refrigerate.

27. Black Pepper Angel Hair With Smoked Salmon Recipe

Serving: 4 | Prep: | Cook: 20mins |Ready in:

Ingredients

- 1 quart heavy cream
- 1 cup clam juice
- 1 cup dry white wine
- 6 whole garlic cloves peeled
- 2 teaspoons whole black peppercorns
- 2 teaspoons salt
- 2 tablespoons dill weed
- 1 tablespoon champagne vinegar
- 16 ounces fresh black pepper angel hair pasta
- 3/4 cup grated parmesan cheese
- Topping:
- 8 ounces heavy cream
- 1 cup sour cream
- 8 ounces smoked salmon
- 4 sprigs fresh dill weed

Direction

- In generous saucepot reduce heavy cream at a gentle simmer until it is half its original volume.
- In a separate smaller pot combine clam juice, wine, garlic, peppercorns, salt, dill and vinegar.
- Reduce at boil to half its original volume then strain and dispose of garlic and peppercorns.
- Add wine reduction to reduced cream and reserve.
- In boiling lightly salted water cook fresh pasta for 45 seconds.
- Drain in colander and cool by running cold water through it to halt cooking.
- For topping whip heavy cream to medium peaks then add sour cream and whip until blended.
- In large sauté pan heat sauce to boil then whisk in parmesan until well blended.
- Sauce will continue to reduce quickly.
- Add cooked pasta to sauce and toss to coat evenly.
- Divide between 4 dishes topping each with 2 ounces smoked salmon, a dollop of cream and dill.

28. Bourbon Marinated Smoked Salmon Recipe

Serving: 4 | Prep: | Cook: 180mins | Ready in:

Ingredients

- 1 1/2 pounds fresh salmon -- skinned and boned
- vegetable oil
- 1 cup bourbon
- 1 cup soy sauce
- 2 2/3 tablespoons fresh ginger
- 2 2/3 tablespoons black pepper
- 1/2 teaspoon chili powder
- 1 1/2 teaspoons garlic -- minced
- 3/4 ounce sesame oil

Direction

- Place salmon in large shallow dish; cover with vegetable oil. Mix all other ingredients together to make marinade; marinate 6 hours or overnight.
- Grill over mesquite until flaky.

29. Bourbon Orange Grilled Salmon Recipe

Serving: 4 | Prep: | Cook: 12mins | Ready in:

Ingredients

- ¼ C bourbon
- ¼ C orange juice
- ¼ C low sodium soy sauce
- ¼ C brown sugar
- 2 Lrge green onions chopped
- 3 T chives
- 2 T lemon juice
- 2 T garlic
- 2 lbs of salmon fillets with skin cut into 4 pieces

Direction

- Place all ingredients in a resealable plastic bag and add salmon
- Marinate 30 minutes to several hours
- Remove from marinade, grill over medium high heat about 12 to 15 mins. Depending on the thickness of the fish, turning 1/2 way through.
- Fish is done when it flakes easily with a fork.
- Skin may be removed prior to serving.

30. Bourbon Salmon Recipe

Serving: 2 | Prep: | Cook: 12mins | Ready in:

Ingredients

- 1/4 cup bourbon or brandy
- 1/4 cup fresh orange juice
- 1/4 cup low-sodium soy sauce
- 1/2 cup packed brown sugar
- 2 Tbl honey
- 1/4 cup chopped green onion
- 1/2 tsp orange zest
- 3 tablespoons chopped fresh chives
- 2 tablespoons fresh lemon juice
- 2 cloves garlic, chopped
- 4 (6 ounce) salmon fillets (about 1 inch thick)
- cooking spray

Direction

- Combine first 8 ingredients in a large zip-top plastic bag, and add salmon to bag. Seal and marinate in refrigerator 1-1/2 hours, turning bag occasionally.
- Prepare grill or broiler.
- Remove salmon from bag, reserving marinade. Place salmon on a grill rack or broiler pan coated with cooking spray. Cook 6 minutes on each side or until fish flakes easily when tested with a fork, basting frequently with reserved marinade.

31. Bourbon Glazed Salmon Recipe

Serving: 4 | Prep: | Cook: 8mins | Ready in:

Ingredients

- 3 tbsp brown sugar
- 3 tbsp bourbon
- 2 tbsp soy-sauce
- 1 tbsp ginger, fresh grated
- 1 tbsp lime juice
- 3 cloves garlic, minced

- ¼ tsp freshly ground pepper
- 4 skinless salmon fillets
- Topping:
- ¼ cup thinly sliced green onions
- 1 tbsp sesame seeds, toasted

Direction

- Combine first 7 ingredients (through pepper) in a large plastic bag
- Add fish and marinate in fridge for 1 ½ hours turning
- Heat a skillet over medium high heat
- Coat with cooking spray
- And fish and marinate to the pan
- Cook for 4 minutes per side or till fish is flaky
- To serve spoon sauce over fish and top with onions and sesame seeds

32. Bow Tie Pasta With Salmon Olives And Capers Recipe

Serving: 4 | Prep: | Cook: 20mins | Ready in:

Ingredients

- 1-1/2 pounds salmon cut into 1" thick steaks
- 1/2 cup extra-virgin olive oil divided
- 1/4 teaspoon salt
- 1/2 teaspoon freshly ground black pepper
- 3 leeks thinly sliced white part only
- 1 cup thinly sliced red onions
- 2 garlic cloves pressed
- 2/3 cup pitted olives halved
- 3 tablespoons capers rinsed
- 4 teaspoons grated lemon peel
- 1 tablespoon fresh lemon juice
- 1 pound bow tie pasta cooked according to package directions
- 6 tablespoons chopped flat leaf parsley

Direction

- Heat a grill pan over high heat then rub salmon with 2 tablespoons olive oil.

- Sprinkle with salt and pepper then grill 2 minutes per side.
- Transfer to a cutting board and break into 1" chunks then set aside.
- Heat remaining oil then sauté leeks, onions and garlic in remaining oil approximately 5 minutes.
- Stir in salmon, olives, capers, lemon peel and juice until heated through about 5 minutes.
- Toss with hot pasta and sprinkle with parsley.

33. Broiled Honey Lime Salmon Recipe

Serving: 4 | Prep: | Cook: 6mins | Ready in:

Ingredients

- marinade
- 2 tbsp Dijon mustard
- juice of one freshly squeezed lime
- 2 tsp olive oil
- 1 tbsp honey
- 1 1/2 tsp dried tarragon
- 2 tbsp dry sherry
- 1/4 tsp salt
- 1 1/4 lb salmon fillets 1/2 to 5/8 thick
- non stick cooking spray

Direction

- Combine marinade ingredients thoroughly.
- Place salmon fillets in shallow non-metal dish and top with Marinade turning to coat other side.
- Marinate in refrigerator for 1 hour turning once or twice.
- Preheat broiler.
- Coat broiler pan with cooking spray.
- Broil fish 4-6 inches from heating element for 5-6 minutes until fish is done (no need to turn).
- Serve with lime wedges (if desired).

34. Broiled Salmon And Miso Glaze Recipe

Serving: 4 | Prep: | Cook: 10mins | Ready in:

Ingredients

- 1 green onion, minced
- 2 tablespoons red miso
- 1 tablespoon rice vinegar
- 1 tablespoon honey
- 1 teaspoon minced fresh ginger
- 4 portions of center-cut salmon fillet
- 1 teaspoon toasted sesame seeds

Direction

- Whisk green onion, miso, vinegar, honey and ginger in a medium bowl until the honey is dissolved.
- Place salmon in a sealable plastic bag, add 3 tablespoons of the sauce and refrigerate; let marinate for 15 minutes.
- Reserve the remaining sauce.
- Preheat broiler. Line a small baking pan with foil and coat with cooking spray.
- Transfer the salmon to the pan, skinned-side down. Discard the marinade.
- Broil the salmon 4 to 6 inches from the heat source until cooked through, 6 to 10 minutes.
- Drizzle with the reserved sauce and garnish with sesame seeds.

35. Broiled Salmon Recipe

Serving: 4 | Prep: | Cook: 15mins | Ready in:

Ingredients

- 1/2 cup hot tomato salsa
- 1/4 cup fresh lime juice
- 1 teaspoon Dijon mustard
- 1 garlic clove minced
- 4 salmon steaks
- 1/4 cup butter softened

- 3/4 teaspoon lime zest grated
- 1/4 teaspoon cumin ground
- 1/2 teaspoon salt
- 1 teaspoon freshly ground black pepper
- 1 tablespoon vegetable oil
- lime wedges

Direction

- Set aside two tablespoons of salsa.
- In medium bowl combine remaining salsa, lime juice, mustard and garlic.
- Coat salmon steaks in marinade then cover and refrigerate for at least 1/2 hour.
- In medium bowl combine butter with lime zest, cumin and reserved salsa.
- Mix well and set aside.
- Preheat broiler on high.
- Remove salmon steaks from marinade and discard marinade.
- Season with salt and pepper then arrange side by side in oiled oven proof dish.
- Place salmon under broiler 4" from heat source.
- Broil 3 minutes per side then bone and skin salmon steaks.
- Arrange salmon steaks on warm plates.
- Spoon a teaspoon of salsa butter on top of each steak.
- Garnish plates with lime wedges then serve hot.

36. Broiled Salmon With Peppercorn Lime Rub Recipe

Serving: 4 | Prep: | Cook: 7mins | Ready in:

Ingredients

- 4(6oz) salmon fillets(about 3/4" thick)
- cooking spray
- 2 tsp grated lime rind
- 1/2 tsp kosher salt
- 1/2 tsp cracked black pepper

- 1 garlic clove m,minced
- lime wedges

Direction

- Preheat broiler.
- Place fish, skin side down, on broiler pan coated with cooking spray. Combine remaining ingredients except lime wedges; sprinkle over fish. Broil 7 mins or till fish flakes easily when tested with a fork or until desired degree of doneness. Serve with lime wedges.

37. Broiled Salmon With Marmalade Dijon Sauce Recipe

Serving: 4 | Prep: | Cook: 10mins | Ready in:

Ingredients

- 1/2 cup orange marmalade
- 1 tablespoon Dijon mustard
- 1/2 teaspoon garlic powder
- 1/2 teaspoon salt
- 1/4 teaspoon black pepper
- 1/8 teaspoon ground ginger
- 4 (6-ounce) salmon fillets
- cooking spray

Direction

- Preheat broiler.
- Combine first 6 ingredients in a small bowl, stirring well. Place fish on a jelly-roll pan coated with cooking spray. Brush half of marmalade mixture over fish; broil 6 minutes. Brush fish with remaining marmalade mixture; broil for 2 minutes or until fish flakes easily when tested with a fork or until desired degree of doneness.

38. Broiled Salmon With Tarragon Garlic Butter Recipe

Serving: 2 | Prep: | Cook: 10mins | Ready in:

Ingredients

- 1/4 cup butter
- 2 garlic cloves, minced
- 2 tablespoons fresh lemon juice
- 1 1/2 tbsp minced fresh tarragon or1 tsp dried, crumbled
- Freshly ground pepper to taste
- 2 (1-inch-thick) salmon fillets
- salt to taste

Direction

- Preheat broiler.
- Melt butter in small saucepan on the stove top over medium-low heat and sauté garlic for a few seconds.
- Remove from heat and add lemon juice, tarragon and pepper.
- Arrange salmon skin side down on broiler-proof pan.
- Brush with half of butter mixture.
- Season with salt.
- Broil until nearly cooked; turn over and a cook until done to personal preference.
- Transfer to plates. Reheat remaining lemon/butter sauce; spoon over salmon and serve.

39. Broiled Sour Cream And Dill Salmon Recipe

Serving: 4 | Prep: | Cook: 15mins | Ready in:

Ingredients

- 2 medium cucumbers,cut into thin slices
- 1 Tbsp. red wine vinegar
- 4 tsp. olive oil
- 1 tsp. lemon pepper seasoning
- 1/2 tsp. gradulated garlic
- 1/2 tsp. fresh dill, chopped (plus sprigs for garnish)
- 1/2 small onion, thinly sliced into rings
- 1 tsp. extra virgin olive oil
- 4 (7 oz) boneless, skin-on salmon fillets
- 1/4 cup fresh lemon juice
- 1/2 tsp. onion salt
- 1/4 cup light sour cream
- lemon slices for garnish
- salt and pepper to taste

Direction

- Using a vegetable peeler, cut cucumber into thin slices (slice up to the seed portion) and place in a small bowl.
- Add onions, vinegar, and extra virgin olive oil and mix well, season with salt and pepper to taste. Refrigerate until ready to serve.
- Place oven rack 4 to 5" from top of oven. Preheat broiler to high.
- Coat both sides of salmon fillets with olive oil.
- Place salmon, skin side up, in a shallow baking dish. Broil salmon until skin is lightly browned, about 4 to 5 minutes.
- Turn salmon over, pour lemon juice over salmon, and sprinkle with granulated garlic, onion salt and lemon pepper seasoning. Broil salmon, checking the oven often, until lightly browned, about 4 to 5 minutes.
- Combine the sour cream and dill and spread evenly over the top of each salmon fillet. Broil approximately 3 to 4 minutes or until the sour cream topping is lightly browned.
- Remove skin from fillets and serve over cucumber mixture, garnished with dill sprigs and lemon slices.

40. Brown Sugar Glazed Salmon Recipe

Serving: 0 | Prep: | Cook: 10mins | Ready in:

Ingredients

- 2 large salmon fillets
- 2/3 cup brown sugar
- 2 Tbs honey
- 2 Tbs Dijon mustard
- 1/2 tsp salt
- chopped fresh dill to garnish

Direction

- Mix the sugar, honey, mustard and salt well. Place salmon skin side down on baking tray. Brush over the salmon.
- Broil 3 to 4 inches from heat source and broil 8 to 10 minutes or until golden glazed and done.
- Garnish with dill and lemon slices if desired
- May be served warm or room temperature
- Note: may also use salmon steaks for the recipe

41. Brown Sugar Salmon Recipe

Serving: 4 | Prep: | Cook: 20mins | Ready in:

Ingredients

- 4 salmon fillets.
- ½ cup of brown sugar.
- 4 tablespoons of margerine, melted.
- 3 tablespoons of freshly squeezed lemon juice.
- 2 tablespoons of dry white wine.

Direction

- Put all of the ingredients in a large baking dish and allow to marinade for about three hours.
- Bake at 360°F (180°C) for about 20 minutes, basting occasionally.
- Serve immediately.

42. Carb Friendly Salmon Welly Style Recipe

Serving: 4 | Prep: | Cook: 10mins | Ready in:

Ingredients

- 4 - six ounce portions of salmon fillets
- brined jarred grape leaves, rinsed and patted dry
- 1 4 ounce log of goat cheese
- 2 ounces of cream cheese
- 2 tbsp of extra virgin olive oil
- 1 large fat leek, cleaned, halved and sliced into moons
- 1 lb of crimini mushrooms, brushed and sliced
- 1 tbsp non-paraeil capers, drained and chopped
- 1 tsp of dried dill weed
- 1 tsp of lemon pepper seasoning
- extra virgin olive oil for brushing outside of grape leaves
- 1/2 stick of melted butter, mixed with the juice on one lemon and a dash of cayenne pepper and two to three scrapes of fresh nutmeg
- 3 small zucchini, washed and shaved into wide noodle shape with mandolin, or use the vegetable peeler

Direction

- In a large skillet, heat the olive oil and add the leeks (lower carb count than yellow onions, shallots and green onions are even less than leeks) and the mushrooms and cook until soft and limp.
- Reserve and cool.
- Mix the cooled veggies into the soft cream cheese and goat cheese until well combined. Add capers and seasonings (dill & lemon pepper).
- Place 3 grape leaves slightly overlapping in a triangle pattern, no holes please. Top with a piece of salmon and evenly divide the filling between each fillet.

- Fold in sides of grape leaves, then the bottom and finally roll into a neat log shape. Completely enclosing salmon and filling mix.
- Refrigerate while you shave the zucchini into wide faux pasta noodles.
- Preheat oven 425 degrees. Place salmon bundles on foil lined cookie sheet, brush foil with oil. Brush bundles with so they barely glisten with the oil. Bake for 10 minutes. Let rest for five.
- While the salmon oven roasts, melt half the butter in a large skillet and toss in the zucchini ribbons, cooking quickly over high heat.
- Melt remaining butter in microwave and season to taste with cayenne, lemon juice and nutmeg.
- Serve salmon bundle with zucchini ribbons, drizzle with flavored lemon butter. Blasted tomatoes (previous post) also make a great side dish for this meal.

43. Cedar Plank Salmon On Puff Pastry With Lemon Dill Sauce Recipe

Serving: 4 | Prep: | Cook: 20mins | Ready in:

Ingredients

- 4 portions of salmon skinned and boned
- 1-2 cedar planks soaked in water for min 3 hours best is 12hours submerged.
- 1 bunch fresh dill (one sprig for each salmon portion balance for the sauce)
- 1Shallot minced
- 2-3 lemons (1 for the sauce)
- 1 package of thawed puff pastry
- lemon dill sauce (Emeril Lagasse)
- # 1/2 cup minced shallots
- # 1 teaspoon minced garlic
- # 1/2 cup dry white wine
- # juice of one lemon(included above)
- # 1/4 cup chopped fresh dill (included above)
- # 1 teaspoon Dijon mustard
- # 1/2 cup heavy cream
- # 5 tablespoons unsalted butter, cubed
- # salt and pepper

Direction

- Take one sheet of puff pastry and cut into half vertically and horizontally
- You should now have 4 equal squares, cut these in half to make 2 triangles from each square. Bake according to instructions on box.
- These can be made in advance and the triangles reheated when served.
- To get a nice golden color paint with an egg wash prior to baking.
- Drizzle olive oil on plank
- Place Salmon pieces on cedar plank with 1/2 inch space in between.
- Turn on Barbeque to hi heat
- Place one sprig of dill on each piece of salmon.
- Sprinkle each salmon with minced shallots.
- Season with sea salt and pepper
- Drizzle fish with E V olive oil
- Slice one lemon and place a slice on each piece of salmon
- Place plank on grill close lid
- If plank starts burning blow out and turn that side of barbeque off
- It will cook through convection with heat from other side as well.
- While fish is cooking prepare lemon dill sauce as follows:
- In a saucepan, combine the shallots, garlic, wine, and lemon. Bring the liquid up to a boil. Stir in the dill and cook for 3 minutes. Whisk in the mustard and cream, continue to cook for 2 minutes. Whisk in the butter a cube at a time, until all the butter is incorporated. Season with salt and pepper.
- Check Salmon, fish is cooked when it flakes in the thickest part and is no longer translucent.
- Place the cooked salmon on the Pastry triangles.
- If you like put another triangle on top but it is not required. Drizzle the sauce over the salmon. Enjoy

- I usually serve these with dill, creamed new potatoes but wild rice and garlic mashed are equally well received

44. Cedar Plank Salmon Recipe

Serving: 4 | Prep: | Cook: 15mins | Ready in:

Ingredients

- 2 tbsp grainy mustard
- 2 tbsp ketchup
- 1 tbsp chopped fresh rosemary
- 2 tbsp olive oil
- 1/2 tsp chili powder
- salt and freshly ground pepper
- One 2 lb piece of raw salmon

Direction

- Combine mustard, ketchup, rosemary, olive oil, chili powder, salt and pepper.
- Spread over salmon and marinate for 30 minutes.
- Heat grill to high heat.
- Place soaked cedar plank on grill and leave for 3 to 4 minutes or until you can smell or see smoke.
- Immediately turn plank, salt it liberally and place fish on top, skin-side down.
- Close cover and cook for 12 to15 minutes or until fish is just cooked.
- Remove plank from grill and slip salmon off, onto serving platter.

45. Cedar Plank Salmon With Orange Balsamic Glaze Recipe

Serving: 4 | Prep: | Cook: 20mins | Ready in:

Ingredients

- 1/2 cup freshly squeezed orange juice

- zest of 1 orange
- 1/4 cup sugar
- 1/4 cup balsamic vinegar
- 1 tablespoon extra-virgin olive oil
- 2 cloves garlic, finely chopped
- 1 tablespoon finely chopped fresh rosemary
- kosher salt & freshly ground black pepper to taste
- 4 salmon steaks or filets (about 6 ounces each)

Direction

- Place orange juice, zest and sugar in a saucepan over high heat and bring to boil. Reduce by half and cool.
- Place reduction along with the rest of the ingredients in a large sealable plastic bag. Shake well. Add salmon and refrigerate 1 hour. Meanwhile, soak a cedar plank for 1 hour and preheat charcoal grill.
- Remove steaks/filets from marinade. Position salmon on soaked cedar plank and place over hottest part of your grill. Close lid and grill until salmon to 120 degrees internal. Remove from grill, cover with foil and rest for 5 minutes.
- Note: while the salmon is grilling, we like to throw down fresh corn on the cob that has been rubbed with olive oil and sprinkled with kosher salt. The corn picks up the wonderful flavor from the cedar. After it's nicely caramelized, take the cobs off the grill and rub butter all over them... enjoy!

46. Cedar Planked Alaskan Salmon With Citrus Rub Recipe

Serving: 3 | Prep: | Cook: 40mins | Ready in:

Ingredients

- Ingredients
- cedar plank
- 3 wild Alaska salmon filets
- Zest of one each orange, lemon, and lime

- 1/4 cup kosher salt
- 1 Tbsp black pepper, ground fresh
- 1/2 tsp Alder-smoked salt, ground fine
- 1/4 tsp ground ginger

Direction

- On individual (easier to serve) or on one cedar plank
- Place your filets skin side down on planks
- Season with above seasoning
- Grill med high 40 minutes
- Method for seasoning
- Combine all the ingredients in a small zip-top bag and shake to combine.
- Set aside for at least three hours to allow the flavors to marry.
- Use as you would any other seasoning.

47. Cedar Planked Salmon

Serving: 4 | Prep: | Cook: 20mins | Ready in:

Ingredients

- 3 (12 inch) untreated cedar planks
- ⅓ cup vegetable oil
- 1 ½ tablespoons rice vinegar
- 1 teaspoon sesame oil
- ⅓ cup soy sauce
- ¼ cup chopped green onions
- 1 tablespoon grated fresh ginger root
- 1 teaspoon minced garlic
- 2 (2 pound) salmon fillets, skin removed

Direction

- Soak the cedar planks for at least 1 hour in warm water. Soak longer if you have time.
- In a shallow dish, stir together the vegetable oil, rice vinegar, sesame oil, soy sauce, green onions, ginger, and garlic. Place the salmon fillets in the marinade and turn to coat. Cover and marinate for at least 15 minutes, or up to one hour.

- Preheat an outdoor grill for medium heat. Place the planks on the grate. The boards are ready when they start to smoke and crackle just a little.
- Place the salmon fillets onto the planks and discard the marinade. Cover, and grill for about 20 minutes. Fish is done when you can flake it with a fork. It will continue to cook after you remove it from the grill.

48. Cedar Planked Salmon Recipe

Serving: 4 | Prep: | Cook: 30mins | Ready in:

Ingredients

- 1 medium plank soaked in water for at least one hour but better if 2 or 3hours.i put mine in the kitchen sink and then i put a heavy can in plastic bag and weigh it down
- 4 skinless salmon fillets about 6 oz each
- 1 c fresh dill, chopped
- 2 Tbsp bbq spice (see below)
- 1/2 c shallots, chopped
- 2 clove garlic, minced
- 2 green onions,finely chopped
- 2 Tbsp planking spice (see below)
- 1 lemon , juiced
- 2 Tbsp olive oil
- sea salt
- 1 lemon
- BONEDUST BBQ seasoning
- 1/2 c paprika
- 1/4 c chili powder
- 3 Tbsp salt
- 2 Tbsp ground coriander
- 2 Tbsp garlic powder
- 2 Tbsp sugar
- 2 Tbsp curry powder
- 2 Tbsp dry mustard powder
- 1 Tbsp black pepper
- 1 Tbsp dried basil
- 1 Tbsp dried thyme
- 1 Tbsp ground cumin

- 1 Tbsp cayenne pepper
- PLANKING spice
- 1/2 c light brown sugar
- 1/4 c coarsely ground pepper
- 1/4 c kosher salt
- 2 Tbsp mustard seeds cracked
- 1 Tbsp dried dill weed
- 1 Tbsp dill seed
- 1 Tbsp coriander seed
- 1 Tbsp lemon pepper seasoning
- 3 Tbsp granulated onion powder
- 2 tsp granulated garlic powder

Direction

- Preheat your grill to medium-high.
- Season salmon with BBQ seasoning and set aside.
- Mix together the dill, shallots, garlic, green onions, planking spice, lemon juice, and olive oil.
- Spread the mixture evenly over the salmon fillets.
- Season the plank with sea salt and place on grill and close the lid. Heat for 3 - 5 mins till the plank starts to crackle.
- Open lid and place the salmon fillets on the plank.
- Close the lid and plank-grill for 12 - 15 mins until cooked or until salmon flakes.
- Remove plank from grill and allow to cool one minute.
- Squeeze the lemon over top and serve.
- * There are so many flavored planks out there... oak, maple, cherry or apple ...so don't just stick to cedar. Apple is so good. My fav!!
- *If your plank catches fire which it can and I have had this happen, spray with a spray water bottle...be careful of not spraying the salmon.

49. Cedar Planked Salmon With Seasoned Butter Recipe

Serving: 8 | Prep: | Cook: 45mins | Ready in:

Ingredients

- 8 Tbs. (1 stick) unsalted butter, at room
- temperature
- 1 1/2 Tbs. poultry and fish grilling rub
- Finely grated zest of 1/2 lemon
- 3 to 4 lb. salmon fillet, skin intact
- 2 Tbs. potlatch seasoning
- 1/2 lemon, thinly sliced

Direction

- In the bowl of an electric mixer fitted with the flat beater, beat the butter on medium speed until smooth, about 1 minute. Add the grilling rub and lemon zest and beat until well blended, about 1 minute more. Spoon the butter mixture onto a sheet of waxed paper and form into a log about 1 inch thick. Twist the ends to seal the butter, then wrap in plastic wrap. Refrigerate for at least 1 hour or up to 2 days.
- Soak a cedar plank in water for at least 20 minutes or up to 4 hours.
- Prepare a medium fire in a grill. Have ready a spray bottle of water to extinguish any flare-ups on the plank. Bring the seasoned butter to room temperature.
- Place the plank on the grill, close the lid, and heat until the plank begins to smoke and crackle. Rub the skinless side of the salmon with the potlatch seasoning. Place the salmon, skin side down, on the plank and arrange the lemon slices on top of the sh. Close the lid and grill until the salmon is cooked through, 8 to 10 minutes.
- Transfer the plank with the salmon to a heatproof platter, or carefully transfer the salmon directly to a warmed platter. Cut as much of the seasoned butter as desired into slices 1/4 inch thick and place on the salmon,

reserving any remaining butter for another use. Serve immediately. Serves 6 to 8.

50. Champagne And Basil Grilled Salmon Recipe

Serving: 4 | Prep: | Cook: 2mins | Ready in:

Ingredients

- 4 fresh salmon steaks or filets
- 1/4 cup fresh basil chopped
- 2 tablespoons Dijon mustard
- 2 tablespoons champagne vinegar
- 1/3 cup extra virgin olive oil

Direction

- Combine all marinade ingredients to use as baste for grilling. Place salmon on a hot lightly oiled grill skin side down. Baste frequently with the marinade. When salmon is done baste with remaining marinade. Serve immediately.

51. Char Siu Salmon Recipe

Serving: 3 | Prep: | Cook: 3hours | Ready in:

Ingredients

- 4 x 80g fillets salmon, mid-cut, skin on
- olive oil, for frying
- For the Char Siu Sauce :
- 1/3 cup honey
- 1/3 cup Shaoxing (Chinese rice wine)
- 2 tbs soft brown sugar
- 2 tbs light soy sauce
- 2 tbs hoi sin sauce
- 2 tbs garlic powder
- 1 tsp five-spice powder
- A few drops of red food colouring
- 2 tbs red bean paste

- 1 tbs Chinese black vinegar
- For the Winter melon and Wood Ear mushroom Stir-Fry :
- 1 tbs hoi sin sauce
- 1 tbs light soy sauce
- 1/4 cup Shaoxing (Chinese rice wine)
- 1/4 cup black rice vinegar
- 2 tsp caster sugar
- 2 tbs peanut oil
- 1 tbs grated ginger
- 1 tbs finely chopped garlic
- 100g winter melon, skin and seeds removed, cut on an angle into 3cm pieces
- 2 wood ear mushrooms, root removed, torn into 3-4cm pieces
- 1 cucumber, alternate strips of skin peeled off, halved lengthways, seeds removed,
- cut on an angle 1cm thick
- 3 spring onions, sliced into 4cm lengths on the diagonal
- 1 bunch garlic chives, cut into 4cm lengths
- Handful of mung bean sprouts
- 1 tbs sesame oil
- 1/4 cup chopped peanuts
- 1/2 cup coriander leaves, to serve

Direction

- Mix all char siu sauce ingredients together, whisk well and strain through a fine sieve to remove any lumps, if necessary.
- Coat the salmon in the marinade in a ceramic dish. Cover with cling wrap, pressing wrap onto the surface of the marinade to eliminate any air. Place in the fridge to marinate for at least 2 hours and up to 12 hours.
- Remove salmon from the fridge, pat excess marinade off with paper towel so it doesn't burn in the pan.
- Heat a non-stick frying pan over medium-high heat. Add olive oil and place salmon in the pan, skin-side down. Season with salt and cook for 1-2 minutes on each side until slightly charred or until cooked to your liking.
- To make the stir-fry, combine the hoi sin sauce, light soy sauce, Shaoxing rice wine, black vinegar and caster sugar in a bowl until

the sugar dissolves. Heat a wok over high heat, add peanut oil, then add garlic and ginger, and cook for 30 seconds until fragrant. Add winter melon and wood ear mushrooms, then toss or stir-fry for 30 seconds. Add 3-4 tablespoons of sauce to the wok, then allow to cook for 1-2 minutes to let the flavours combine and soak into the melon. Add cucumber, spring onion and garlic chives, mung beans and sesame oil and cook for 30 seconds. Scatter with peanuts and drizzle with another tablespoon of sauce. Reserve the remaining sauce in the fridge for up to 1 week.

- To serve, place a piece of salmon in serving bowls with some of the stir-fry.

52. Chinese Style Barbecued Salmon Recipe

Serving: 4 | Prep: | Cook: 10mins | Ready in:

Ingredients

- Marinade;
- 3Tbs molasses
- 3 Tbs mirin,dry sherry or chicken broth
- 1Tbs soy sauce
- 1Tbs dark sesame oil
- 2 garlic cloves,minced
- 1 tbs minced fresh ginger
- Salmon:
- 4(6 to 8 oz) skin-on center-cut salmon fillets(1 to 11/2" thick)
- 4 fresh pineapple rings(3/4" thick) if desired

Direction

- Combine all marinade ingredients in small bowl. Place salmon in a single layer in glass baking dish. Pour marinade over salmon, turning to coat. Refrigerate 1 hour, turning at least once.
- Heat grill, oil grate. Remove salmon from marinade. Grill salmon skin-side up, covered, over med-high heat 3 to 4 mins or till salmon

can be turned without sticking; turn. Grill additional 3 mins or till salmon begins to flake. Remove skin.

- Brush pineapple with 1 tsp. of reserved marinade; grill 2 mins. or till browned, turning once. Cut in quarters, arrange over salmon.
- Bring remaining marinade to a boil in small saucepan, boil 2 to 3 mins. or till slightly reduced. Drizzle over salmon.

53. Chipotle Cedar Salmon Recipe

Serving: 4 | Prep: | Cook: 10mins | Ready in:

Ingredients

- 4-5 T. soft lite butter (Land o Lakes makes a great product.)
- 1 t. sweet Hungarian paprika, or for a smokier variety, sweet Spanish smoked paprika
- 1 t. medium chipotle chili
- 2 T. ground cumin
- 1 T. garlic powder
- 1 t. onion powder
- ½ t. sea salt
- 4 T. dark brown sugar
- 2 T. unsalted butter, melted
- Large fillet of salmon, skinless, about 2-2/12 lbs
- 1 sweet onion, sliced thin
- A cedar plank (you can get them at any BBQ supplies store)

Direction

- Prepare medium hot fire for indirect cooking. Soak cedar plank for at least 2 hours before grilling. Combine all ingredients except salmon and onion into a paste. Put salmon on cedar plank and slather on paste. Cover lightly with onion slices. Grill for 10-12 minutes until salmon flakes with a fork, onion slices soften.

54. Cinnamon Apricot Glazed Salmon Recipe

Serving: 4 | Prep: | Cook: 8mins | Ready in:

Ingredients

- 2 tbl low sodium soy sauce
- 1 tbl minced fresh peeled ginger
- 2 (3inch) cinnamon sticks
- 1 12 oz can apricot nectar
- 4 6oz salmon fillets about 1 inch thick

Direction

- Combine the first 4 ingredients in a saucepan and bring to a boil
- Reduce heat and simmer mix until reduced to 3/4 cup (about 30 minutes)
- Strain the apricot mixture thru a sieve over a bowl and discard solids
- Preheat broiler
- Place salmon fillets on a broiler pan lined with foil and broil for 5 minutes
- Brush fish with 1/4 cup apricot mixture
- Broil for 3 minutes or until lightly brown and fish flakes easily when tested with a fork
- Serve the fish with the remaining mixture

55. Citrus Marinated Salmon Recipe

Serving: 4 | Prep: | Cook: 10mins | Ready in:

Ingredients

- Ingredients for salad:
- 1 cup grated carrots
- ½ cup chopped capsicum
- 1 cup of cos lettuce, washed and shredded
- ¼ cup parsley, finely chopped
- ¼ cup coriander, finely chopped
- 1 spanish onion, roughly chopped
- 1 tsp of lemon juice
- 1 tsp of lime juice
- 1-2 garlic cloves
- 1 tbsp tamari soy sauce
- 2 tbsp olive oil
- 1 tsp fresh ginger
- 1 tsp of fresh chilli, deseeded
- Marinate for the salmon:
- 1 tbsp lemon juice
- 1 tsp lemon zest
- 1 tbsp of lime juice
- 1 tsp lime zest
- 4x100g salmon

Direction

- Mix the carrots, cos lettuce, capsicum, parsley, coriander and Spanish onion in a bowl. Whisk together the lemon and lime juice, tamari, ginger, garlic and chilli.
- Pour over the vegetable mixture.
- Place all the citrus ingredients in a bowl including the salmon and let it marinate for 10 minutes.
- Lightly pan-fry the salmon until slightly pink in the middle.
- Serve the salmon on a bed of the vegetable mixture or a green a salad.

56. Citrus Salmon Recipe

Serving: 2 | Prep: | Cook: 12mins | Ready in:

Ingredients

- 2 ea 8 oz. salmon fillets
- 1 lemon, zested and segmented
- 1 orange, zested and segmented
- ½ cup orange juice
- ¼ cup lemon juice
- 1 jalapeño pepper
- 2 tablespoons fresh cilantro, chopped
- 2 sprigs fresh cilantro for garnish
- 2 tablespoons olive oil or vegetable oil

Direction

- Remove skin from salmon fillets; discard.
- Slice 8-10 very thin rounds from the tip of the jalapeño; set aside. Cut remaining pepper in half, remove and discard seeds, then mince.
- Mince lemon and orange zest, then combine in a 1-quart-size Ziploc storage bag with lemon juice, orange juice, jalapeño and cilantro; add salmon fillets, close bag, and set on a plate – marinate in refrigerator for 30 minutes.
- While salmon marinates, heat oven to 400ºF and segment lemon and orange.
- To segment, cut top and bottom off of lemon and orange; stand upright. Using a very sharp knife, run the blade down from top to bottom, removing the white pith. Turn and continue until all pith has been removed. Lay citrus on its side; use blade to cut segments of flesh from between the white membrane; reserve.
- After salmon has marinated, heat 2 tablespoons olive oil in an oven-safe skillet over medium heat. Remove salmon from Ziploc, shake loose excess marinade, and carefully lay each fillet in pan (be careful – oil will pop and sizzle). Cook for 2 minutes, then turn each fillet over; top each with even amounts of lemon and orange segments, then transfer skillet to oven to finish cooking (about 8-10 minutes).
- Remove from oven; use spatula to lift each fillet from pan; place on a plate. Garnish with a fresh sprig of cilantro and thin-shaved pieces of jalapeño. Serve while hot!

---

57. Citrus Salmon With Orange Relish Recipe

Serving: 4 | Prep: | Cook: 15mins | Ready in:

Ingredients

- Citrus Salmon:
- 1/4 cup orange juice
- 2 Tbs. olive oil
- 1 1/2 tps. thyme leaves, divided

- 4 salmon fillets (about 1 pound)
- 1 Tbs. brown sugar
- 1 tps. paprika
- 1/2 tps. salt
- orange Relish:
- 1/2 tps. grated orange peel
- 2 seedless oranges, pelled, sectioned and cut into 1/2 -inch pieces
- 2 Tbs. chopped red bell pepper
- 1 Tbs. honey
- 1 Tbs. chopped red onion
- 1 Tbs. chopped fresh parsley
- 1/2 tps. ground ginger

Direction

- For the Salmon, mix orange juice, oil and 1 tsp. of the thyme in a small bowl. Place salmon in a large resealable plastic bag or glass dish. Add marinade; turn to coat well. Refrigerate 30 minutes or longer for extra flavor. For the Relish, mix all ingredients in medium bowl. Cover. Refrigerate until ready to serve.
- Preheat oven to 400F. Mix brown sugar, paprika, remaining 1/2 tsp. thyme and salt in small bowl. Remove salmon from marinade. Discard any remaining marinade> Rub salmon evenly with paprika mixture. Place salmon on foil-lined baking pan.
- Bake 10 to 15 minutes or until fish flakes easily. Serve salmon with the relish.
- Recipe McCormick & Co ENJOY

---

58. Classic Poached Salmon Recipe

Serving: 10 | Prep: | Cook: 20mins | Ready in:

Ingredients

- Two 2 lb center-cut salmon pieces, bones removed, skin on
- salt and freshly ground pepper
- 12 cups Court Bouillon (recipe follows)
- ==============================
- Garnish

- seedless cucumber
- lemon slices
- watercress
- =============================
- Court Bouillon
- Use this for salmon or other large fish.
- Court Bouillon can be strained after using, refrigerated or frozen up to six months.
- Add water to top it up.
- 12 cups water
- 1 cup dry white wine
- 1/2 cup wine vinegar
- 2 onions, sliced
- 2 carrots, sliced
- 2 bay leaves
- 6 stalks parsley
- 1 tsp dried thyme
- 1 tbsp whole peppercorns

Direction

- Preheat oven to 450°F
- Season each piece of salmon with salt and pepper, and place one on top of the other.
- Measure salmon horizontally at its thickest part.
- Wrap salmon in cheesecloth and place in buttered baking dish.
- Bring court bouillon to boil and pour over fish. It should come three-quarters of the way up the fish.
- Cover dish with foil and place on baking sheet.
- Transfer to oven and cook for 5 minutes per inch.
- Remove from oven, uncover and cool in broth.
- Place on serving platter, using the cheesecloth to help with the transfer.
- Undo cheesecloth and remove top layer of skin.
- Using cheesecloth again, turn salmon over and place skinned side down on serving platter.
- Remove the cheesecloth and top layer of skin.
- Thinly slice cucumber on a mandolin or slicer.
- Bring a pot of water to a boil, immerse cucumber slices and bring back to boil.
- Immediately drain.

- Pat cucumber slices dry.
- Overlap on top of fish to simulate scales.
- Decorate platter with lemon slices and watercress.
- Slice and serve with Green Herb Mayonnaise.
- =============================
- Court Bouillon
- In a large pot on high heat, bring all the ingredients to a boil.
- Reduce heat and simmer for 15 minutes.

59. Coulibiac Of Salmon Recipe

Serving: 8 | Prep: | Cook: 40mins | Ready in:

Ingredients

- Brioche Dough: or use packaged puff pastry sheets if desired.
- 4 to 5 cups flour sifted, I used bread flour
- 1 pkg dry yeast dissolved in 1/2 cup warm water
- 1 Tbs sugar
- 4 eggs
- 1 tbs salt
- 3/4 cup butter, softened to same consisitency of the dough
- Fish:
- One whole poached or baked salmon, seasoned as you like ,about 12 inches long, head, tail removed, deboned and skinned when cold(it will be then about 8 inches of usable fish)
- or use about 6 to 8 salmon filets of even size and thickness
- Mushrooms:
- 1 box, 10 oz mushroooms
- 1 shallot
- butter or olive oil to saute
- salt and pepper and herbs as desired
- Spinach:
- 1 small bunch of fresh spinach: steam or saute with garlic
- salt and pepper

- 1 container of herbed boursin cheese
- 1 cup quinoa prepared and seasoned butter and salt, pepper, fresh grated ginger to taste
- champagne cream sauce: or any hollandaisse or cream sauce of choice
- 1 1/2 cup champagne
- juice of 3 lemons
- 2 tbsp. shallots
- 2 pints heavy cream
- salt, pepper, dash of sugar to taste if desired
- Melted egg wash or butter to brush the dough before baking
- coarse salt to sprinkle over dough (optional)

Direction

- Make the brioche:
- Combine 1 cup flour, dissolved yeast and the sugar adding 1 to 2 more tbsp. of water to make a soft and pliable dough.
- Form into a ball, cut a cross in the top of the dough sand place in bowl, cover with towel and allow to rise in a warm place until double, about 1 hour.
- Meanwhile, in a large mixing bowl with electric mixer with dough hook, combine the remaining 3 cups flour, the eggs, salt and mix low speed until thoroughly blended.
- Then add the softened butter a few pieces at a time until all is well blended into the dough.
- You may need to stop and scrape the dough several times with a spatula when mixing.
- When the yeast mixture has doubled, remove from the bowl; add to the egg mixture and mix to combine either by hand, with a wooden or machine until well combined.
- This dough is not kneaded!
- It will be soft and possible, a bit sticky.
- Cover the dough bowl, and let rise double in a warm place.
- When double punch down, and cover and refrigerate several hours or overnight.
- Under refrigeration, the dough texture becomes more solid and workable.
- Meanwhile, cook the whole fish by your favorite method, cool and chill
- Mushrooms:

- Clean mushrooms, slice and sauté in butter or oil along with some chopped shallots.
- Season to taste.
- Cool and set aside or chill.
- Spinach:
- Wash spinach, drain very well.
- Either sauté in butter or oil with garlic and herbs and set aside or chill.
- Quinoa:
- Cook per package directions, season to taste.
- I like to add some fresh grated ginger, butter, salt and pepper.
- Sauce:
- In a heavy sauce pan over high heat, reduce the first 3 ingredients by half.
- Add cream and reduce until thick.
- Turn down sauce to low heat.
- I also added a dash of sugar to tone down the acidity and added some salt and pepper.
- Assembly: Remember one can prepare all the things a day before.
- Remove the pastry from the refrigerator.
- Roll out to a large rectangle.
- In the center of the rectangle, spread on some of the cooled cook quinoa.
- Add a layer of mushrooms and then some spinach.
- Place on the fish and fill the cavity with the boursin cheese.
- If using fillets, stack the fillets and fill the cheese in between.
- Top the fish again with layers of the quinoa, spinach and mushrooms.
- Now carefully enclose the whole thing with the pastry by bringing one side to the other end to completely cover the fish.
- One can place the pastry stuffed fish seam side down (roll it over), or have the seam in the middle or top; it does not matter as long as the whole thing is well sealed.
- If any brioche dough is leftover, use to decorate top if desired.
- Slit one or two place on top so a bit of steam can escape.

- Brush the whole pastry with either melted butter or an egg wash (egg mixed with cold water.)
- If desired, sprinkle some coarse salt over top of egg wash.
- Carefully lift and place the Coulibiac on a baking pan.
- Let sit about 20 minutes so dough can rise just a bit.
- Bake in a 365 to 375F oven about 30 to 40 minutes or until pastry is golden and puffed.
- To serve: let cool a few minutes.
- Carefully remove to a large serving platter with wide spatulas and present to guests.
- Then carefully slice pieces with a serrated knife and carefully lift pieces onto guests' plates.
- Either pour the sauce of the pieces or serve and pass the pitcher of sauce on the side.
- Leftovers can be gently reheat in the micro or wrapped in foil and oven heated and it's just as wonderful!!!
- Makes 8 *good servings.

60. Creamed Salmon And Asparagus On Garlic Toast Recipe

Serving: 2 | Prep: | Cook: 20mins | Ready in:

Ingredients

- 3 to 6 oz. cooked salmon (or a 3 to 4 oz can)
- 5 tbsp butter, separated (2,1,2)
- I clove garlic, minced
- 1 tbsp olive oil
- 1/2 lb asparagus, trimmed and cut into 1" pieces
- 1 small shallot, chopped
- 2 tbsp flour
- 1 1/2 cup milk
- 1 tbsp Dijon mustard (nice spicy one! I used a horseradish dijon)
- 3/4 tsp dried dill (or 1 tbsp chopped fresh)

- salt and pepper to taste
- 2 thick slices Italian bread
- 2 tbsp chopped fresh parsley or fresh dill

Direction

- Place 2 tbsp. butter in a small saucepan or microwave safe bowl with the garlic. Melt butter and set aside.
- In skillet, melt another 1 tbsp. of butter with 1 tbsp. olive oil. Add chopped shallot and cook for 2 or 3 minutes. Add asparagus and cook until asparagus is tender, but still bright green. Remove asparagus with slotted spoon and set aside. Add remaining 2 tbsp. butter to skillet. When melted, whisk in flour to create a roux. Whisk in milk slowly, and bring to a boil, stirring often. Add mustard, dill, flaked salmon and asparagus, and heat through.
- Meanwhile, brush bread with butter-garlic mixture and toast in toaster oven, under broiler or on a grill pan/griddle until golden.
- Place a slice of bread on each plate, top with some of the asparagus and spoon creamed salmon mixture over top. Garnish with chopped parsley or dill.

61. Creamy Salmon Pockets Recipe

Serving: 4 | Prep: | Cook: 20mins | Ready in:

Ingredients

- 4 fresh salmon steaks
- 4 Tbsp light cream
- 1 tsp fresh dill
- white pepper and salt to taste

Direction

- Rinse salmon steaks under cold running water. Pat dry and season with dill, pepper and salt.
- Prepare 4 aluminum foil, each big enough to largely hold one piece of fish.

- Arrange seasoned fish in the middle of the aluminum foil and pour 1 Tbsp. of cream on top of each steak.
- Loosely close foil over the fish, forming pockets.
- Place pockets on a baking sheet and bake in preheated 375°F oven for about 20 minutes, until fish flakes easily with a fork.

62. Creamy Salmon With Green Beans Recipe

Serving: 4 | Prep: | Cook: 20mins | Ready in:

Ingredients

- 1 large salmon fillet (about 3/4 pound)
- 2 tablespoons butter or margarine
- 1 large ripe tomato, cut into 1/2-inch pieces
- 1 small onion, coarsely chopped
- 2 tablespoons all-purpose flour
- 1 cup vegetable or chicken broth
- 1 package (9 ounces) frozen cut green beans, partially thawed
- 1 cup half-and-half
- 1/4 teaspoon salt
- 1/4 teaspoon white pepper
- 5 tablespoons grated parmesan cheese, divided
- Hot cooked angel hair pasta

Direction

- 1. Rinse salmon and pat dry with paper towels. Remove skin and bones; discard. Cut salmon into 3/4-inch pieces.
- 2. Heat wok over medium-high heat 1 minute or until hot. Add butter. Swirl to coat bottom; heat 30 seconds. Add salmon; stir-fry gently 3 to 4 minutes or until fish flakes easily when tested with fork. Remove to large bowl; cover and keep warm.
- 3. Add tomato and onion to wok; stir-fry about 5 minutes or until onion is tender. Stir in flour until well mixed. Increase heat to high. Stir in

broth and beans; cook until sauce boils and thickens. Add salmon, half-and-half, salt and pepper; cook until heated through. Add half of cheese; toss until well mixed. Spoon salmon mixture over angel hair pasta. Sprinkle with remaining cheese. Garnish as desired.

63. Crispy Grilled Salmon Recipe

Serving: 6 | Prep: | Cook: 10mins | Ready in:

Ingredients

- 2 Pounds fresh salmon fillet, skin on
- 1 cup light cream
- 2 tbs. mayo
- salt and pepper
- 1 tsp. dried dill weed
- lemons
- Seasonings:
- 2 tbs peppercorn melody
- 1 tsp. coriander seed
- 1 tsp. dill seed
- 2 tsp. kosher salt

Direction

- Preheat grill
- Soak fish in cream for 30 minutes. Meanwhile place all the seasonings (only the seasonings under seasoning category) in a plastic bag and pound them with a mallet to crack them open. Remove fish from cream. Spread mayo on both sides of the fish. On the skin side season with salt and pepper. On the flesh side sprinkle with the dill weed and rub the crushed seasoning into the flesh. All the flesh should be covered with mayo and seasonings generously.
- Grill fish first seasoned side down 5-7 minutes, then 5-7 minutes on other side. Fish is done when it flakes with a fork. Remove and squeeze desired amount of lemon juice on it....and enjoy!

64. Crispy Baked Salmon Recipe

Serving: 4 | Prep: | Cook: 12mins | Ready in:

Ingredients

- 1 cup cornflakes, crushed
- 1/3 cup flour
- 1 egg
- 1/4 cup skim milk
- 4 (4 ounce) salmon fillets
- salt and pepper

Direction

- Preheat oven to 450-degrees.
- Cut each filet into two or three pieces.
- Place flour and Cornflakes in two, separate shallow containers.
- Whisk egg and milk and place in another shallow container.
- Season fish with salt and pepper.
- Dredge in flour and shake off excess.
- Dip fish in the milk mixture, then coat with Cornflakes on all sides.
- Place fish on baking sheet sprayed with nonstick cooking spray and bake at 450-degrees for eight to ten minutes per 1-inch of thickness or until flakes easily with fork.

65. Crock Pot Salmon Bake Recipe

Serving: 6 | Prep: | Cook: 360mins | Ready in:

Ingredients

- 3 pounds canned salmon
- 4 cups bread crumbs
- 1 pound canned tomatoes in puree
- 1 green pepper chopped
- 3 teaspoons lemon juice
- 1 can condensed cream of onion soup
- 2 chicken bouillon cubes crushed
- 6 eggs well beaten
- 1 can condensed cream of celery soup
- 1/2 cup milk

Direction

- Grease removable liner well. Combine all ingredients except celery soup and milk then place in liner pan then place liner in base. Cover and cook on low for 6 hours. Combine cream of celery soup with 1/2 cup milk and heat in saucepan. Use as sauce for salmon bake.

66. DEVILED SALMON CAKES Recipe

Serving: 4 | Prep: | Cook: 20mins | Ready in:

Ingredients

- 1 14 oz. can pink salmon, drained, skin and bones removed
- 2 Large eggs
- ½ cup diced sweet onion
- ½ cup diced yellow bell pepper (or any other color)
- 1 tsp minced garlic
- ½ tsp ground cumin
- ¼ to ½ tsp sea salt
- 1/8 to ¼ tsp ground cayenne pepper
- 2 cups cooked jasmine rice (or any sticky rice, leftover rice that will bind well)
- vegetable oil, or lard for frying - ¼ inch in frying pan or enough to cover half of your patty …I use lard…no apologies…

Direction

- Heat oil in skillet on Medium High heat.
- Mix salmon and rice together until thoroughly blended then add eggs.
- Add onion and pepper and mix well.
- Add spices.

- I use my hands and fingers to make sure everything is evenly distributed.
- When oil is hot form into patties in the palm of your hand.
- I made mine about 3 inches in diameter and not very thick (about the thickness of a hamburger patty)
- Place in hot oil and fry about 7 minutes on each side or until golden brown.
- When served fresh they are very crispy on the outside and moist on the inside.
- Awesome with Pinto Beans and Creamed Potatoes and skillet corn bread.
- Would also be great with a black bean and corn salsa.
- Serves 4 as main course or 12 as appetizers, depending on size of cake.

67. Dijon Salmon Recipe

Serving: 2 | Prep: | Cook: 20mins | Ready in:

Ingredients

- 1/4 cup of butter (melted)
- 3 Tblsp of Dijon mustard
- 1 1/2 Tblsp of honey
- 1/4 cup of dry bread crumbs
- 1/4 cup of finely chopped pecans
- 4 tsp chopped fresh parsley
- 4 (4oz.) fillets of salmon
- 1 lemon for garnish (optional)
- salt & pepper to taste

Direction

- (Preheat oven to 400F.)
- In a small bowl, stir together butter, mustard and honey, set aside.
- In a food processor or blender put together the breadcrumbs, the pecans and the parsley.
- Hit the chop first to crumble the pecans and then grind to reach a thinner texture (like sand) or like a thick powder.

- Once you reach that point, transfer to a bowl and set aside.
- Season the salmon fillets with salt & pepper and then brush each one lightly with honey mustard mixture.
- Sprinkle evenly the top of the fillets with the prepared breadcrumb mixture.
- Bake salmon uncovered in preheated oven until it flakes easily with a fork, approximately 10 to 15 minutes. (Always remember that salmon cooks really quick).
- Garnish with a wedge of lemon if desired.
- Serve with mashed potatoes, steamed veggies, creamed spinach or pasta salad.

68. Dill Salmon Topped Potatoes Recipe

Serving: 4 | Prep: | Cook: 30mins | Ready in:

Ingredients

- dill salmon Topped potatoes
- 15-1/2 ounce can salmon with liquid
- 2 tablespoons butter
- 2 tablespoons flour
- 3/4 cup evaporated milk undiluted
- 1/3 cup water
- 1 tablespoon instant minced onion
- 2 teaspoons spicy mustard
- 1/2 teaspoon dill weed
- 1/4 teaspoon salt
- 1/2 cup grated swiss cheese
- 4 baked potatoes

Direction

- Drain salmon reserving 1/4 cup liquid.
- Remove skin and bones from salmon and set aside.
- Melt butter in medium saucepan then stir in flour until well blended.
- Gradually stir in evaporated milk, water and reserved salmon liquid into butter mixture.

- Stir in onion, mustard, dill weed and salt then cook over medium heat stirring constantly until mixture comes to a boil and thickens.
- Stir in cheese until melted.
- Stir reserved salmon into cheese sauce and heat to serving temperature.
- Serve over split baked potatoes.

69. Earl Grey Salmon Recipe

Serving: 2 | Prep: | Cook: 10mins | Ready in:

Ingredients

- 2 6-ounce salmon steaks or fillets
- 3 ounces Earl Grey tea leaves
- 4 cups boiling water
- salt and pepper
- fresh lemon wedges (optional)

Direction

- Steep the tea in the boiling water for 10 minutes.
- Strain half of the tea leaves into a marinating container of some sort (with lid is great) and place the salmon pieces on top of the tea leaves.
- Strain the other half of the tea leaves on top of the salmon pieces.
- Spoon about 6 tbsps. of the steeped tea into the marinating container and cover.
- Marinate in the fridge for about 6 hours, turning the salmon pieces once or twice.
- The salmon can then be seasoned with salt and pepper and grilled, broiled or pan fried. A 6-ounce salmon fillet takes approximately 3 minutes per side to cook; a steak takes less than that, so watch carefully and don't overcook. It is cooked when it is no longer transparent in the middle.
- Serve with fresh lemon wedges. Anything else would mask the subtle flavour of the tea.

70. Easy Salmon Patties Recipe

Serving: 4 | Prep: | Cook: 10mins | Ready in:

Ingredients

- 1 15 oz. can red or pink salmon, bones removed
- 2 Tbs minced onion
- 1 Tbs. minced fresh parsley
- 1 large egg
- salt, pepper, dry dillweed to taste
- some fresh squeezed lemon juice
- Enough fresh bread crumbs to bind: try Japanese honey flavored panko breadcrumbs
- oil to sauté (peanut oil is nice)

Direction

- Combine everything and add enough breadcrumbs to bind mixture.
- Form into patties. These may be made ahead of time and chilled.
- Tip: chilling recommended so patties hold together better
- They fry in hot oil until golden on both sides. Turning carefully
- Serve with tartar sauce or mango mayo
- Note: by changing the herbs and spices (example add cilantro, ginger) one can easily change flavor

71. Easy Alaskan Salmon Teriyaki Bowl Recipe

Serving: 3 | Prep: | Cook: 15mins | Ready in:

Ingredients

- 1 (14.75-ounce) can Alaska salmon
- 1 cup instant or quick-cooking rice
- 1 tablespoon canola oil
- 1 (16-ounce) package frozen stir-fry vegetables

- 1/2 cup prepared thick teriyaki sauce
- 1/4 teaspoon red pepper flakes
- 1/4 teaspoon sesame oil
- 1/4 teaspoon ground ginger

Direction

- Prepare Rice according to package
- Drain salmon, dry and break into chunks, reserve 1 tablespoon of the liquid
- In a skillet or wok heat up the oil, and add veggies
- After about a minute add teriyaki sauce and salmon liquid and stir
- Add sesame oil, ginger, and red pepper flakes and salmon. Cook until vegetables are tender (about 3-5 minutes)
- Serve with rice

72. Easy Baked Alaska Salmon Recipe

Serving: 4 | Prep: | Cook: 25mins | Ready in:

Ingredients

- 1 whole salmon fillet
- 1 lemon
- 1 tbs dill
- 1 Tbs fresh parsley
- 1/4 cup mayonnaise
- salt & pepper to taste
- 1 onion, sliced
- 1 cup of your favorite white wine

Direction

- Spray large baking dish with Pam.
- Put fillet in pan; salt and pepper lightly. Season with dill and parsley. Spread mayonnaise over fillet. Place onion slices on top and squeeze fresh lemon over top.
- Pour your favorite wine in the bottom of the pan and cover.

- Bake at 350 for approximately 20-30 minutes or until salmon flakes.

73. Easy Brown Sugar Salmon Recipe

Serving: 2 | Prep: | Cook: 15mins | Ready in:

Ingredients

- 2 salmon filets, fresh or frozen (thawed)
- 2 Tablespoons olive oil
- 2 Tablespoons dark brown sugar
- dash of cajun seasoning
- salt and pepper to taste

Direction

- Salt, pepper, and dash of Cajun seasoning on each side of salmon filets. Then pack the brown sugar on all sides of meat. In a skillet (I use cast iron), heat olive oil on medium heat, then add the salmon filets. Add about 1/2 cup water and cover and turn to med/low heat...as the water/brown sugar mixture thickens, spoon onto to salmon while cooking. Turn salmon once during cooking and cover again.

74. Easy Country Salmon Cakes Croquettes N Lemon Sauce Recipe

Serving: 4 | Prep: | Cook: 10mins | Ready in:

Ingredients

- Easy Country salmon cakes Croquettes n lemon Sauce
- 1 - 7 1/2 ounce can salmon, drained and flaked
- 1/3 cup of saltine cracker crumbs
- 1 egg, slightly beaten
- 2 tablespoons of chopped onion

- 2 tablespoons of milk
- 1 tablespoon of lemon juice
- 2 tablespoons butter or margarine
- In medium bowl, combine all ingredients except the butter, and blend well. Shape the mixture into 4 patties. Melt
- the butter in a skillet and fry the patties on both sides until golden brown and heated throughout
- lemon SAUCE:
- 1 c. lemon or orange juice
- 2 tbsp. cornstarch diluted in 1/4 c. cold water
- Bring all ingredients to a rolling boil in saucepan. Cook until sauce is clear. Serve hot over salmon croquettes.

Direction

- In medium bowl, combine all ingredients except the butter, and blend well.
- Shape the mixture into 4 patties.
- Melt the butter in a skillet and fry the patties on both sides until golden brown and heated throughout.
- LEMON SAUCE:
- 1 c. lemon or orange juice
- 2 tbsp. cornstarch diluted in 1/4 c. cold water
- Bring all ingredients to a rolling boil in saucepan. Cook until sauce is clear. Serve hot over or with salmon croquettes.

75. Easy Grilled Whole Salmon Recipe

Serving: 6 | Prep: | Cook: 30mins | Ready in:

Ingredients

- Whole salmon, cleaned, head and tailed removed
- Fresh sliced lemons to cover length of fish
- Fresh lemon wedges for serving
- mayonnaise (not Miracle Whip -- too sweet)

Direction

- Preheat grill to medium-high.
- Slather the inside of the fish with mayonnaise and stuff with lemon slices and wrap in two layers of heavy aluminum foil.
- Grill for 20 to 30 minutes, depending on size of fish. (Fish is done when no longer opaque.) Do not overcook (although mayo will keep the fish from drying out).
- To serve, remove from tinfoil, lay fish open on a large platter and remove lemon slices. Garnish the platter with fresh lemon slices and allow guests to serve themselves.

76. Easy Roast Salmon With Veggies Recipe

Serving: 3 | Prep: | Cook: 35mins | Ready in:

Ingredients

- 3 salmon steaks
- 9 onions
- 3 carrots
- 1 c. marinated mushrooms
- 1/2 c. olive oil
- glass of water
- juice of 1 lemon
- salt
- pepper
- 2 tblsp Trinidad hot sauce
- oregano

Direction

- Place the 3 salmon steaks on the tray
- Cut the 9 onions in halves place face down around the steaks, together with three carrots sliced in half across the center, and a cup of marinated mushrooms.
- pour half a cup of Olive Oil, a glass of water, the juice of one lemon, salt and pepper, 2 tablespoons of Trinidad Hot Sauce and a pinch of oregano over the salmon

- Cover the tray with foil and bake for 30 minutes at 375 degrees. When just about ready turn the salmon upside down
- Separate the layers of the onions and bake a little bit more until the water evaporates and the steaks are a golden colour

77. Elaines Bbqd Salmon Steaks With Key Lime Balsamic Honey Reduction Recipe

Serving: 4 | Prep: | Cook: 20mins | Ready in:

Ingredients

- 4 salmon steaks
- 10 key limes
- 1 clove garlic, minced
- 3 tbsp honey
- 2 tbsp balsamic vinegar
- salt and pepper
- key lime for garnish
- fresh parsley

Direction

- In a cooking pot, combine:
- 10 halved key limes
- Minced garlic
- Honey
- Vinegar
- Bring to a boil and reduce this liquid to ½ the original volume
- The salmon steaks:
- Drizzle the salmon steaks with olive oil, salt and pepper
- On high heat setting, grill the steaks, giving a one-quarter turn after 5 minutes for the grate marks
- Turn the fish, and drizzle with olive oil, salt and pepper, on the other side
- Pour the reduction over the finished salmon steaks
- Garnish:

- Halved key lime with fresh sprig of parsley

78. Elaines HEALTHY Salmon Tortilla Wraps Recipe

Serving: 2 | Prep: | Cook: | Ready in:

Ingredients

- 1 can red salmon
- butter for spreading
- 1 whole lemon, peeled and cut thinly into slices
- 2 green onions, finely chopped
- 1 baby red onion, finely chopped
- 1 tbsp Zesty Italian salad dressing
- 2 large leaves romaine lettuce, trimmed of center leaf vein
- 2 10 inch tortillas, whole wheat

Direction

- Butter the tortillas
- Add to the salmon:
- The onions
- The salad dressing
- Combine well.
- Spread the salmon over the tortilla, leaving about 1 inch free space around the edges. This makes it easier to roll, and eliminates spill over.
- Now, add three thin slices of fresh lemon
- Add the trimmed Romaine lettuce
- Roll the tortilla into a neat, tight bundle.
- Refrigerate until ready to use, or serve immediately.
- Delicious

79. Elaines Skewered Salmon And Whitefish With Steak Recipe

Serving: 4 | Prep: | Cook: 60mins | Ready in:

Ingredients

- ½ lb wild Pacific salmon fillets
- ½ lb Whitefish fillets
- ¼ lb beef fillets
- ½ lb chinese noodles (vermicelli)
- salt & pepper to taste
- 1 cup chicken broth
- lemon wedges or 'Real Lemon juice' to taste

Direction

- Place the fillets on top of parchment paper.
- Place beef fillets in a separate piece of parchment
- Cook both together as illustrated…. @ 325*F until fish is opaque and beef is tender
- In the interim, cook the vermicelli in the chicken broth until tender.
- Turn the pieces of fish and beef only once.
- NOTE:
- The reason I cook these in separate parchment pieces is to prevent allergy crossing. Some people are allergic to beef, and some are allergic to fish.
- This method ensures even cooking without danger of cross-contamination of either ingredient.
- Served on a bed of fresh Vermicelli, this dish is a hearty, healthy, delicious main!
- Veggies alongside could well include leafy greens, with fresh carrots, your imagination is the only thing you need!
- ENJOY!
- NOTE:
- Vermicelli can be boiled, deep-fried, sautéed, whatever you desire.
- In this recipe, I cooked it in chicken broth.

80. Elegant Salmon Recipe

Serving: 8 | Prep: | Cook: 15mins | Ready in:

Ingredients

- 1Tbs. chopped chives
- 1Tbs herbs de provence
- 1tsp salt
- 1/2tsp black pepper,divided
- 2tsp chopped garlic
- 1c sparkling wine
- 1tsp dried thyme
- 2Tbs capers

Direction

- Heat oven to 450. In small bowl, combine chives, herbes de provence, salt and 1/4tsp black pepper. Place salmon, skin side down, on greased broiler rack; sprinkle with herb mixture. Roast 15 mins. or till salmon fillet flakes easily with a fork.
- Meanwhile, in large non-stick skillet over med-high heat, cook 1Tbs butter 30 seconds or till melted. Add chopped garlic. Cook 1 min or till golden brown, stirring occasionally. Stir in sparkling wine; cook 2 mins. Add dried thyme and remaining black pepper
- Remove skillet from heat. Add capers and remaining butter stirring till butter is completely melted. Arrange salmon on serving platter. Top with sauce
- Wine tip: A white like the 2007 Columbia Winery Cellar master's Riesling ($12) accentuates the herb notes of the salmon but any Riesling will do.

81. FIRECRACKER SALMON STEAKS Recipe

Serving: 4 | Prep: | Cook: 20mins | Ready in:

Ingredients

- Ingredients:
- ¼ cup balsamic vinegar
- ¼ cup chili sauce
- ¼ cup packed brown sugar
- 3 garlic cloves, minced
- 2 tsp. Minced fresh parsley

- ¼ tsp. ground ginger or 1tsp. Minced fresh gingerroot
- ¼ to ½ tsp. cayenne pepper
- ¼ to ½ tsp. crushed red pepper flakes, optional
- 4 salmon steaks (6-oz each)

Direction

- In a small bowl, combine the first 8 ingredients. If grilling the salmon, coat grilling rack with non-stick cooking spray before starting the grill. Grill salmon, un-covered, over medium heat or broil 4 – 6-inches from the heat for 4 – 5 minutes on each side or until fish flakes easily with a fork, brushing occasionally with sauce.
- Serving size: 1 steak
- Nutrition Values: Calories per serving: 373, Fat: 17g, Cholesterol: 106mg, Sodium: 565mg, Carbohydrate: 22g, Protein: 32g
- Diabetic Exchanges: 5 lean meat, 1 ½ starch
- NOTE: This recipe is Diabetic Friendly, Gastric Bypass friendly, and for anyone.

82. Fabulous Salmon Provencal Recipe

Serving: 4 | Prep: | Cook: 12mins | Ready in:

Ingredients

- Here's a salmon dish made for summer.
- salmon Provencal Recipe
- 3 large plum tomatoes
- 3 shallots, coarsely chopped
- 1 Tbsp coarsely chopped fresh tarragon
- 1 Tbsp coarsely chopped fresh basil
- 1 Tbsp coarsely chopped fresh chives
- 1 Tbsp fresh lemon juice
- 1 Tbsp balsamic vinegar
- salt
- 2 Tbsp olive oil
- 4 salmon fillets, about 5-6 ounces each

Direction

- Preheat oven to 400°F.
- Blanch the tomatoes by plunging them into a pot of simmering salted water for 15-30 seconds, then plunging them into ice water for 1 minute. Drain the tomatoes and peel off and discard the skin. Cut the tomatoes into quarters, remove the core, seeds, and dice the flesh.
- In a large bowl combine the tomatoes, shallots, tarragon, basil, and chives. In another bowl, whisk together the lemon juice, vinegar, olive oil and salt to taste. Add to the tomato mixture, toss to coat.
- Arrange salmon fillets on an oiled baking sheet without crowding. Drizzle with olive oil and season lightly with salt. Bake until salmon is barely cooked through and lightly browned on the edges, 10-12 minutes.
- To serve, spoon a couple tablespoons of the tomato mixture over each fillet. Serve immediately.

83. Farfalle With Smoked Salmon And Lemon Sauce Recipe

Serving: 6 | Prep: | Cook: 15mins | Ready in:

Ingredients

- 1/2 c. canola oil
- 6 cloves garlic, finely chopped
- 1/2 c. chopped onion
- 1 lb. farfalle pasta (bow tie)
- 3 TB fresh lemon juice
- 1/2 c. chopped scallions
- 1/4 c. chopped Italian parsley
- 1/2 lb. sliced smoked salmon
- salt and pepper
- Thin sliced lemons

Direction

- Heat canola oil in a skillet over low heat.
- Add the garlic and onion; cook until soft; set aside.

- Cook farfalle according to package directions and drain well.
- Put the pasta back into the pot it was cooked in.
- Add the garlic and onion mixture and mix well.
- Add lemon juice, scallions, parsley and salmon and mix well again.
- Season to taste with salt and pepper.
- Garnish with a sprig of parsley and thin lemon slices.

84. Firecracker Grilled Alaskan Salmon Recipe

Serving: 4 | Prep: | Cook: 20mins | Ready in:

Ingredients

- 4 salmon steaks
- 1/4 cup peanut oil
- 2 tablespoons soy sauce
- 2 tablespoons balsamic vinegar
- 2 tablespoons chopped scallions
- 1-1/2 teaspoons brown sugar
- 1 clove garlic minced
- 3/4 teaspoon grated fresh ginger root
- 2 teaspoons red chili flakes
- 1/2 teaspoon sesame oil
- 1/8 teaspoon salt

Direction

- Place the salmon steaks in a glass dish.
- Whisk together the remaining ingredients and pour over salmon.
- Cover with plastic wrap and marinate in refrigerator for 6 hours.
- Heat grill then remove salmon from marinade.
- Brush grill with oil and place salmon on grill.
- Grill salmon over medium for 10 minutes per inch of thickness.
- Turn halfway through cooking.

85. Firecracker Salmon Steaks Recipe

Serving: 4 | Prep: | Cook: 10mins | Ready in:

Ingredients

- 1/4 cup balsamic vinegar
- 1/4 cup chili sauce
- 1/4 cup packed brown sugar
- 3 garlic cloves, minced
- 2 teaspoons minced fresh parsley
- 1 teaspoon minuced fresh gingerroot
- 1/4 to 1/2 teaspoon cayenne pepper
- 1/4 to 1/2 teaspoon crushed red pepper flakes, optional
- 4 salmon steaks (6 oz each)

Direction

- Coat grill rack with non-stick cooking spray before starting the grill. In a small bowl, combine the vinegar, chili sauce, sugar, garlic, parsley and seasonings.
- Grill salmon, covered over medium heat for 4-5 minutes on each side or until fish flakes easily with a fork, brushing occasionally with sauce.

86. Fish In Tomato Rhubarb N Blood Orange Sauce Recipe

Serving: 8 | Prep: | Cook: 65mins | Ready in:

Ingredients

- For the sauce
- 3 medium blood oranges (or 2 large, juicy navel oranges)
- 2 tablespoons olive oil
- 2 cups finely chopped onion
- 1 1/2 teaspoons fresh ginger, peeled and finely minced

- 1 tablespoon honey, orange blossom or other light floral flavor
- salt and freshly ground black pepper
- 1 pound rhubarb, ends trimmed (discard leaves, which can be toxic), tough strings removed with a vegetable peeler, and stalks cut into 1-inch pieces (4 cups)
- 1 cup fresh orange juice
- Generous pinch of ground cinnamon
- 2 cups canned, peeled plum tomatoes (about a pound), coarsely chopped, and 1/2 cup of their liquid.
- juice of 1/2 lemon
- -----------------
- For the fish
- ---------------
- 3 pounds fish fillets or steaks (salmon, red snapper, grouper, sea bass, halibut, cod or sole)
- 1/3 to 1/2 cup mint leaves, finely minced for garnish

Direction

- Make the sauce

87. Five Spice Salmon With Cabbage And Bacon Recipe

Serving: 4 | Prep: | Cook: 20mins | Ready in:

Ingredients

- FIVE spice salmon WITH cabbage & bacon
- 4 8oz skinless salmon filets
- 3 T. extra virgin olive oil
- 1 t. crushed garlic
- 1 T. crushed ginger
- 1 T. dark brown sugar
- 2 t. five-spice powder
- sea salt to taste
- cayenne pepper to taste
- 1 T. butter
- 6 slices bacon

- 1 head of green cabbage
- ½ c. chicken stock

Direction

- 1) Make a paste of 3T Olive Oil
- 1 t Crushed Garlic
- 1 T Crushed Ginger
- 1 T Brown Sugar
- 2 t Five Spice Powder
- Salt & Cayenne to taste
- 2) Coat 4 Salmon Filets with the marinade. Cover and refrigerate for 1hour, making sure that the paste is all over the filets during the marinating process
- 3) Melt 1 T Butter and pan fry 6 slices Bacon until chewy.
- 4) Remove half of the Bacon Fat and the Bacon. Drain and chop the Bacon and add back.
- 5) Add ½ c Chicken Stock.
- 6) Add 1 head Cabbage, cored and thinly shredded.
- 7) Add Salt & Pepper to taste. And cook covered over low heat for about 5 minutes, stirring a couple of times. The Cabbage should be crisp, tender.
- 8) Grill salmon with paste adhered on a George Foreman indoor grill for 4 minutes. Alternatively, you could broil the salmon. The George Foreman is better as it cooks both sides at the same time and thus keeps it moister.
- 9) Serve Salmon on a bed of Baconated Cabbage.
- Serves 4

88. Flaked Salmon Tartare Recipe

Serving: 6 | Prep: | Cook: 15mins | Ready in:

Ingredients

- 1 large egg
- 1 pound salmon fillet, skinned
- 1 tablespoon extra-virgin olive oil
- 1 ¼ teaspoons coarse salt

- freshly ground pepper
- 2 teaspoons fresh lemon juice, plus wedges for garnish
- dash of hot sauce
- 1 small shallot, finely chopped
- 1 tablespoon chopped drained capers
- 3 cornichons, coarsely chopped
- 2 tablespoons finely chopped chives
- 1 tablespoon finely chopped fresh flat-leaf parsley

Direction

- Place egg in a small saucepan, and cover with cold water by 1 inch. Bring to a boil. Remove from heat. Cover, and let stand 13 minutes. Using a slotted spoon, remove egg, and rinse under cold water until cool. Gently press against a hard surface to crack shell; peel. Cut egg in half lengthwise. Grate each half on the small holes of a grater into a small bowl. Cover with plastic wrap; set aside.
- Preheat oven to 350 degrees. Place salmon in a 13x9 inch baking dish. Brush with 1 teaspoon oil; season with 1 teaspoon salt and ¼ teaspoon pepper. Cover with foil; bake until salmon is cooked through and flakes easily, about 15 minutes. Uncover partially, and let cool slightly in dish on a wire rack. Using a fork, gently flake salmon into large pieces. Transfer to a large bowl.
- Whisk together lemon juice, hot sauce, and remaining ¼ teaspoon salt in a bowl. Add remaining 2 teaspoons oil, whisking until emulsified. Drizzle dressing over salmon, and toss gently. Divide among plates. Scatter shallot, capers, cornichons, chives, parsley, and egg over each dividing evenly, season with pepper. Serve with lemon wedges.

89. Fresh Caught Recipe

Serving: 4 | Prep: | Cook: 13mins | Ready in:

Ingredients

- 4 salmon steaks,thick cut(do not skin,leave it on)
- 4 Tablespoons butter,melted
- 2 Tablespoons fresh lemon juice
- ~Sauce~
- 1 green onion,chopped,fine
- fresh tarragon leaves,small handful,chopped,fine
- 3 Tablespoon white wine vinegar
- 1 Fresh egg
- 1 teaspoon Dijon mustard
- 1 Tablespoon fresh lemon juice
- 1 Tablespoon tomato paste(gives a nice color)
- 1 Cup butter,hot
- Chopped fresh herbs(your choice)

Direction

- Pat salmon dry, brush each side with butter; drizzle with lemon juice.
- Place in baking dish, bake in a 375-degree oven for about 7 minutes, turn carefully and brush with pan drippings.
- Bake for another 5 minutes (do not cook too long).
- Combine the green onion, tarragon and vinegar in saucepan.
- Boil until reduced to about 2 teaspoons, to really intensify the flavor.
- With blender going, combine the onion mixture, egg, mustard, lemon juice and tomato paste.
- Slowly drizzle in the hot butter, and process until thick and smooth.
- ~Serve Salmon steaks with the sauce, buttered and dilled, small red potatoes, wakame salad, fresh lemon slices~

90. Fresh Salmon Burgers Recipe

Serving: 4 | Prep: | Cook: 15mins | Ready in:

Ingredients

- 1 1/2 pounds skinless salmon filet, cut into large chunks
- 2 tablespoons capers, chopped
- Grated peel of half a lemon (lemon half reserved for squeezing)
- 1/3 cup finely chopped flat-leaf parsley (a generous handful)
- 2 teaspoons seafood seasoning
- salt and pepper
- 1 tablespoon extra-virgin olive oil (EVOO)
- 1/4 seedless cucumber, chopped
- 2 plum tomatoes, seeded and chopped
- 1/2 small red onion, finely chopped
- 1/2 cup Dijon mustard
- 3 tablespoons fresh dill, finely chopped
- 4 kaiser rolls, split
- 4 red-leaf lettuce leaves
- Hot stuff
- Add horseradish to the dill mustard.

Direction

- Using a food processor, coarsely chop the salmon; transfer to a bowl. Mix in the capers, lemon peel, parsley and seafood seasoning and season with salt and pepper. Form into 4 patties.
- Preheat the broiler. In a non-stick skillet, heat the EVOO, 1 turn of the pan, over medium-high heat. Add the patties and cook for 4 minutes on each side.
- Meanwhile, in a small bowl, combine the cucumber, tomatoes and red onion. In another small bowl, mix the mustard with the dill.
- Toast the rolls under the broiler and slather each side with the mustard-dill sauce. Squeeze the lemon half over the cooked burgers. Set a lettuce leaf and burger on each roll bottom and top with tomato-cucumber relish and a roll top.

91. Garam Masala Seared Salmon With A Coconut Curry Butter Recipe

Serving: 8 | Prep: | Cook: 25mins | Ready in:

Ingredients

- 8 ea., 7 oz. salmon fillets
- 2 Tbsp. prepared garam masala spice mixture
- kosher salt to taste
- 3-4 Tbsp. oil for frying
- For the sauce:
- 3/4 c. dry white wine
- 1/3 c. heavy cream
- 2/3 c. Premium unsweetened coconut milk
- 2 Tbsp. Indian curry powder
- 2 bay leaves
- 3-4 cloves
- 1 c. cold unsalted butter, cut into small cubes
- kosher salt to taste

Direction

- In a saucepan, combine all of the ingredients for the sauce except for the butter and salt. Bring to light boil, then reduce to a simmer and cook until the sauce reduces to 1/2 cup. Turn the heat down to low, then whisk in the butter until it is incorporated into the sauce. Do NOT let the sauce boil at this point. Season to taste and reserve.
- Keep the sauce warm.
- Pre-heat oven to 400 F. In an oven proof sauté pan or heavy skillet, heat the oil until lightly smoking. Season both sides of the fish with salt and sprinkle with the garam-masala. Pan sear for approximately 1 minute per side, then finish cooking in the oven for about 6-7 minutes, or until desired doneness is achieved. Serve immediately with the coconut-curry butter.

92. Garlic Salmon Linguine Recipe

Serving: 6 | Prep: | Cook: 30mins | Ready in:

Ingredients

- 1 package (16 oz) linguine
- 3 garlic cloves, minced
- 1/3 cup olive or vegetable oil
- 1 can (14 3/4 oz) salmon, drained, bones and skin removed
- 3/4 cup chicken broth
- 1/4 cup minced fresh parsley
- 1/2 teaspoon salt
- 1/8 teaspoon cayenne pepper

Direction

- Cook linguine according to package directions. Meanwhile, in a large skillet, sauté garlic in oil. Stir in salmon, broth, parsley, salt and cayenne. Cook until heated through. Drain linguine; add to the salmon mixture and toss to coat.

93. Gingered Salmon In Carrot And Orange Sauce Recipe

Serving: 4 | Prep: | Cook: 15mins | Ready in:

Ingredients

- 1.5 lb salmon fillet skinned and without bones
- 1 + 1/4 cups fresh carrot juice*
- 1/2 cup (minus 1 Tbsp) freshly squeezed orange juice
- Juice of 1/2 lemon
- 1/2 cup butter, cold
- 3 inch fresh ginger root
- 3 scallions
- 1/4 cup unsalted peanuts, coarsely chopped
- 1 Tbsp canola oil
- 1 Tbsp olive oil
- A dash of cayenne pepper
- Fleur de sel (or seasalt)
- 2 cups cleaned snow peas, or sugar snap peas and rice to accompany
- 1 cup bean sprouts to garnish
- Note
- ____
- It's advised that you make your own fresh carrot juice if you have a juicer (mine is the Juiceman Juicer), it is so much better. You will never go back to store-bought carrot juice!

Direction

- To prepare the sauce, start by slicing half of the ginger in small pieces.
- Pour the carrot juice in a small pot with the slices of ginger.
- Bring to a light boil, then simmer and cook until the juice is reduced by half.
- Add the orange juice and repeat the process.
- Remove from the heat and take out the ginger slices.
- Add the cold butter in small pieces mixing with a whip and add the lemon juice. Keep warm on the side.
- To prepare the garnish, start by cleaning the scallions. Cut them in diagonal. Blanch them in salted boiling water for 2 min. Remove and strain on paper towels.
- Chop the nuts coarsely and chop the ginger thinly.
- Mix all ingredients with 1 Tbsp. canola oil and keep on the side.
- To prepare the fish, dice the salmon in one inch squares.
- Heat 1 to 2 Tbsp. of olive oil in a non-stick frying pan. When the oil is hot, add the pieces of fish and cook lightly for 1 min on one side, then on the other. Do not overcook the fish as it should actually stay rosé, that is a little undercooked.
- Add a pinch of cayenne pepper.
- To assemble your dish, take warm plates and place some fish pieces in the middle. Pour some orange sauce around.
- Sprinkle with fleur de sel (sea salt) and add the peanut/scallions mixture on top.

- Serve with jasmine rice and steamed snow (or sugar snap) peas.

GROUND BLACK PEPPER AND GARNISH WITH PARMESAN SHAVINGS AND HERS.
- ENJOY!

94. Gnocchi With A Gorgonzola And Smoked Salmon Sauce Recipe

Serving: 4 | Prep: | Cook: 25mins | Ready in:

Ingredients

- 30ML butter
- 180G gorgonzola, CRUMBLED
- PINCH ground nutmeg
- 45ML brandy (OPTIONAL)
- 190ML chicken stock
- 250 CREAM
- 500G READY-MADE gnocchi
- olive oil, FOR DRIZZLING
- 100G smoked salmon, SLICED
- PARMESON cheese AND fresh herbs, TO SERVE

Direction

- MELT THE BUTTER IN A LARGE POT
- ADD THE GORGONZOLA CHEESE AND STIR UNTIL IT HAS MELTED
- ADD THE NUTMEG, BRANDY AND THE CHICKEN STOCK, THEN WHISK IN THE CREAM
- BRING TO THE BOIL
- PLACE THE GNOCCHI IN A LARGE PAN AND DREIZZLE WITH OLIVE OIL
- COVER WITH A LID AND COOK UNTIL SOFT IN THE CENTRE
- REMOVE THE LID AND FRYN UNTIL CRISP AND GOLDEN
- ADD THE SALMON TO THE SAUCE AND LEAVE IT TO SIMMER FOR TWO MINUTES
- POUR A LITTLE SAUCE INTO EACH DISH AND TOP WITH GNOCCHI
- SEASON TO TASTE WITH SALT (BE CAREFUL WITH THE SALT) AND FRESHLY

95. Golden Baked Salmon Recipe

Serving: 4 | Prep: | Cook: 45mins | Ready in:

Ingredients

- 1 lb salmon (or substitute any other fish)
- 1/3 cup mayonnaise
- 1/2 teaspoon salt
- 1 onion, sliced thin
- 1/2 cup Grated cheese (your favorite) **
- 1 tomato, sliced thin
- dash paprika or black pepper
- ** I like to use 1/2 block cream cheese, 1/2 t capers and 1/2 - 1 t. chives mixed with the mayo before spreading

Direction

- Place fish in oven-proof baking dish.
- Sprinkle with salt.
- Spread with mayonnaise like you are frosting a cake.
- Best to create a seal to lock in moisture.
- Top with onion, tomato & cheese.
- Add paprika or pepper.
- Bake at 375 for 45 min.
- Add small amount of water to dish if necessary.

96. Grilled Cilantro Salmon Recipe

Serving: 4 | Prep: | Cook: 20mins | Ready in:

Ingredients

- 1 bunch cilantro leaves, chopped
- 2 cloves garlic, chopped
- 2 cups honey

- juice from one lime
- 4 salmon steaks
- salt and pepper to taste

Direction

- 1. In a saucepan over medium-low heat, stir together cilantro, garlic, honey, and lime juice. Heat until the honey is easily stirred, about 5 minutes. Remove from heat, and let cool slightly.
- 2. Place salmon steaks in a baking dish, and season with salt and pepper. Pour marinade over salmon, cover, and refrigerate 10 minutes.
- 3. Preheat grill for high heat. Lightly oil grill grate. Place salmon steaks on grill, cook 5-to 6 minutes on each side, or until fish is easily flaked with a fork.

97. Grilled Jack Daniels Salmon Recipe

Serving: 4 | Prep: | Cook: 15mins | Ready in:

Ingredients

- 2 salmon fillets (enough for 3 to 4 servings. 6-8 oz each)
- 1/2 c Jack Daniels Whiskey
- 1/2 c brown sugar
- 1/4 c soy sauce
- 2 tablespoons honey
- 1/2 tsp ground ginger
- salt & pepper, to taste
- aluminum foil

Direction

- Preheat grill.
- Meanwhile, in a small saucepan combine Jack Daniels, brown sugar, soy sauce, honey, & ginger.
- Bring to boiling.

- Lower heat to medium setting, continually stirring mixture until liquid is thickened and caramelized.
- Remove from heat. Salt and pepper the salmon fillets.
- Create a foil platter for your Salmon to grill upon by folding all 4 edges of the foil such that it creates a 1/2" lip around the platter.
- Place fillets skin side down on foil and grill on a low heat setting. Brush Jack sauce on fillets.
- Cook for about 7 minutes.
- Flip the Salmon fillets; the skin should stick to the foil platter.
- Continue to baste fillets with the caramelized Jack sauce about every 3 minutes until fillets are cooked thoroughly.
- (About 15 minutes or until Salmon has a light pink color in the middle.)
- Serve immediately

98. Grilled King Salmon Roasted Fennel And Goat Cheese Feta Hash Lemon Cucumber Vinaigrette Recipe

Serving: 6 | Prep: | Cook: 40mins | Ready in:

Ingredients

- #
- roasted fennel & goat cheese Hash
- Ingredients:
- 1 Large bulb of fennel
- 1 large red pepper, roasted and peeled
- 1 cup sliced onions (red, Spanish, shallots or cipollini can be used)
- 3 Lbs. potatoes (redskin, Yukon gold or any variety can be used)
- 3 T. fresh oregano
- Blended oil
- salt & pepper
- 1/2 cup Vermont goat cheese feta
- Lemon cucumber Vinaigrette
- Ingredients:

- 1 cup minced seedless cucumber
- 3 T. chopped shallots
- 1 T. chopped fresh garlic
- 3 T. capers
- 1/4 cup fresh lemon juice
- 2 cups blended oil
- salt and pepper

Direction

- Directions Roasted Fennel & Goat Cheese Hash
- Ingredients:
- Cut the leaves off of the fennel bulb and reserve. Cut the bulb in half and separate. Place the fennel on a sheet pan. Coat the fennel in oil and lightly salt and pepper. Place the sheet pan in a preheated 400-degree oven. Roast the fennel until it is soft. When the fennel is cool, slice and reserve.
- Roast the red peppers using the above procedure. When the peppers are soft, remove them from the pan into a bowl and cover with plastic wrap for 15-20 minutes. This process will allow the pepper skin to steam off. When the peppers are ready, remove the plastic and peel the skins off, chop the peppers and reserve.
- Sauté the onions until translucent, reserve.
- In a large mixing bowl, toss the fennel, peppers, potatoes and onions together. Chop the fresh oregano and add to the mixture. This mixture can be made a day ahead of time and keep in the refrigerator for up to 3 days.
- When you reheat the hash, add the goat cheese at the last minute so it does not melt all the way. Adjust the seasoning with salt and pepper.
- Procedure
- Mince the cucumbers and set aside.
- In a food processor fitted with a metal blade, place the shallots, garlic and capers. Pulse quickly for a few seconds.
- Add the lemon juice and process. Slowly add the oil. Remove the mixture to a small mixing bowl.
- Add the cucumbers and adjust the seasoning with salt and pepper.
- To Serve
- Grill or sauté a piece of salmon (you may substitute any fish, but the richness of the salmon holds up well with the stronger flavors in the hash and vinaigrette).
- Heat a skillet over medium-high heat and add 1 T. of oil. When the oil is hot. Add the hash mixture, toss frequently until the mix is hot, turn the heat off and add the feta cheese.
- Place a mound of hash in the center of the plate. Place the Salmon on top of the hash.
- Surround the hash with some cucumber vinaigrette.
- Garnish the Salmon with some micro greens or some herb salad.

99. Grilled Miso Salmon Recipe

Serving: 2 | Prep: | Cook: 15mins | Ready in:

Ingredients

- (A) Main Ingredients::
- 2 salmon fillets
- 1 cup frozen vegetables/peas, cooked in microwave or steamer according to package instructions.
- some stalks of aspragus, remove hard skin along lower stalk using a butter knife
- bonito flakes (for garnishing)
- (B) Paste for miso marinate::
- 2 tbsp miso paste
- 1 tsp light soy sauce
- 1 tbsp mirin
- 1 tsp sesame oil
- 1 tsp grated ginger
- 1/2 tsp sake or white cooking wine
- a bit of black pepper

Direction

- Add the ingredients listed at (B) in a small bowl. Mix well.

- Pull out the bones from the salmon fillet using your fingers or a tweezer.
- Marinate the salmon fillets with the ingredients you mixed in step 1. Leave in fridge for at least half an hour, and longer if you can.
- Season the asparagus with some salt and pepper, then grill.
- Grill the salmon fillets, skin side down first, for about 4 minutes each side (or till lightly browned) over medium fire.
- Serve cooked salmon fillets with the asparagus and mixed vegetables, and topped with bonito flakes.

100. Grilled Pecan Crusted Salmon Recipe

Serving: 4 | Prep: | Cook: 10mins | Ready in:

Ingredients

- 2 8oz. salmon fillets
- 2Tbs butter
- 1/2tsp lemon pepper
- 1tsp italian seasoning
- 1/4c brown sugar
- 1/4c crushed pecans
- non-stick cooking spray
- 1tsp herbs de Provence

Direction

- Heat grill to med-high. Spray large piece of aluminum foil with spray.
- Place salmon on foil, skin side down. Melt the butter. Remove from heat and mix in Italian seasoning and herbs de Provence. Brush on the fillets.
- Seal the aluminum foil, do not wrap tightly, leave a bit of breathing room. Place on grill and cook 6 to 10 mins, until salmon is flakey not dry. When cooked, remove from heat and open packet. Sprinkle with brown sugar.

Close packet and heat from the fish will melt it. Pat on pecans and serve.

101. Grilled Salmon Fillet With Honey Mustard Sauce Recipe

Serving: 4 | Prep: | Cook: 10mins | Ready in:

Ingredients

- 1/4 cup Dijon mustard
- 2 tablespoons whole-grain mustard
- 3 tablespoons honey
- 2 tablespoons prepared horseradish, drained
- 2 tablespoons finely chopped fresh mint leaves
- kosher salt and freshly ground black pepper
- 2 pound fillet salmon, skin on
- 2 tablespoons canola oil
- 1 bunch watercress, coarsely chopped
- 1 small red onion, halved and thinly sliced
- 2 tablespoons aged sherry vinegar
- 2 tablespoons extra-virgin olive oil

Direction

- Whisk together the mustards, honey, horseradish, mint and 1/4 teaspoon of salt and 1/4 teaspoon of pepper in a small bowl. Let sit for at least 15 minutes before using. Can be made 1 day in advance and refrigerated but do not add the mint until just before using. Bring to room temperature before using.
- Heat the grill to high.
- Brush the salmon with the oil and season with salt and pepper. Place the salmon on the grill, skin side down, and grill until golden brown and slightly charred, about 3 minutes.
- While the salmon is cooking, place the watercress and onion in a medium bowl, add the vinegar and oil and salt and pepper and toss to combine. Transfer the salad to a platter, top with the salmon fillet and drizzle each fillet with the mustard sauce.

102. Grilled Salmon Fillets Recipe

Serving: 2 | Prep: | Cook: 15mins | Ready in:

Ingredients

- 1 pound fresh salmon fillets (wild salmon preferred)
- 2 cloves minced garlic
- 1 T olive oil
- 1/4 c chopped fresh parsley
- salt/pepper

Direction

- Heat grill.
- Prepare salmon fillets by placing them on a sheet of aluminum foil. Salt liberally, then add pepper, garlic, olive oil and parsley.
- Once the grill reaches a medium-high heat, place foil containing salmon onto grill.
- Close lid.
- Keep a close watch on the salmon.
- Depending on the thickness, it should be done in 10-15 minutes.
- Test for doneness with a fork.
- If fish flakes easily, it is done.
- Can cook on an indoor grill 5-7 minutes or 5-7 minutes per side, depending on the type of grill used.

103. Grilled Salmon Oriental Recipe

Serving: 6 | Prep: | Cook: 10mins | Ready in:

Ingredients

- 1-1/2 pounds salmon steaks or fillets
- 1 6 ounces c unsweetened pineapple
- juice
- 1 tablespoon light soy sauce
- 1 teaspoon hot pepper oil
- 1 tablespoon vegetable oil
- 2 cloves garlic
- 1/2 cup onion finely chopped
- 1 tablespoon grated fresh ginger
- 1/2 teaspoon grated lime rind
- 2 tablespoon fresh lime juice
- vegetable oil spray

Direction

- Rinse fish and pat dry. Arrange fish in a rectangular non aluminum baking dish. Combine all remaining ingredients in a small bowl, stir and pour over steaks, turning to coat evenly. Cover and refrigerate overnight. Preheat grill. Lightly spray grill top or grill pan with vegetable oil. Remove steaks from marinade and place steaks over hot coals or under grill, 4 to 5 inches from heat. Grill 5 to 7 minutes on each side, or until fish flakes easily with a fork.
- NOTE:
- DO NOT use vegetable oil spray near Open Flame or a heat source

104. Grilled Salmon Recipe

Serving: 2 | Prep: | Cook: 15mins | Ready in:

Ingredients

- 1 lb salmon
- 3 cloves garlic - minced
- zest of 1 lemon
- juice from 1 lemon (nice how that works out)
- 2 teaspoons fresh dill

Direction

- I prep this dish by mincing the garlic, zesting the lemon, half the lemon and chop the dill. I put all on a plate along with the salmon and give to the grill master.

- He places on the grill over low coals and covers with the garlic, lemon zest, squeezes lemon over salmon and finishes with the dill and grills for about 15 minutes or until salmon flakes. He does not turn the salmon.

105. Grilled Salmon With Citrus Dill Butter Recipe

Serving: 4 | Prep: | Cook: 20mins | Ready in:

Ingredients

- 2 tablespoons butter, softened
- 1 teaspoon chopped fresh chives
- 1 teaspoon chopped fresh dill
- ¼ teaspoon grated lemon peel
- 1 teaspoon fresh lemon juice
- 1/8 teaspoon salt
- 2 (4 oz.) salmon fillets
- 2 sprigs fresh dill

Direction

- Heat grill. In small bowl, combine all ingredients except salmon and dill sprigs; mix until well blended.
- When ready to grill, spread ½ teaspoon butter mixture over each salmon fillet. Place, skin side up, on gas grill over medium heat. Cook 3 minutes. Turn skin side down; spread ½ teaspoon butter mixture over top of salmon. Cook 8 to 10 minutes or until fish flakes easily with fork.
- To serve, spread remaining butter mixture over salmon fillets. Garnish with dill sprigs.
- Notes: I make the butter ahead and then refrigerate. Using a mini scoop (melon ball size) I scoop up the butter and put it into a freezer bag/container and freeze until I need it.

106. Grilled Salmon With Lime Butter Sauce Recipe

Serving: 6 | Prep: | Cook: 15mins | Ready in:

Ingredients

- 6 (6-oz) pieces center-cut salmon fillet (about 1 inch thick) with skin
- 1 1/2 teaspoons finely grated fresh lime zest
- ****
- NOTE: It takes only 5 minutes to make this fantastic Lime butter Sauce. Once you see how versatile it is — it works perfectly with the grilled salmon and the grilled corn on the menu — you'll want to make it for a whole host of your summer favorites.
- **
- Lime butter Sauce: (You'll need 6 tablespoons for the salmon - reserve the rest for the Grilled corn with herbs or some other lucky dish.)
- 1 large garlic clove, chopped
- 1/4 cup fresh lime juice
- 1 teaspoon salt
- 1/2 teaspoon black pepper
- 1 stick (1/2 cup) unsalted butter, melted

Direction

- Lime Butter Sauce:
- Purée garlic with lime juice, salt, and pepper in a blender until smooth.
- With motor running, add melted butter and blend until emulsified, about 30 seconds.
- Reserve 6 tablespoons for salmon.
- Lime Butter Sauce Note: Lime butter sauce can be made 1 day ahead and chilled, covered. Stir before using.
- Makes about 3/4 cup.
- ****
- Prepare grill for cooking over medium-hot charcoal (moderate heat for gas).
- Season salmon all over with salt and pepper, then grill, flesh sides down, on lightly oiled grill rack (covered only if using gas grill) for 4 minutes.

- Turn fillets over and grill (covered only if using gas grill) until just cooked through, 4 to 6 minutes more.
- Sprinkle fillets with zest and top each with 1 tablespoon prepared Lime Butter Sauce.
- ****
- STOVETOP INSTRUCTIONS:
- Salmon Note: If you aren't able to grill outdoors or don't care to, the salmon can be cooked in a hot well-seasoned large pan on the stovetop over moderately high heat. As follows -
- Heat large sauté pan over medium-high heat.
- When hot, add 1-2 tablespoons of olive oil and 1 tablespoon of unsalted butter. When the butter melts completely into the olive oil, add the salted and peppered salmon fillets, flesh side down.
- Watch the salmon closely. You do not want to overcook it.
- I would estimate 4-6 minutes per side. HOWEVER, I don't time the process as much as I watch the "cook line" of the salmon. In that I mean, you can see the salmon turning a lighter pink as it cooks and it will move up the fillet from the pan surface. Watch the center sides where the thickness is.
- As the cook line gets almost half way up the center thickness of the fillet, flip the fillet into the skin side. Cook another 4 minutes or until the cook line gets close to the done line above.
- What you want: To leave about 1/8 inch of uncooked salmon in the very center of the thickness part of the fillet. Remove from pan and place on serving platter.
- **The salmon will continue to cook after it is removed from the heat. But the perfectly cooked salmon fillet here is still a tiny bit on the just-barely-cooked side in the dead center. That way it remains moist and flaky and perfect throughout
- Sprinkle fillets with zest and top each with 1 tablespoon lime butter sauce.

Serving: 2 | Prep: | Cook: 15mins | Ready in:

Ingredients

- Prepare at least one hour ahead:
- English or seedless cucumber, finely chopped
- green onion, thinly sliced
- tablespoon fresh cilantro or parsley, minced
- 4 tablespoons wine vinegar
- cups fresh strawberries, hulled and diced small
- yellow bell pepper
- Sauce:
- 1 stick unsalted butter or margarine
- 1 teaspoon minced garlic
- 1 tablespoon honey
- 1 tablespoon ketchup (or soy sauce when its not Pesach)
- 1 tablespoon fresh lemon juice
- 1 salmon fillets (or fish of your choice), skinless

Direction

- In a bowl, mix together the cucumbers, green onion, cilantro and vinegar.
- Cover and chill at least one hour.
- Just before serving, add strawberries.
- In a small saucepan, melt butter with garlic over low heat.
- Stir in honey, ketchup and lemon juice and cook 2 minutes; set aside.
- Preheat a grill pan.
- When ready to cook, brush sauce on salmon pieces and place in pan.
- Grill approximately 4 to 5 minutes on each side.
- Brush with the sauce again after turning, and again when done.
- Transfer to warm platter and top with salsa.

108. Grilled Salmon With Thai Curry Sauce And Basmati Rice Recipe

Serving: 4 | Prep: | Cook: 25mins | Ready in:

Ingredients

- For rice
- 1 cup basmati rice
- 1 1/2 cups water
- 2 tablespoons unsalted butter
- For sauce
- 1 1/8 teaspoons minced peeled fresh gingerroot
- 1 1/8 teaspoons minced garlic
- 2 1/4 teaspoons peanut oil
- 3/4 teaspoon ground coriander seeds
- 1 1/2 teaspoons curry powder
- 1 1/2 teaspoons Thai red curry paste
- 1 1/2 teaspoons paprika
- 3/4 teaspoon ground cumin
- 1 1/4 cups well-stirred unsweetened coconut milk
- 3 tablespoons tomato purée
- 1 tablespoon soy sauce
- 1 1/2 tablespoons packed dark brown sugar
- For vegetables
- 3 cups finely shredded green cabbage
- 3/4 cup julienne strips of seeded peeled cucumber
- 3 tablespoons finely chopped fresh coriander
- 3 tablespoons finely chopped fresh mint leaves
- 1 tablespoon soy sauce
- 3 tablespoons rice vinegar (not seasoned)
- four 6-ounce pieces salmon fillet
- olive oil for brushing salmon
- 1/4 cup roasted peanuts

Direction

- Make rice:
- Preheat oven to 400°F.
- In a saucepan with an ovenproof lid bring rice, water, and butter to boil. Bake rice, covered, in middle of oven 12 minutes. Keep rice warm.
- Make sauce:
- In a heavy saucepan sauté gingerroot and garlic in oil over moderately high heat, stirring, until golden. Add coriander, curry powder, curry paste, paprika, and cumin and sauté, stirring, 1 minute, or until fragrant. Whisk in coconut milk, tomato purée, soy sauce, and brown sugar and bring just to a boil. Remove pan from heat and keep warm.
- Prepare vegetables:
- In a bowl, toss together all vegetable ingredients.
- Prepare grill.
- Brush salmon with oil and sprinkle with salt and pepper to taste. Grill salmon on an oiled rack set 5 to 6 inches over glowing coals until just cooked through, about 5 minutes on each side.
- Put each in center of 4 plates and arrange salmon on top. Top salmon with vegetables and spoon sauce around it. Sprinkle vegetables with peanuts.

109. Grilled Salmon With Bacon Recipe

Serving: 4 | Prep: | Cook: 10mins | Ready in:

Ingredients

- 4 salmon fillets, about 1 pound
- salt & freshly ground pepper, to taste
- 4 slices bacon, pre-cooked about 3/4's of the way done
- 2 T. balsamic vinegar
- 2 T. dark brown sugar

Direction

- Cut bacon in half and distribute evenly over tops of fillets.
- Mix vinegar and brown sugar in small bowl.
- Gently lay fish on prepared grill or use a grill basket, brush with basting mixture several times until salmon is done to your liking.

110. Grilled Salmon With Lemon And Ginger Recipe

Serving: 5 | Prep: | Cook: 10mins | Ready in:

Ingredients

- For a perfectly simple dinner, serve this salmon with grilled or broil asparagus and a mix of California brown and wild rices.
- 6 tablespoons Meyer lemon juice (or regular juice if Meyer lemons are not available)
- 3 tablespoons low-sodium soy sauce
- 1 1/2 tablespoons canola oil
- 1 1/2 teaspoons sugar
- 1 1/2-inch piece fresh ginger, peeled and grated
- 1 1/2 pounds wild king salmon fillets (preferably skinless)
- Freshly ground pepper

Direction

- In a small bowl or measuring cup whisk together lemon juice, soy sauce, oil, sugar and ginger. Set aside 1/3 of the mixture in a small bowl. Place salmon in a shallow dish and pour the rest of the marinade over the top. Let marinate at room temperature for 20 minutes, turning once or twice. Grill or broil salmon over medium heat, turning once with a wide spatula and brushing with excess marinade until salmon is cooked to your liking (about 10 minutes depending on thickness.) Sprinkle with pepper and serve with reserved marinade for drizzling. Makes 4 to 6 servings.

111. Grilled Salmon With Nectarine Red Onion Relish Recipe

Serving: 4 | Prep: | Cook: 12mins | Ready in:

Ingredients

- 2 1/2 cups coarsely chopped nectarines (about 3 medium)
- 1 cup coarsley chopped red bell pepper
- 1 cup coarsely chopped red onion
- 1/4 cup thinly sliced fresh basil
- 1/4 cup white wine vinegar
- 1/2 tps. grated orange peel
- 1/4 cup fresh orange juice
- 2 TBSP. minced seeded jalapeno pepper
- 2 TBSP. fresh lime juice
- 2 tps. sugar
- 2 garlic cloves minced
- 1/4 tps. salt, divded
- 1/2 tps. freshly groun pepper
- 4 (6-ounce) fillets
- 1/2

Direction

- 1. Combine first 11 ingredients and 1/8 tsp. salt in a medium bowl, and stir well. Let nectarine mixture stand 2 hours.
- 2. Sprinkle pepper and 1/8 teaspoon salt over salmon fillets. Prepare grill. Place fillets on a grill rack coated with cooking spray, and grill 5-6 minutes on each side or until fish flakes easily when tested with a fork. Serve immediately with nectarine-red onion relish.
- 3. Serving size: 1 fillet and 1 cup relish.

112. Grilled Salmon With North African Flavors Recipe

Serving: 4 | Prep: | Cook: 12mins | Ready in:

Ingredients

- 1/4 cup(s) low-fat or nonfat plain yogurt
- 1/4 cup(s) chopped fresh parsley
- 1/4 cup(s) chopped fresh cilantro
- 2 tablespoon(s) lemon juice
- 1 tablespoon(s) extra-virgin olive oil
- 3 clove(s) garlic, minced

- 1 1/2 teaspoon(s) paprika
- 1 teaspoon(s) ground cumin
- 1/4 teaspoon(s) salt, or to taste
- Freshly ground pepper , to taste
- 1 pound(s) center-cut salmon fillet, cut into 4 portions
- 1 lemon, cut into wedges

Direction

- Directions
- Stir together yogurt, parsley, cilantro, lemon juice, oil, garlic, paprika, cumin, salt and pepper in a small bowl.
- Reserve 1/4 cup for sauce; cover and refrigerate.
- Place salmon fillets in a large sealable plastic bag.
- Pour in the remaining herb mixture, seal the bag and turn to coat.
- Refrigerate for 20 to 30 minutes, turning the bag over once.
- Meanwhile, preheat grill to medium-high.
- Oil the grill rack
- Remove the salmon from the marinade, blotting any excess.
- Grill the salmon until browned and opaque in the center, 4 to 6 minutes per side.
- To serve, top each piece with a dollop of the reserved sauce and garnish with lemon wedges.

113. Grilled Salmon With Peach Salsa Recipe

Serving: 4 | Prep: | Cook: 8mins | Ready in:

Ingredients

- 4 salmon steaks (6 ounce)
- 2 diced, pelled, pitted peaches
- 3/4 cup thawed frozen corn kernels
- 1/2 cup chili sauce
- 1/4 cup each finely diced red onion and sweet red pepper

- 1/4 cup each chopped freah mint and cilantro
- 2 tbsps. each honey and lime juice, 1/2 tps. salt

Direction

- 1. Preheat the grill. Generously oil grill to prevent fish from sticking. Grill over moderately heat 8 inches from the heat until cooked through, 3 to 4 minutes on each side.
- 2. Spoon salsa over fish.

114. Grilled Salmon With Strawberry Salsa Recipe

Serving: 6 | Prep: | Cook: 10mins | Ready in:

Ingredients

- Strawberry Salsa:
- 1 seedless cucumber, finley chopped
- 1 green onion, thinly sliced
- 1 yellow bell pepper, seeded and cut into strips
- 1 TBS. chopped cilantro
- 3 TBS. seasoned rice wine vinegar
- 2 cups fresh strawberries, hulled and diced small.
- Sauce:
- 1/2 cup unsalted butter
- 1 clove garlic, minced
- 1 TBS. honey
- 2 TBS. soy sauce
- 1 TBS. freah lemon juice
- 6 salmon fillets, skinless

Direction

- 1. Mix cucumbers, green onions, cilantro and vinegar. Cover and chill at least one hour. Just before serving, add strawberries.
- 2. In a small saucepan melt butter with garlic over low heat. Stir in honey, soy and lemon juice and cook 2 minutes, set aside.
- 3. Prepare a charcoal grill, when ready brush sauce on salmon pieces and place on a well-

oiled fish grilling rack. Place rack over coals about 4 inches from fire and grill approximately 4 to 5 minutes on each side. Brush with the sauce again after turning, and again when done. Transfer to warm platter and top with salsa.

115.   Grilled Salmon With Tomatoes Spinach And Capers Recipe

Serving: 4 | Prep: | Cook: 20mins | Ready in:

Ingredients

- 4 salmon fillets(6oz ea.),skin on
- 1Tbs extra virgin olive oil
- 1 med. onion,chopped
- 2 cloves garlic,minced
- 1lb. plum tomatoes,chopped
- 3c baby spinach
- 1Tbs rinsed and drained capers
- 4 lemon wedges

Direction

- Heat oven to broil. Lightly coat baking dish with cooking spray
- Place salmon, flesh side up, in baking dish and lightly season with salt and pepper. Broil without turning until salmon is cooked through 8 to 10 mins.
- Meanwhile, heat oil in large saucepan over med heat. Add onion and garlic and cook, stirring occasionally, until softened, about 7 mins. Stir in the tomatoes, spinach and capers. Cook 2 mins. longer. Remove pan from heat.
- Remove salmon from broiler and transfer to 4 serving plates. Spoon tomato mixture over salmon, squeeze lemon wedges over top and serve warm.

116.   Grilled Salmon In Tinfoil Recipe

Serving: 2 | Prep: | Cook: 8mins | Ready in:

Ingredients

- 2 salmon steaks
- 2 chopped green onions
- 2 tsp balsamic vinegar
- 1 tbsp olive oil
- coarse salt
- fresh pepper
- fresh herbs

Direction

- Lay out two pieces of tinfoil
- Put fish in centre
- Sprinkle green onions over top
- Drizzle with vinegar
- Drizzle with olive oil
- Sprinkle with salt and pepper to taste
- Pick whatever fresh herbs you have on hand that work nicely with fish (I like basil, oregano, and lemon grass) chop up a bit and sprinkle on the fish
- Fold the tinfoil and make nicely sealed packages
- Bbq over low heat on the top rack of your grill for about 8 minutes. Don't overcook!

117.   Healthy Baked Salmon Recipe

Serving: 2 | Prep: | Cook: 15mins | Ready in:

Ingredients

- 6 ounce salmon fillet (can use any portion based on how many ppl)
- cayenne pepper
- ground black pepper
- pinch of garlic powder
- 2 Tablespoons olive oil, divided

- 1 lemon
- 2 cloves minced garlic
- 1 bag baby spinach
- fresh basil

Direction

- Salmon:
- Preheat oven to 375
- Place fillet(s) on a cookie sheet sprayed with cooking spray (or on non-stick foil)
- Poke tiny holes in the salmon with a fork just in center and on ends
- Sprinkle pepper, garlic powder and cayenne pepper on fillet
- Brush 1 Tablespoon of olive oil on fillet
- Juice 1/2 a lemon and pour over salmon
- Slice a few lemon slices and place on top
- Bake 12-15 minutes, until salmon flakes easily...varies based on ovens and portion of fish
- Spinach
- While Salmon is baking (start about 7 mins before it is finished)
- Place 1 TBSP olive oil & garlic in a large sauté pan
- Add spinach and sauté for about 2 mins
- Add juice from 1/2 a lemon and sauté until spinach is slightly welted
- When Salmon is finished baking use a spatula to separate the skin from the bottom of the fish and place on top of the spinach on a platter
- Garnish with fresh basil
- Cook on MED heat for about 30 seconds
- Add spinach

118.   Herb Crusted Salmon Recipe

Serving: 2 | Prep: | Cook: 35mins | Ready in:

Ingredients

- extra virgin olive oil

- 2 salmon filets, 4 ounces each
- 1/4 cup plain dry bread crumbs
- 1 tbsp salted butter, melted
- 1/2 cup fresh basil, chopped
- 1 clove garlic, chopped
- 1/2 tsp dried rosemary
- 1/2 tsp dried oregano
- 1/2 tsp kosher salt
- fresh ground black pepper

Direction

- Preheat oven to 400 degrees.
- Prepare on a baking sheet 2 foil sheets large enough to cover each salmon completely.
- Spray both sheets of foil with cooking spray and sprinkle lightly with kosher salt before placing each salmon filet on the foil.
- In a small bowl combine breadcrumbs, basil, garlic, rosemary, oregano, salt, and pepper.
- Coat both salmon filets with melted butter.
- Top each filet with dry mixture and drizzle olive oil over the top.
- Wrap the salmon filets by pulling the longer sides of the foil and joining them so they stay together.
- Fold the ends upward to prevent leakage once cooked. Bake for 35 minutes.

119.   Herbed Salmon Steaks Recipe

Serving: 4 | Prep: | Cook: 35mins | Ready in:

Ingredients

- 1/4 cup butter or margarine, melted
- 2/3 cup crushed saltines (about 20 crackers)
- 1/4 cup grated parmesan cheese
- 1/2 tsp salt
- 1/2 tsp dried basil
- 1/2 tsp dried oregano
- 1/4 tsp garlic powder
- 4 salmon steaks (6-8 oz each)

Direction

- Place melted butter in a shallow dish
- In another dish, combine the cracker crumbs, parmesan cheese, salt, basil, oregano and garlic powder.
- Dip salmon into butter, then coat both sides with crumb mixture
- Place in a greased 13x9x2 baking dish
- Bake, uncovered at 350 degrees or until fish flakes easily with fork

120.   Hoisin Baked Salmon Recipe

Serving: 2 | Prep: | Cook: 10mins | Ready in:

Ingredients

- 2 (6 ounce) salmon, pieces
- 2 tablespoons hoisin sauce
- 2 teaspoons soy sauce
- 5 drops dark sesame oil
- 1/4 teaspoon chili paste (optional) or hot sauce (optional)
- 1-2 teaspoon sesame seeds (light or black)

Direction

- Preheat oven to 375 degrees.
- Place salmon on baking dish or tray.
- Thin hoisin with a little soy sauce and flavor with a few drops of sesame oil.
- Stir in chili paste, if desired.
- Brush or spoon mixture on salmon.
- Sprinkle with sesame seeds.
- Bake for 8 to 10 minutes, or until it flakes with a fork.
- Makes 2 servings.
- Serve with rice or pasta that has been tossed with a little sesame oil, and steamed green vegetables like broccoli, bok choy or green beans, drizzled with bottled oyster sauce.

121.   Hoisin Glazed Salmon With Plum Ginger Relish Recipe

Serving: 4 | Prep: | Cook: 10mins | Ready in:

Ingredients

- Plum-ginger relish:
- 4 ripe plums, diced
- 2 Tbl fresh ginger, minced
- 1/4 c. rice wine vinegar
- Hoisin glazed Salmon:
- 1/4 c. hoisin sauce
- 2 tsp soy sauce
- 2 tsp sesame oil
- 1 tsp honey
- 1 tsp fresh garlic, minced
- 1/2 tsp fresh ginger, minced
- 4 salmon fillets
- 2 tsp sesame seeds

Direction

- Combine the plums, ginger and rice wine vinegar. Cover and refrigerate at least eight hours.
- Preheat oven to 425°. Line a baking sheet with aluminum foil and spray with cooking spray.
- Combine Hoisin, soy sauce, sesame oil, honey, garlic and ginger.
- Lay salmon, skin side down, on baking sheet and spread half the mixture over fish. Reserve the other half to serve on the side.
- Sprinkle fish with sesame seeds, and bake on center rack for 10 minutes per inch thickness. Salmon is ready when it easily flakes with a fork.
- Remove salmon from oven. Using a flipper, plate each fillet, leaving the skin on the baking sheet. (Easy clean up .... who doesn't like this?) Garnish with plum-ginger relish and enjoy.

122. Honey Ginger Grilled Salmon Recipe

Serving: 4 | Prep: | Cook: 15mins | Ready in:

Ingredients

- 1 teaspoon ground ginger
- 1 teaspoon garlic powder
- 1/2 cup soy sauce
- 1/3 cup orange juice
- 1/4 cup honey
- 1 green onion, chopped
- 1 1/2 pounds salmon fillets (4 6 oz. fillets)

Direction

- In a large zip top plastic bag, combine first 6 ingredients; mix well.
- Place salmon in bag and seal tightly.
- Turn bag gently to distribute marinade.
- Refrigerate 15 minutes or up to 30 minutes for stronger flavor.
- Turn bag occasionally.
- Lightly grease cold grill rack.
- Preheat grill for medium heat.
- Remove salmon from marinade; reserved marinade.
- Grill 12 to 15 minutes per inch of thickness or until fish flakes easily with fork.
- Brush with reserved marinade up until the last 5 minutes of cooking time.
- Discard leftover marinade.
- Serves 4

123. Honey Ginger Salmon Recipe

Serving: 4 | Prep: | Cook: 15mins | Ready in:

Ingredients

- 1/3c orange juice
- 1/3c soy sauce
- 1/4c honey

- 1tsp. ground ginger
- 1tsp garlic powder
- 1 green onion
- 4 6oz. salmon fillets

Direction

- In a small bowl, combine orange juice, soy sauce, honey, ground ginger, garlic powder and green onion. Place salmon in a large glass dish and pour marinade over them. Turn to coat and refrigerate 15 mins.
- Preheat grill. Discard marinade and grill salmon over med-high heat for 6-8 mins a side or till fish flakes easily with a fork.

124. Honey Glaze For Salmon Or Fish Recipe

Serving: 4 | Prep: | Cook: 20mins | Ready in:

Ingredients

- honey
- rosemary vinegar
- dry mustard
- brown sugar
- fresh garlic pressed
- Fresh lemon juice
- olive oil
- Fresh Tri-colored cracked pepper
- 4 salmon steaks

Direction

- Mix all of the above to taste.
- Sauté salmon in olive oil until almost done, then brush with glaze, this will caramelize in the pan, when done and on a serving dish, pour additional glaze over salmon, but not too much.

125. Horseradish Asiago Encrusted Salmon Recipe

Serving: 6 | Prep: | Cook: 15mins | Ready in:

Ingredients

- 4-6 oz. skinless salmon fillets
- 3/4 C fresh shredded horseradish root
- 3/4 C shredded asiago cheese
- 1/4 C butter (melted)
- 1/4 C olive oil
- salt
- pepper
- 2 tsp. minced fresh rosemary
- 1 lemon
- Grated parmesan for garnish
- Sauce
- 1 C sour cream
- 1 bunch cilantro
- 1/4 tsp. ground coriander

Direction

- Mince 2 tbsp. fresh cilantro, reserve remaining cilantro for garnish. Combine sour cream, cilantro, and coriander.
- Mix well and set aside.
- In a bowl combine grated horseradish, asiago, butter and rosemary.
- Brush each salmon fillet with olive oil then a dash of salt and pepper.
- Coat with asiago cheese mixture
- Place each fillet on a well-oiled baking sheet and bake at 350 until golden brown (about 15 minutes)
- Remove and garnish with sour cream mixture, fresh squeezed lemon and cilantro leaves.
- Dust with parmesan and enjoy!

126. Horseradish Crusted Salmon With A Whole Grain Mustard Beurre Blanc And Sweet Riesling Emulsion Recipe

Serving: 8 | Prep: | Cook: 7mins | Ready in:

Ingredients

- For the Salmon:
- 8 ea., 7-8 oz. salmon fillets
- 2-3 oz. Prepared horseradish, drained
- 1 cup. panko (Japanese breadcrumbs)
- 1-2 Tbsp. clarified butter
- 1 Tbsp. finely minced Italian parsley
- kosher salt
- fresh cracked pepper
- cooking oil as needed
- For the Beurre Blanc:
- 8 oz. dry white wine
- 2 shallots, thinly sliced
- 4 oz. heavy cream
- 3 Tbsp. whole grain mustard
- 1 Tbsp. Dijon mustard
- 12 oz. unsalted butter
- kosher salt to taste
- For the Rielsing Emulsion:
- 8 oz. Late Harvest Rielsing
- 6 oz. unsalted butter
- 3 oz. Elderflower
- 1 tsp. Lecithin
- kosher salt to taste

Direction

- For the Beurre blanc:
- In a saucepan, combine the white wine and shallots, and reduce until au sec. Add the heavy cream and gently reduce by half. Strain out the liquid with a fine chinois into another saucepan, and whisk in the butter over low heat until emulsified. Whisk in the mustards (add more whole grain if needed), and season to taste with salt. Reserve and keep warm.
- For the Riesling Emulsion:

- In a sauce pan, gently simmer the Riesling for about 5-7 minutes to remove the harshness from the alcohol. Dissolve the butter, and add the elderflower, lecithin, and a fair amount of salt. Using an immersion blender, aerate the sauce until it foams, then taste the foam and add more salt if needed. If the Riesling is still too harsh from the alcohol, balance it with more elderflower and butter. Reserve and keep warm.
- For the Salmon:
- In a sauté pan, heat the clarified butter on medium heat. When hot, turn the heat down to low, add the panko, and sauté until it starts to turn golden brown. Add the parsley and sauté until the parsley dries out. Season the mixture to taste with kosher salt and cool (this can be made 1-2 days in advance). Pre-heat oven to 400 degrees. Heat some oil in a sauté pan on high until smoking. Season the salmon with kosher salt and pepper, and sear, top side first, until golden brown. Flip the salmon over and cook on the second side for just a few seconds and remove from the pan. Crust the salmon with an even, but light amount of horseradish and top with the panko crust. Roast in the oven until medium doneness, about 2-4 minutes depending on the thickness of the fish. Serve with the beurre blanc and the Riesling emulsion.

127.   Horseradish Salmon Recipe

Serving: 4 | Prep: | Cook: 8mins | Ready in:

Ingredients

- 1 english cucumber,cut in half lengthwise and then in 1/4" thick half-moons
- 2 Tbs. white vinegar
- 2 Tbs chopped fresh dill
- 2 Tbs olive oil
- 1/2 c panko

- 2 Tbs prepared horseradish,drained
- 4 skinless,boneless salmon fillets(5 to 6 oz ea.)
- 6 oz. baby spinach

Direction

- In large bowl, toss cucumber, vinegar, 1 Tbsp. dill, 1 Tbsp. oil and 1/8 tsp each salt and pepper.
- In small bowl, combine panko, horseradish and remaining dill and oil. Sprinkle salmon with 1/8 tsp. each salt and pepper; place on cookie sheet, smooth side up. Press panko mixture evenly on top of fillets. Bake salmon 8 mins or till golden brown on top and opaque throughout.
- Toss spinach with cucumber mixture in bowl, serve with salmon.

128.   Incredibly Creamy Salmon Melt Recipe

Serving: 2 | Prep: | Cook: 5mins | Ready in:

Ingredients

- 2 salmon fillets cooked
- 2 eggs hard boiled peeled and chopped
- 1/2 teaspoon chopped garlic
- 1/4 cup tartar sauce
- 1/4 cup plus 2 tablespoons mayonnaise divided
- 4 slices rye bread
- 2 roma tomatoes sliced
- 4 slices swiss cheese

Direction

- Preheat oven to broil. In a medium bowl crumble salmon. Add eggs, garlic, tartar sauce and 1/4 cup of the mayonnaise. Mix thoroughly and lightly season with salt and pepper. Spread remaining 2 tablespoons mayonnaise on the 4 slices of bread then lay them on a baking sheet. Evenly distribute salmon mixture onto the bread slices. Place 3 slices of tomato on each piece of bread followed by 1 slice of cheese then cut into 2 triangles. Place under preheated broiler for 3 minutes. Serve immediately.

129. Indian Spiced Roast Salmon Recipe

Serving: 4 | Prep: | Cook: 15mins | Ready in:

Ingredients

- 1 teaspoon ground cumin
- 1 teaspoon ground coriander
- 1/2 teaspoon ground turmeric
- 1/2 teaspoon dried thyme
- 1/2 teaspoon fennel seeds, crushed
- 1/2 teaspoon black pepper
- 1/4 teaspoon ground cinnamon
- 1/8 teaspoon ground cloves
- 4 (6-ounce) salmon fillets (about 1 1.4-inches thick)
- 1/2 teaspoon olive oil
- 1/4 cup plain fat-free yogurt
- 4 lemon wedges

Direction

- Heat oven to 400.
- Combine first 8 ingredients in a shallow dish. Sprinkle fillets with salt, dredge fillets in spice mixture. Heat oil in a large skillet over medium-high heat. Add fillets, skin side up; cook 5 minutes or until bottoms are golden. Turn fillets over. Wrap handle of skillet with foil; bake at 400 for 10 minutes or until fish flakes easily when tested with a fork. Remove skin from fillets; discard skin. Serve with yogurt and lemon wedges.

130. Jack Daniels Salmon Patties Recipe

Serving: 5 | Prep: | Cook: 6mins | Ready in:

Ingredients

- 1, 15 oz canned salmon, drained and bones removed
- panko bread crumbs, enough to bind or any other dried white bread crumbs or even cracker crumbs.
- 1 egg
- 2 Tbs Jack Daniels barbecue sauce
- 1 tsp Jack Daniel's whiskey or to taste
- cajun seasoning to taste or use salt and pepper
- 1 Tbs fresh minced parsley
- cracker crumbs (season with a bit of cajun seasoning)
- oil to fry

Direction

- Combine salmon, egg, parsley, Jack Daniel's barbecue sauce and whiskey and enough dried breadcrumbs to bind mixture so it will be firm enough to shape into patties.
- I usually get about 5 nice size ones.
- After forming in patties dust both sides well with cracker crumbs.
- Fry golden both sides in hot oil (I used peanut).
- Place absorbent paper a few minutes and then remove and serve.
- Serve as is with assorted salads and sides or place in buns for a salmon burger.

131. Jetts Bourbon Marinated Salmon Recipe

Serving: 3 | Prep: | Cook: 60mins | Ready in:

Ingredients

- 3 salmon fillets*

- 1/2 cup bourbon
- 1/2 cup low sodium soy sauce
- 1 cup lightly packed brown sugar
- 1/4 cup orange juice
- 1 teaspoon garlic
- 1/2 teaspoon ginger
- 1 large jar with tight fitting lid

Direction

- Place all ingredients except salmon into the jar. Shake well.
- Put salmon fillets in a container that will allow enough room for marinade to completely cover.
- Pour marinade over the fish, leaving some to brush over the fish when baking.
- Let it all get happy in the refrigerator for at least 3 hours.
- Preheat oven to 375 degrees F
- Prepare a broiler pan by lining with foil and spraying the pan with a non-stick cooking spray.
- Place salmon fillets skin side down.
- Brush with marinade.
- Enjoy!
- ~Be anxious for nothing, but in everything by prayer and supplication, with thanksgiving, let your requests be made known to God. ~ Phil 4:6

132. Jetts Salmon Patties Recipe

Serving: 5 | Prep: | Cook: 20mins | Ready in:

Ingredients

- 1- 2 cans good quality salmon (15 oz)
- 1/2 small onion chopped(optional)
- 1 egg
- worcestershire sauce
- Franks hot sauce
- Ritz crackers(1/2 sleeve or more)

- baggie for crushing crackers
- seasoned salt
- pepper
- garlic powder
- oil for frying

Direction

- Drain juice out of the salmon can.
- Pour salmon into a bowl and remove the skin and the bones.
- With a fork, break up the salmon.
- Add seasonings to your liking. You can taste it before adding the egg to make sure it's not too salty.
- Add crackers to the baggie and crush up.
- After you have seasoned the salmon to your liking, add the egg and cracker crumbs. The consistency should not be too sticky. You should be able to spoon out the mixture and make patties.
- Have your oil hot in a large cast iron skillet.
- Carefully, carefully add the salmon patties into the hot oil and let brown on one side before turning over. Have a plate with paper towels ready to put patties on after they are removed from oil.
- *** Swallowing your pride seldom leads to indigestion ***

133. Jewel Studded Salmon With Cilantro Cream Cheese Recipe

Serving: 4 | Prep: | Cook: 10mins | Ready in:

Ingredients

- 2 large salmon filets, skinned
- 2 cloves garlic
- 4 tablespoons softened cream cheese
- 4 stalks of fresh cilantro, chopped
- 1-teaspoon kosher salt

Direction

- Peel and mince the garlic.
- Mince the cilantro.
- Thoroughly mix the garlic, cilantro, and cream cheese, and then set aside.
- Butterfly the salmon filets.
- Spread the cream cheese mixture into the salmon and fold it back up.
- Place on hot grill and cook for about 6 minutes on each side.
- Sprinkle with salt during cooking.

134.   Kind Of Asian Flavored Marinated Salmon Recipe

Serving: 2 | Prep: | Cook: 6mins | Ready in:

Ingredients

- 2 6 ounce pices of salmon
- garlic
- hot mustard (Coleman's recommended)
- soy sauce
- hoisin sauce
- sherry vinegar
- extra virgin olive oil
- lemon
- black pepper
- scallions

Direction

- Combine 3 parts soy sauce with one part hoisin sauce (or so!)
- Add a bit of mustard and a dash of vinegar
- Add minced garlic
- Squeeze in the juice of one quarter of the lemon
- Stir in olive oil
- Pepper the salmon
- Marinate the salmon in the mixture for around 45 min
- Get a pan heated on med. to high heat

- Cook the salmon about 2-3 minutes on both sides, be careful not to overcook
- Serve topped with chopped scallions

135.   Kitchen Disaster Salmon With Lemon Herb Sauce Recipe

Serving: 4 | Prep: | Cook: 20mins | Ready in:

Ingredients

- 3 shallots, very finely chopped
- 1 1/2 oz. butter
- Zest and juice of 1 1/2 lemons
- 1 1/2 generous teaspoons garlic powder
- 1 1/2 generous teaspoons onion powder
- 2 1/2 generous teaspoons Italian style dried herb mix
- 1 1/2 pints hot chicken stock
- 1 1/2 generous teaspoons chicken bouillon granules
- juice of another lemon, a smallish one
- 1 1/2 generous teaspoon cornstarch
- 1 1/2 tablespoons parsley, finely chopped
- More chicken stock if needed
- 2 tablespoons bland flavoured oil (I used groundnut)
- 4 good sized salmon fillets
- lemon wedges to serve
- parsley to garnish

Direction

- Heat butter in a frying pan.
- Add the shallots and sauté gently until soft but not browned, about 5-7 minutes.
- Add lemon zest and stir in well. Cook briefly.
- Add the garlic powder, onion powder and dried herbs. Stir in well and cook gently for half a minute or so.
- Add the lemon juice and chicken stock, and add the bouillon granules. Stir well, turn up the heat and reduce the liquid a bit.

- Transfer to a saucepan. Bring back up to the simmer.
- Make a slurry with the lemon juice and the cornstarch. Add to the sauce and cook until thickened.
- Add the parsley and stir well in.
- Turn off the heat and set aside while cooking the salmon.
- Wipe out the frying pan.
- Add the oil and heat.
- Put in the salmon fillets and pan fry on a low-medium heat, turning once, till just done - about 15-20 minutes total depending on thickness.
- Cook your veg of choice.
- Just before salmon is ready to serve, reheat the sauce. Add more stock if it is too thick.
- Put the salmon on the plates and pour over the fish juices from the pan. Then pour over the sauce.
- Serve with plain boiled new potatoes and veg of choice, and garnish with lemon wedge and parsley.
- Then get someone else to do the washing-up.

136. Lemon Glazed Salmon Fillet Recipe

Serving: 6 | Prep: | Cook: 30mins | Ready in:

Ingredients

- 1 1/2 c. brown sugar
- 6 Tbsp. butter or marg., melted
- 3 to 6 Tbsp. lemon juice
- 2 1/4 tsp. dill weed
- 3/4 tsp. cayenne pepper
- _____
- 1 salmon fillet (about 2 pounds)
- lemon-pepper seasoning

Direction

- Small bowl- Combine first 5 ingredients; mix well.

- Remove 1/2 c. to saucepan; simmer until heated through.
- Set aside remaining for basting.
- _____
- Sprinkle salmon with lemon pepper.
- Place on grill with skin side down.
- Grill covered, medium heat, 5 mins.
- Brush with reserved brown sugar mixture.
- Grill 10-15 mins. longer, basting occasionally.
- _____
- Serve with warm sauce.

137. Lemon Herb Salmon Recipe

Serving: 6 | Prep: | Cook: 20mins | Ready in:

Ingredients

- 6 tablespoons extra virgin olive oil
- 2 tablespoons fresh lemon juice
- 2 teaspoons minced fresh lemon zest
- 1-1/2 teaspoons finely minced fresh rosemary
- 1-1/2 teaspoons minced fresh basil
- 1 tablespoon minced fresh parsley
- 1/8 teaspoon crushed red pepper flakes
- 1/2 teaspoon minced fresh garlic
- 1/4 teaspoon salt
- 6 fresh thick cut salmon fillets

Direction

- Mix all ingredients except fish and set aside.
- Preheat oven to 450 then season fish with salt and pepper.
- Heat 1 tablespoon olive oil in a large heavy skillet over moderately high heat.
- Add fish and cook until golden brown about 4 minute then turn and cook 2 minutes more.
- Place skillet with fish in preheated oven and roast fish 5 minutes.
- Place fish on plates and splash each piece with 1 tablespoon or more of the lemon splash.

138. Lemon Rice With Crispy Salmon Recipe

Serving: 4 | Prep: | Cook: 35mins | Ready in:

Ingredients

- • 2 pouches (125 g each) Minute Rice Jasmine Rice
- • 3/4 cup (175 mL) frozen peas, thawed
- • 1/4 cup (60 mL) sliced green onion
- • 2 tbsp (30 mL) lemon juice
- • 4 skin-on salmon fillets (5 to 6 oz/140 to 170 g each)
- • 1/2 tsp (2 mL) salt
- • 1/4 tsp (1 mL) pepper
- • 2 tbsp (30 mL) canola oil
- • Lemon wedges

Direction

- Step 1: Cook rice according to package directions. Add peas during the last minute of cooking; stir in half of the green onion, and lemon juice.
- Step 2: Meanwhile, using a sharp knife, score skin side of salmon, slicing 1/2-inch (1 cm) across and about 1/4-inch (5 mm) deep; season all over with salt and pepper.
- Step 3: In large, heavy-bottom skillet, heat oil over medium-high heat; cook salmon skin side down for about 5 minutes or until skin is golden brown and crispy. Turn over; cook for 2 or 3 minutes or until fish is just cooked through and flakes easily with a fork. Serve with rice and lemon wedges. Sprinkle with remaining green onion.
- Nutrition Facts. Per 1/4 recipe: Calories 410, Fat 18g, Cholesterol 80mg, Sodium 450mg, Carbohydrate 29g, Fibre 2g, Sugars 2g, Protein 33g

139. Lemon Salmon Linguini Recipe

Serving: 4 | Prep: | Cook: 10mins | Ready in:

Ingredients

- 1Tbs. olive oil
- 1 pound salmon (boneless and skinless), cut into 2-inch chunks
- 1 tps. kosher salt
- 1/2 tps. fennel seed
- 1/4 tps. ground black pepper
- 1 1/2 cups thinly sliced red onion
- 1 1/2 cups cherry tomatoes, halved
- 1 cup ripe olives. halved
- 3/4 cup chicken broth
- 1/4 cup lemon juice
- 2 Tbs. Chopped dill
- 1 1/2 Tbs. minced lemon zest
- 1 quart (1 1/4 pound) cooked linguini pasta
- 6 ounces baby spinach

Direction

- Heat 1 Tbs. of olive oil in a large high-sided sauté pan over medium-high heat. Place salmon in pan, season with salt, fennel seed and pepper and cook for 4-5 minutes, turning occasionally, until golden and cooked through. Using a slotted spatula, transfer to a clean bowl and set aside.
- Heat remaining oil in pan, add onions and cook over medium heat for 3-4 minutes until tender. Stir in tomatoes, ripe olives, chicken broth, lemon juice, dill and lemon zest and bring to a boil.
- Mix in linguini and continue cooking until heated through. Gently toss with salmon and baby spinach and serve immediately.

140. Lime And Ginger Grilled Salmon Recipe

Serving: 2 | Prep: | Cook: 18mins |Ready in:

Ingredients

- 1 teaspoon finely grated lime rind
- 1/4 cup lime juice (about 1 large lime)
- 2 teaspoons vegetable oil (Becel)
- 1 teaspoon minced fresh ginger
- 1 jalapeno pepper, seeded and finely minced
- 2 (6 ounce) salmon steaks

Direction

- Whisk together lime rind, lime juice, oil, ginger and jalapeno. Set aside a teaspoon of the mixture. Place salmon steaks in a dish just large enough to hold them. Pour remaining lime juice mixture over salmon and turn to coat. Marinate at room temperature for 15 minutes, turning once (Do not marinate longer than 30 minutes or the salmon will go mushy). Preheat bbq to medium high and grease grill. Bbq salmon turning once, until cooked through, about 3 to 4 minutes on each side. Remove to platter and spoon reserved lime juice mixture over salmon. Serve immediately. If you wish to broil salmon, place on a rack set over a pan. Broil about 4 inches from heat, turning once, until salmon is cooked through, about 3 to 4 minutes per side.

141. Lime Marinated Grilled Salmon Recipe

Serving: 4 | Prep: | Cook: 10mins |Ready in:

Ingredients

- 1/4 cup fresh lime juice
- 1 tablespoon olive oil
- 2 teaspoons Dijon mustard
- 1 teaspoon Fresh ginger; grated
- 1 clove Garlic; crushed
- 1/4 teaspoon cayenne pepper
- 1/8 teaspoon black pepper
- 4 salmon steaks; 1 inch thick

Direction

- Combine marinade ingredients in a small bowl.
- Place fish in a flat glass pan or pie plate or into a large zip bag, pour marinade over top. Turn to coat.
- Marinate for 45-60 minutes, turning several times.
- Have grill heated to white coals or gas grill heated to medium.
- Brush grill with additional olive oil.
- Grill fish until cooked through and opaque in center.
- Turn after about 4-5 minutes.
- Total grilling time will depend on heat of the grill and thickness of fish.
- Fish may also be done on a broiler pan brushed with oil. Turn after 5 minutes for about 10 minutes total broiling time.

142. Linguine With Smoked Salmon And Peas Recipe

Serving: 10 | Prep: | Cook: 30mins |Ready in:

Ingredients

- 3 cups whipping cream
- 3 cups bottled clam juice
- 2 1/2 tsp grated lemon peel
- 2 pounds linguine
- 2 10 ounce packages frozen petite peas
- 1 1/2 pound thinly sliced smoked salmon, cut into 1/2 inch wide strips
- 8 tbsp. chopped fresh dill
- Chopped green onions

Direction

- Combine cream, clam juice and 1 1/2 tsp. lemon peel in heavy medium saucepan. Boil until reduced by half, about 15 minutes. Season with salt and pepper.
- Cook pasta in a large pot of boiling salted water until almost tender. Add peas and cook until pasta is tender but still al dente and peas are tender, about 2 minutes. Drain pasta and peas. Divide between 2 serving bowls.
- Bring sauce to simmer. Pour over pasta in bowls; toss gently. Add 3/4 pounds of smoked salmon, 3 tbsp. dill and 1/2 tsp. lemon peel to each bowl and toss gently. Season with salt and pepper.
- Divide pasta among plates. Garnish with remaining 2 tbsp. dill and green onions and serve.

143.   Linguini With Salmon And Mushrooms Recipe

Serving: 4 | Prep: | Cook: 20mins | Ready in:

Ingredients

- 1/4 cup olive oil
- 12 ounce skinless salmon fillet cut into 3/4" pieces
- 1/2 teaspoon salt
- 1 teaspoon freshly ground black pepper
- 3 large garlic cloves chopped
- 1/2 pound fresh mushrooms sliced
- 5 green onions chopped
- 1 large tomato seeded and diced
- 1/3 cup dry white wine
- 3 tablespoons drained capers
- 1/2 pound dried linguine freshly cooked
- 1/4 cup chopped fresh dill
- 1 tablespoon fresh lemon juice

Direction

- Heat oil in heavy large skillet over medium high heat.

- Season salmon with salt and pepper then add to skillet and sauté 3 minutes.
- Using slotted spoon transfer salmon to plate.
- Add garlic to same skillet and sauté 30 seconds then add mushrooms and sauté 2 minutes more.
- Add green onions, tomato, wine and capers then cook 5 minutes.
- Add linguine, dill, lemon juice and salmon then toss well and season to taste.

144.   Lomi Lomi Salmon Recipe

Serving: 4 | Prep: | Cook: 20mins | Ready in:

Ingredients

- 1-1/2 pounds salmon fillets
- 1 teaspoon kosher salt
- 3 tomatoes diced
- 1 small white onion diced
- 1 tablespoon lime juice
- 1 teaspoon Tabasco sauce
- 1 teaspoon sugar
- 1 teaspoon pepper

Direction

- Lay salmon on bed of salt in glass dish then cover with salt.
- Cover with plastic wrap and refrigerate overnight.
- The following day rinse off salt and dice salmon.
- Mix tomatoes and onions with salmon then add in other ingredients.
- Chill until ready to serve.

145. Maple Cured Cedar Planked Salmon Or Tofu With Chipotle Glaze And Blueberry Pico Recipe

Serving: 4 | Prep: | Cook: 15mins | Ready in:

Ingredients

- salmon fillet, Trimmed 1 Side (2.5-3#) [For Vegetarian - 1 brick of tofu, pressed of water]
- Serves: 1 salmon side 4-6 people
- Cedar Plank, big enough to fit the fillet, 1 each Clean and unfinished - soak in cool water for 3 hrs.)
- FOR THE BRINE
- water 1 qt
- sugar, Brown 1/2 c
- maple syrup 2 cups
- salt, Kosher 1 ½ cup
- sugar, granulated ½ cup
- rosemary or thyme, fresh 3 sprigs
- FOR THE CHIPOTLE glaze
- chipotle peppers 2-3 peppers with bit of sauce
- maple syrup 1 c
- FOR THE BLUEBERRY pico de gallo
- blueberries, fresh, washed 2 cups
- cucumber, seeded and diced 2 cups
- jalapeno, fresh minced 6 large
- onion, Red, diced small 1 large
- lime, juice and zest 2 large
- olive oil, Extra Virgin ½ cup
- cilantro, fresh, minced ½ bunch
- salt and FGBP to taste
- [I added about 1/8 cup of honey]

Direction

- Put together your Blueberry Pico de Gallo: Mix all ingredients and let sit at room temperature. After 3 hours adjust seasoning and serve. Serve room temperature.
- Yield: 4 cups
- Prepare the Brine for the salmon. Bring water, Brown Sugar, Maple Syrup, salt and granulated sugar to a boil to dissolve sugars;

- Add fresh herbs and chill brine. Once brine is chilli, add the side of salmon to and marinate for 1-hour. [Vegetarian notes: I just divided up the brine and put tofu in one container and salmon in the other]
- Remove from brine, discard brine and pat salmon dry. [No need to pat tofu dry]
- Preheat oven to 450-degrees, or grill to high heat
- Season fish with salt and pepper.
- Place fish on the plank, then place in a heated oven or on a charcoal grill for about 15 minutes, glaze with Chipotle & Maple Glaze, continue cooking to desired doneness
- Serve on plank garnished with fresh lemon wedges or transfer to a serving platter.

146. Maple Salmon Recipe

Serving: 4 | Prep: | Cook: 20mins | Ready in:

Ingredients

- 1/4 cup pure maple syrup
- 2 Tbs. soy sauce
- 1 clove garlic, minced
- 1/4 tsp. garlic salt
- 1/8 tsp. ground black pepper
- 1 pound salmon

Direction

- In a small bowl, mix the maple syrup, soy sauce, garlic, garlic salt and pepper.
- Place salmon in a shallow glass baking dish and coat with the maple syrup mixture. Cover the dish and marinade salmon in the refrigerator 30 minutes, turning once.
- Preheat oven to 400F (200C).
- Place the baking dish in the preheated oven and bake salmon uncovered 20 minutes or until it easily flakes with a fork.

147.   Maple Soy Salmon Filets Recipe

Serving: 24 | Prep: | Cook: 15mins | Ready in:

Ingredients

- real maple syrup
- Low-Sodium soy sauce (or Teryaki if that's what in the cupboard)
- salmon filet (not steak) to fit the crowd

Direction

- Depending on the number you're feeding:
- 1/2 real maple syrup into big ziplock bag
- 1/2 soy sauce poured in
- Shake them together
- Put in salmon filet, slosh it around, and throw in frig 1 hour to overnight, turning over whenever you think about it
- Preheat oven to 350. Into a shallow baking dish, pour everything in.
- Cook until salmon's done -- do a fork-flake test to tell when -- usually 15 minutes (depends on salmon thickness and your oven).
- Pull it out and check the filet through to make sure it's cooked through and through.
- Should have a maple soy caramelized crust, opaque center.
- Carefully extract it from the baking dish with a spatula.
- Cut according to number of servings.
- You won't need a knife to eat this when cooked right.
- Adjust amount of maple syrup and soy marinade according to filet size.
- Enjoy and prepare for the rave reviews from your guests!

148.   Maple Whiskey Salmon Recipe

Serving: 4 | Prep: | Cook: 20mins | Ready in:

Ingredients

- 2cedar planks
- 1 side of Atlantic salmon cut in 8 pieces
- 1/2 cup whiskey
- 6 tbsp maple syrup
- salt and pepper - depending on your taste
- 1sprig thyme
- 1 sprig tarragon
- 1 tbsp corn oil
- dash of lemon juice

Direction

- Soak the cedar plank in water overnight (the better soaked, the smokier it gets).
- 1 hour before barbecuing, mix in one bag the salmon and the rest of the ingredients and let it marinate. Before barbecuing, discard the thyme and tarragon sprigs.
- Preheat Barbecue to 400F.
- Reduce heat to 300F and barbecue salmon on the planks with barbecue lid closed for about 15 minutes.
- This recipe works well if you sear the salmon in the pan instead of grilling it, just in case it is raining outside.
- Bon appetit!

149.   Marinaded Citrus Grilled Salmon With A Maple Glaze Recipe

Serving: 4 | Prep: | Cook: 20mins | Ready in:

Ingredients

- ======Marinade======
- 4 salmon Filets
- 1 tea course salt
- 1 sm. navel orange, zested and juiced
- 1 sm. lemon, zested and juiced
- 2 cloves of garlic, finely chopped
- 2 tea. Dijon mustard
- 2 Tab. chopped tarragon

- 1/2 cup olive oil
- 3 green onions chopped
- ======BBQ Glaze======
- 1/2 sm. red onion finely chopped
- 1 Tab. olive oil
- 3 Tab. red wine vinegar
- 1 cup dark amber maple syrup
- 1 Tab. tomato paste
- 1 tea. curry powder
- 1/8 tea. liquid smoke
- 1 tea black pepper

Direction

- ======Marinade======
- Mix all ingredients together and put in large plastic zip lock bag along with the salmon filets. Keep in fridge overnight.
- ======Glaze/Grill======
- Mix all ingredients together in bowl.
- Grill the salmon skin side down first and add glaze to meaty part. Flip over and cook other side and glaze. Cook until desired doneness.
- Leftover salmon is wonderful on top of salad the following day with a citrus dressing.

150.   Maui Sunset Salmon Recipe

Serving: 6 | Prep: | Cook: |Ready in:

Ingredients

- 2lbs salmon(whole or fillets)
- 1/2 cup chopped macadamia nuts
- 1/2 cup shredded or flaked coconut(unsweetened)
- 2/3 cups panko
- 1t ground cumin
- 1/2t ground coriander
- 1/2 stick butter, melted
- juice from 1 large or 2 small limes
- fresh ground pepper

Direction

- Lay salmon, skin side down, in baking pan.
- Combine melted butter and lime juice and brush about 3/4 of the mixture over the salmon. Reserve the remainder.
- Combine nuts, coconut, cumin, coriander and Panko with fresh ground pepper.
- Sprinkle liberally over top of salmon.
- Drizzle with remaining butter mixture.
- Bake at 375 for 15-20 minutes, until fish flakes easily and top is browning.
- Serve with lime wedges.

151.   Melissa DArabians Salmon Cakes Recipe

Serving: 4 | Prep: | Cook: 8mins |Ready in:

Ingredients

- 2 strips bacon, cooked until crispy, crumbled, bacon fat reserved
- 1/4 cup chopped onion
- 1 egg
- 1/2 cup mayonnaise
- 2 teaspoons Dijon mustard
- 1/2 teaspoon sugar
- 1/2 lemon, zested
- 1 (14-ounce) can wild salmon, checked for bones
- 1 baked or boiled russet potato, peeled, and fluffed with a fork
- 1/4 cup bread crumbs
- 2 tablespoons grated Parmesan
- Freshly ground black pepper
- 1/2 cup vegetable oil, divided

Direction

- Heat 1 tablespoon of the reserved bacon fat in a small sauté pan over low heat.
- Add the onions and cook until translucent.
- Set aside to cool.
- Mix the bacon, onion, egg, mayonnaise, mustard, sugar, and lemon zest in a bowl.

- Add the salmon and potato, mixing gently after each addition.
- Form the mixture into 12 small patties. (Use an ice cream scoop to make them uniform.)
- In a shallow dish, combine the bread crumbs, parmesan, and pepper, to taste.
- Coat the patties in the bread crumb topping.
- Heat 1/4 cup of the oil in a large sauté pan over medium heat.
- Cook the salmon cakes in batches until golden, about 3 to 4 minutes per side.
- Serve immediately

152. Miso Glazed Salmon Recipe

Serving: 4 | Prep: | Cook: 10mins | Ready in:

Ingredients

- 1/4 c. packed brown sugar
- 2 tbsp low-sodium saoy sauce
- 2 tbsp hot water
- 2 tbsp miso (soybean paste)
- 4 (6-ounce) salmon fillets (about 1 inch thick)
- cooking spray
- 1 tbsp chopped fresh chives

Direction

- Preheat broiler
- Combine first 4 ingredients, stirring with a whisk. Arrange fish in a shallow baking dish coated with cooking spray. Spoon miso mixture evenly over fish.
- Broil 10 minutes or until fish flakes easily when tested with a fork, basting twice with miso mixture. Sprinkle with chives.

153. Miso Salmon With Sake Butter Recipe

Serving: 4 | Prep: | Cook: 30mins | Ready in:

Ingredients

- 1/4 cup brown sugar, packed
- 2 tablespoons low sodium soy sauce
- 2 tablespoons hot water
- 2 tablespoons miso (soybean paste)
- 4 (6 ounce) salmon fillets (about 1 inch thick)
- cooking spray
- 1 tablespoon fresh chives, chopped
- cooked rice
- sake butter ingredients
- 2 tablespoons peeled and julienned ginger
- 1 tablespoon minced shallots
- 1 tablespoon unsalted butter
- 1/2 cup plus 1 teaspoon quality sake (Momokawa)
- 1 tablespoon heavy cream
- 1/2 cup (1 stick) cold unsalted butter, cut into large dice
- 1/2 teaspoons fresh lime juice
- Kosher salt

Direction

- Preheat broiler.
- Combine first 4 ingredients, stirring with a whisk.
- Arrange fish in a shallow baking dish coated with cooking spray.
- Spoon miso mixture evenly over fish.
- Broil 10 minutes or until fish flakes easily when tested with a fork, basting twice with miso mixture.
- Sprinkle with chives.
- Sake Butter
- In a small saucepan over medium-high heat, sweat the ginger and shallots in the one tablespoon butter for two to three minutes.
- Add 1/2 cup of the sake, bring to a boil, and reduce by two-thirds, about three minutes.
- Add the heavy cream, bring to a boil, and reduce by half, about two minutes.

- Add the pieces of cold butter to the sauce, bit by bit, whisking constantly over medium-high heat. The butter will emulsify, creating a thick creamy sauce.
- Once all the butter has been incorporated, remove the pan from the heat. Whisk in the remaining one teaspoon sake and the lime juice.
- Season to taste with salt.
- Place Sake butter on plate, top with a bed of rice, place salmon on top of rice.

154. Miso Glazed Salmon Recipe

Serving: 4 | Prep: | Cook: 20mins | Ready in:

Ingredients

- 1/4 cup packed brown sugar
- 2 Tbsp low sodium soy sauce
- 2 Tbsp hot water
- 2 Tbsp miso (soybean paste)
- 4 (6oz.) salmon fillets (about 1 inch thick)
- 1 Tbsp toasted sesame seed
- 2 Tbsp thinly sliced green onions (green parts)
- canola oil

Direction

- Start by mixing the first 4 ingredients (brown sugar, soy sauce, hot water, and miso) in a bowl. Stir until completely mixed.
- Set broiler on high and set rack about 6 inches from the flame.
- Salt and pepper you fish filets on both sides. Pan Searing the salmon - Before you put your fish in the pan you want it to be very very hot to the point where it just begins to smoke. Then add enough canola oil to coat the pan evenly.
- *TIP the best pan to use for this process is a cast iron pan or a skillet that has a metal handle. This will allow you to move it from the stove top to the broiler.

- Cook your filet for about 2 minutes on each side then baste it with a coating of the miso glaze then move to the broiler. Let cook for about 3 minutes then baste the fish again with glaze.
- Let cook for about 5 minutes once the fish is nice and flaky and the glaze bubbly take it out.
- Garnish with green onion, sesame seed.

155. Miso Marinated Salmon With Cucumber Daikon Relish Recipe

Serving: 6 | Prep: | Cook: 15mins | Ready in:

Ingredients

- 1/4 cup white miso (fermented soybean paste)
- 1/4 cup mirin (sweet Japanese rice wine)
- 2 tablespoons unseasoned rice vinegar
- 2 tablespoons minced green onions
- 1 1/2 tablespoons minced fresh ginger
- 2 teaspoons oriental sesame oil
- 6 6-ounce Alaskan salmon fillets, with skin
- Nonstick vegetable oil spray
- ~~~~
- cucumber-Daikon Relish:
- 2 English hothouse cucumbers, peeled, halved, seeded, cut crosswise into 1/4-inch-thick slices
- 2 teaspoons sea salt
- 8 ounces daikon (Japanese white radish), peeled, cut into 2x1/4-inch sticks
- 2/3 cup unseasoned rice vinegar
- 2/3 cup sugar
- 1 tablespoon minced fresh ginger
- 1/8 teaspoon cayenne pepper
- ~~~~
- 1 1/2 teaspoons sesame seeds, toasted
- 1/2 cup radish sprouts
- 1/2 8x8-inch sheet dried nori,* cut with scissors into matchstick-size strips

Direction

- Make Cucumber-Daikon Relish:
- Toss cucumbers with sea salt in colander. Place colander over bowl and let stand 15 minutes. Rinse cucumbers. Drain and pat dry with paper towels.
- Place radish sticks in medium bowl. Cover with water. Soak 15 minutes. Drain and pat dry with paper towels.
- Stir vinegar and next 3 ingredients in large bowl to blend. Add cucumbers and radish; toss to coat. Cover and chill at least 30 minutes and up to 2 hours.
- ~~~~
- Whisk first 6 ingredients in 13x9x2-inch glass baking dish to blend for marinade. Add salmon; turn to coat. Cover and chill at least 30 minutes and up to 2 hours.
- Preheat broiler. Line heavy large baking sheet with foil; spray with non-stick spray.
- Remove salmon fillets from miso marinade; using rubber spatula, scrape off excess marinade. Arrange salmon, skin side up, on prepared baking sheet.
- Broil 5 to 6 inches from heat source until skin is crisp, about 2 minutes. Using metal spatula, turn salmon over. Broil until salmon is just cooked through and golden brown on top, about 4 minutes.
- Transfer salmon to plates, skin side down. Spoon Cucumber Relish over. Sprinkle with sesame seeds, then sprouts and nori. Serve immediately.

---

156. Moroccan Baked Salmon Recipe

Serving: 1 | Prep: | Cook: 50mins | Ready in:

Ingredients

- spice Mixture (Makes about 6 tbsp)
- 1 tbsp ground coriander
- 1 tbsp cumin
- 1/2 tbsp smoked paprika

- 1 tsp black pepper
- 1 tsp turmeric
- 1/2 tbsp ground ginger
- 1/2 tsp cayenne
- 1 tbsp brown sugar
- 1 tsp kosher salt
- 1 tsp cinnamon
- 1/4 tsp nutmeg
- 1/2 tsp crushed cardamom
- 1/2 tsp crushed anise
- Fish
- 4 oz wild skin-on salmon fillet
- 1 tbsp Moroccan spice (above)

Direction

- Moroccan Spice
- In a small bowl, combine all the "spice mixture" ingredients, stirring well to break up any bits of brown sugar. Remove 1 tbsp. of the mixture for the salmon and store remaining blend in a tightly covered container for later use.
- Moroccan Baked Salmon
- Line a small baking sheet with foil.
- Sprinkle flesh side of the salmon with reserved Moroccan spice mixture and place skin side down on lined sheet.
- Cover and refrigerate 30 minutes.
- Preheat the oven to 450F and bake fish 10 - 13 minutes, to desired level of doneness.
- Serve over rice pilaf or couscous.

---

157. Moroccan Broiled Salmon Recipe

Serving: 0 | Prep: | Cook: 15mins | Ready in:

Ingredients

- Moroccan spice Blend (From Gourmet Magazine) or buy your own
- 1 teaspoon ground cumin
- 1 teaspoon ground ginger

- 1 teaspoon salt
- 3/4 teaspoon freshly ground black pepper
- 1/2 teaspoon ground cinnamon
- 1/2 teaspoon ground coriander seeds
- 1/2 teaspoon cayenne
- 1/2 teaspoon ground allspice
- 1/4 teaspoon ground cloves
- 2 large salmon steaks, about 1 inch thick
- olive oil
- Ras El Hanout: Moroccan spice blend (see above)
- juice from a fresh lemon
- Garnish:
- Sliced toasted almonds
- chopped fresh cilantro
- lemon slices

Direction

- In a broiler pan, place 2 tbsp. olive oil
- Lay steaks down to fit pan.
- Squeeze on lemon juice and dust heavily with the spice
- Carefully flip over fish in oiled pan and repeat with lemon juice and spices
- Broil until cooked through
- When out of the oven, sprinkle with the almonds and cilantro
- Note: to broil broccoli: have broccoli cooked crisp tender.
- Toss in olive oil, lemon juice and fresh minced garlic and S&P
- Broil a few minutes to brown top of broccoli
- This can be done the last few minutes while fish is finishing broiling.

158.   Moroccan Grilled Salmon Recipe

Serving: 4 | Prep: | Cook: 15mins | Ready in:

Ingredients

- 1/2 cup plain yogurt
- juice of 1 lemon, plus lemon wedges for garnish
- 1 tablespoon extra-virgin olive oil, plus more for the grill
- 2 to 3 cloves garlic, smashed
- 1 1/2 teaspoons ground coriander
- 1 1/2 teaspoons ground cumin
- kosher salt and freshly ground pepper
- 4 6-ounce skinless center-cut salmon fillets
- 1/4 cup chopped fresh cilantro or parsley, for garnish

Direction

- Stir together the yogurt, lemon juice, olive oil, garlic, coriander, cumin, 1/4 teaspoon salt, and pepper to taste in a small bowl. Pour half of the sauce into a large resealable plastic bag; cover and refrigerate the remaining sauce. Add the salmon to the bag and turn to coat with the marinade. Refrigerate for 20 to 30 minutes, turning the bag over once.
- Preheat a grill to medium-high. Remove the salmon from the marinade and blot off excess yogurt with paper towels. Lightly oil the grill and add the salmon; cook, turning once, until browned on the outside and opaque in the center, 4 to 6 minutes per side, depending on the thickness. Serve with the reserved yogurt sauce and garnish with the herbs and lemon wedges.

159.   Mustard Crusted Salmon Recipe

Serving: 4 | Prep: | Cook: 10mins | Ready in:

Ingredients

- 1 1/4 pounds center-cut salmon fillets, cut into 4 portions
- 1/4 teaspoon salt, or to taste
- Freshly ground pepper to taste
- 1/4 cup reduced-fat sour cream
- 2 tablespoons stone-ground mustard

- 2 teaspoons lemon juice
- Lemon wedges

Direction

- Preheat broiler. Line a broiler pan or baking sheet with foil, then coat it with cooking spray.
- Place salmon pieces, skin-side down, on the prepared pan. Season with salt and pepper. Combine sour cream, mustard and lemon juice in a small bowl. Spread evenly over the salmon.
- Broil the salmon 5 inches from the heat source until it is opaque in the center, 10 to 12 minutes. Serve with lemon wedges.

---

160. Mustard Crusted Salmon With Asparagus And Linguine Recipe

Serving: 6 | Prep: | Cook: 30mins | Ready in:

Ingredients

- For Salmon
- about 2-2 1/2lbs salmon fillets
- 4-6T butter, softened
- 1 cup bread crumbs
- 2T whole grain mustard
- 1t dry mustard
- 2 cloves garlic, minced
- several dashes hot sauce
- 1T fresh dill, minced(or sub a couple t, dried)
- juice from 1 lemon
- fresh ground pepper
- For asparagus and Linguine
- 1lb linguine(I used a fantastic black pepper variety)
- 1 1/2lb fresh asparagus, trimmed and snapped into about 1 inch sections
- about 1T olive oil
- 4T butter
- 1 small onion, diced(or sub a couple shallots)
- 3 cloves garlic, minced
- 1/2 cup good quality mustard(I used a yellow German with herbs)
- 1/2 pint heavy cream
- juice from 1 lemon
- kosher or sea salt and fresh ground pepper

Direction

- Heat water and boil pasta per package directions. Drain and set aside.
- In small bowl, combine butter, bread crumbs, whole grain mustard, dry mustard,2 cloves garlic, hot sauce, dill and salt and pepper and mix until a crumbly, pasty mixture forms.(use a little more/less butter/breadcrumbs as needed). Set aside.
- In medium sauce pan, melt remaining butter over medium heat and add onion and garlic.
- Cook about 4-5 minutes, until onion begins to get tender.
- Add mustard, and lemon juice and mix well.
- Add cream and bring just to a boil and immediately reduce heat and let simmer, stirring often, while preparing the rest of the meal.
- In large cast iron or similar high heat resistant pan, place asparagus pieces, drizzle with the olive oil and sprinkle with salt.
- Heat in 450 oven for a few minutes, just until tender. Do not overcook.
- Remove asparagus from pan and set aside. Increase oven temp to 500.
- Place salmon fillets in still hot pan and immediately top each with a scoop of the breadcrumb/mustard mixture.
- Bake or broil (just don't get too close to the element or the crumbs will burn! Use your best judgment for your oven :) for about 5 minutes, until top is lightly golden browned and salmon flakes easily. Do not overcook.
- Toss still warm pasta and asparagus with the mustard sauce and serve the salmon on top of a serving of the pasta.

161. Mustard Broiled Salmon With Potato Salad Recipe

Serving: 4 | Prep: | Cook: 10mins | Ready in:

Ingredients

- 1 1/2 lbs new potatoes
- 2 tsp salt, divided
- 1/4 tsp black pepper
- 3/4 cup Crème fraîche or sour cream
- 2 tbs fresh lemon juice
- 1 small fennel bulb, thinly sliced
- 4 6-ounce salmon fillets, skin removed
- 3 tbs Dijon mustard
- 1/4 cup fresh dill, chopped

Direction

- Heat broiler.
- Place the potatoes in a pot, cover with cold water, and bring to a boil. Add 1 teaspoon salt, reduce heat, and simmer until tender, about 15 minutes. Drain, run under cold water to cool, then cut into quarters.
- Meanwhile, in a large bowl, combine the crème fraîche or sour cream, 1 tablespoon of the lemon juice, 1 tsp. salt, and 1/4 tsp. pepper. Stir in the potatoes and fennel; set aside.
- Place the salmon on a foil-lined baking sheet.
- In a small bowl, combine the mustard and the remaining lemon juice. Spread over the top of the salmon. Broil until the salmon is the same color throughout, 6 to 8 minutes, depending on the thickness. Divide the salmon and salad among individual plates and sprinkle with the dill.

162. Nigiri Salmon Recipe

Serving: 4 | Prep: | Cook: 20mins | Ready in:

Ingredients

- 1 pack sushi grade salmon fillet (very fresh)
- 1 cups sort grain rice
- 4 tbs rice vinegar
- 2 tbs sugar(because i don't have mirin)
- 1/2 tsp kombu dashi
- 1.5 cups water
- For the condiment :
- pickle gari(ginger)
- soyu
- wasabi

Direction

- In a microwave rice cooker, cook the rice and water for 15 mins on high heat (rice cooking setting).
- Slice the fish; set aside.
- Mix rice vinegar, sugar, hondashi and pour on top of cooked rice, fan let the steam out.
- Make a rice ball as big as your thumb.
- Smear with a little bit wasabi on the rice and top with salmon fillet.
- Ready to serve.
- And also look in my oldest sushi creation, serunya sushi.

163. Northwestern Salmon Quiche Recipe

Serving: 8 | Prep: | Cook: 60mins | Ready in:

Ingredients

- 1 cup all-purpose flour
- 1 cup grated parmesan cheese, divided
- 1/4 cup chopped hazelnuts (walnuts, almonds, or pecans)
- 1/2 teaspoon salt
- 1/4 teaspoon paprika
- 6 tablespoons extra-virgin olive oil
- 1/2 cup milk
- 3 eggs, beaten
- 1 cup sour cream
- 1/4 cup mayonnaise

- 1 tablespoon finely chopped fresh chives
- 1/4 teaspoon Colgin's Smoke flavoring
- 1/4 teaspoon salt
- 1/4 teaspoon pepper
- 1 1/2 to 2 cups cooked salmon, (ok to used canned) flaked and all skin and bones removed
- sour cream & fresh dill for garnish

Direction

- Preheat oven to 400 degrees. In a medium bowl, combine flour, 3/4 cup parmesan cheese, hazelnuts, salt, paprika, and olive oil. Press mixture onto bottom and sides of a 10-inch pie plate or quiche pan. Bake for 10 minutes; remove from oven and reduce oven temperature to 325 degrees.
- In a large bowl, combine milk, eggs, sour cream, mayonnaise, chives, liquid smoke, salt, and pepper. Stir in flaked salmon and remaining 1/2 cup parmesan cheese. Pour mixture into baked crust. Bake approximately 45 to 50 minutes or until a knife inserted in the center comes out clean. Remove from oven and let cool 12 to 15 minutes.
- To serve, spread a thin layer of sour cream over the top. Cut into wedges and serve.
- Makes 4 dinner-size servings and 6 to 8 lunch or appetizer servings.

---

164.   Oak Plank Atlantic Salmon Filet With Dill Hollandaise Sauce And Lemon Roasted Asparagus Recipe

Serving: 4 | Prep: | Cook: 20mins | Ready in:

Ingredients

- For the Salmon:
- 2 untreated Oak planks (or Cedar), each about 5 by 12-inches, soaked in red wine (or water) to cover for at least 2 hours (see link below for planks we used)
- olive oil
- 4 salmon fillets, 8-ounces each
- brown sugar
- smoked paprika
- fresh orange zest
- kosher salt and freshly ground black pepper, to taste
- ~~~~~~~~~~~~~~~~~~~~~~~~~~~~~~~~~~~~~
- For the Hollandaise Sauce:
- 2 organic egg yolks
- ½ cups warm clarified butter
- 1 Tbsp lemon juice
- 1 tsp dried dill
- kosher salt and freshly ground black pepper, to taste
- ~~~~~~~~~~~~~~~~~~~~~~~~~~~~~~~~~~~~~
- For the Asparagus:
- 20 spears of green asparagus
- zest of one lemon
- olive oil, to drizzle
- kosher salt and fresh ground black pepper to taste

Direction

- For Salmon: Season salmon with brown sugar, smoked paprika, orange zest, salt and freshly ground black pepper, to taste. Take planks out of soaking liquid and dry with paper towel. Lightly oil planks with olive oil, using a paper towel or pastry brush. Place seasoned salmon on planks and grill over in direct charcoal heat for about 20 minutes. Once done, remove salmon from grill, lightly tent with foil and let rest 10-15 minutes.
- For Hollandaise:
- In the top half of a small double boiler, beat egg yolks and 2 tbsp. of the hot water from boiler.
- Place over very hot (not boiling) water and whip constantly to prevent scrambling of the eggs. Cook until the egg yolks become of a sauce consistency.

- Remove from heat. Whisk in clarified butter in a slow stream, whipping constantly to prevent sauce from breaking.
- Whisk in lemon juice, dill, salt and pepper to taste. Hold warm for service (I transfer the sauce to a small bowl, then place bowl in the pan of hot water, covered, until I'm ready to plate).
- For Asparagus:
- Preheat the oven to 400 degrees F.
- Snap or cut the dry stem ends off each asparagus and place on a heavy baking sheet. Drizzle with olive oil, sprinkle with salt, pepper and lemon zest and toss. Roast until the asparagus is tender, about 10-15 minutes, depending on how thick your asparagus is. Cool slightly and serve warm or at room temperature.
- To plate: Spoon sauce on serving plate, top with salmon. Place asparagus next to salmon.

165. Old Bay Grilled Salmon Wraps Recipe

Serving: 6 | Prep: | Cook: 30mins | Ready in:

Ingredients

- 6 4-6oz salmon fillets, grilled with lemon, butter, salt, fresh ground pepper and Old Bay Seasoning
- 6 large flour tortillas
- handful of fresh baby spinach leaves, or Romaine
- 1 sweet onion, sliced thin
- 2 bell peppers, cut into strips
- drizzle of olive oil(if desired)
- 1 cucumber, cut into strips
- 1 cup feta or goat cheese crumbles
- Old Bay dill Sauce
- 1/2 cup plain Greek yogurt
- 1/2 cup mayonnaise
- 1T Fresh dill, minced
- 1 clove garlic, minced

- 1t fresh lemon juice
- 1T Old Bay Seasoning
- dash of hot sauce

Direction

- For Old Bay Dill Sauce
- Combine all ingredients and set aside.
- For Wraps
- In small sauté pan, heat a little olive oil and quickly sauté the onions and peppers, lightly, if desired.
- Spread tortillas with a little of the sauce then layer with spinach, onions, peppers, cucumbers and a salmon fillet.
- Roll up burrito style.

166. Orange Glazed Salmon Fillets With Rosemary Recipe

Serving: 4 | Prep: | Cook: 7mins | Ready in:

Ingredients

- 4 (6 ounce) salmon fillets, 1" thick
- 1/2 teaspoon kosher salt
- 1/4 teaspoon freshly ground black pepper
- cooking spray
- 2 tablespoons minced shallots
- 1/4 cup dry white wine
- 1/2 teaspoon chopped fresh rosemary
- 3/4 cup fresh orange juice (about 2 oranges)
- 1 tablespoon pure maple syrup

Direction

- Sprinkle fillets evenly with salt and pepper.
- Heat a large nonstick skillet over medium high heat.
- Coat pan with cooking spray.
- Add fillets.
- Cook 2 minutes per side OR until fish flakes with a fork.
- Remove from pan.
- Recoat pan with spray.

- Add shallots and sauté 30 seconds.
- Stir in wine and rosemary.
- Cook until liquid almost evaporates, about 30 seconds.
- Add juice and syrup, bring to a boil and cook 1 minute.
- Return fillets to pan.
- Cook 1 minute per side OR until thoroughly heated.

167.   Orange And Fennel Glazed Salmon Recipe

Serving: 4 | Prep: | Cook: 10mins | Ready in:

Ingredients

- 4 six ounce portions of one inch thick salmon fillets
- 1/2 tsp of salt and 1/2 tsp of black pepper
- 2 teaspoons of grated orange rind
- equal portions of fresh rosemary leaves and fennel seeds
- 1/2 cup of fresh orange juice
- cooking spray

Direction

- Combine orange juice, orange rind and crushed rosemary leaves and fennel seeds.
- I use a mortar and pestle for the rosemary and fennel.
- Put fish and marinade in a large resealable plastic bag.
- Refrigerate 20 minutes. Turning at least once.
- Meanwhile preheat broiler.
- Remove fish from marinade, reserving the marinade.
- Place fish skin side down on a broiler pan well coated with non-stick cooking spray.
- Season liberally with salt and pepper.
- Broil about 10 minutes.
- Bring reserved marinade to a boil in a small sauce pan, reduce heat and simmer while the salmon cooks.

- Serve the sauce with the finished salmon.
- I like peas with this dish especially the braised peas with lettuce and a mushroom rice pilaf.

168.   Orange Glazed Salmon Fillets With Rosemary Recipe

Serving: 4 | Prep: | Cook: 10mins | Ready in:

Ingredients

- 4 (6-ounce) salmon fillets (1 inch thick)
- 1/2 tsp kosher salt
- 1/4 tsp freshly ground black pepper
- cooking spray
- 2 Tbs minced shallots
- 1/4 cup dry white wine
- 1/2 tsp chopped fresh rosemary
- 3/4 cup fresh orange juice (about 2 oranges)*
- 1 Tbs maple syrup
- *I used juice from a carton and thought it tasted fine.

Direction

- Sprinkle fillets evenly with salt and pepper. Heat a large nonstick skillet over medium-high heat. Coat pan with cooking spray. Add fillets; cook 2 minutes on each side or until fish flakes easily when tested with a fork or until desired degree of doneness. Remove from pan.
- Recoat pan with cooking spray. Add shallots; sauté 30 seconds. Stir in wine and rosemary; cook 30 seconds or until liquid almost evaporates. Add juice and syrup; bring to a boil, and cook 1 minute. Return fillets to pan; cook 1 minute on each side or until thoroughly heated.

169. Orange Glazed Salmon Recipe

Serving: 4 | Prep: | Cook: 9mins | Ready in:

Ingredients

- 4 (4oz) salmon fillets, 1" thick
- 1/4t salt
- 1/4t pepper
- cooking spray
- 3T soy sauce, low-sodium
- 3T orange juice
- 1/2t dark sesame oil

Direction

- Sprinkle salmon with salt and pepper. Coat a large nonstick skillet with cooking spray; place over high heat until hot. Add fish, and cook, uncovered, 3 minutes on each side. Cover and cook 3 additional minutes or until fish flakes easily when tested with a fork. Remove from skillet; set aside, and keep warm.
- Add soy sauce and orange juice to skillet; cook over high heat 1 minute, stirring to deglaze skillet. Add oil and stir well. Pour sauce over fish, serve immediately.
- 148 calories, 28% from fat.

170. Orange Glazed Salmon And Greens Recipe

Serving: 8 | Prep: | Cook: 30mins | Ready in:

Ingredients

- 1/3 cup frozen orange juice
- concentrate, thawed
- 1/4 cup light soy sauce
- 1/4 cup water
- 1 1/2 teaspoons sesame oil
- 2 tablespoons honey
- 1/2 teaspoon grated fresh ginger
- 4 salmon filets, about 6- to 8-ounces each
- 2 teaspoons canola or peanut oil
- 1/2 cup chopped onion
- 1 red pepper, cut into 1- by- 1/4 -inch strips
- 1 cup sliced mushrooms
- 7 to 8 cups fresh torn greens (such as spinach, mustard, collard, swiss chard, or
- combination)

Direction

- Combine orange juice concentrate, soy sauce, water, sesame oil, honey and ginger.
- Stir to combine well.
- Measure out 1/4 cup mixture to use as a basting sauce on salmon; reserve remaining sauce.
- Place salmon filets on broiler pan and brush with half of the 1/4 cup orange juice mixture.
- Broil 5 to 6 minutes or until browned.
- Turn salmon, brush with orange juice mixture and broil 5 to 6 minutes or until fish is opaque and flakes easily with fork.
- Remove skin.
- Meanwhile, heat oil in large skillet.
- Add onion and sauté, stirring frequently, until onion is translucent.
- Add red pepper and mushrooms and cook, stirring frequently, until vegetables are crisp-tender. Pour reserved orange juice mixture into skillet and heat until sauce boils rapidly.
- Add torn greens, cover and cook 1 minute.
- Using tongs, lift steamed greens from skillet and arrange in deep serving platter.
- Place salmon over greens. Spoon remaining vegetables around salmon, then pour sauce over salmon, coating well.

171. Orange Scented Salmon Saute With Thyme Garlic Dipping Oil Recipe

Serving: 2 | Prep: | Cook: 10mins | Ready in:

Ingredients

- 2 6- to 8-ounces wild salmon steaks cut about an inch thick, or other fish
- Good-tasting extra-virgin olive oil
- salt and fresh ground black pepper
- 1 large garlic clove, thin sliced
- Shredded zest of half a large orange
- herbed Oil: see variations in instructions below
- 2 teaspoons fresh thyme leaves (6 long sprigs more or less)
- 1 clove garlic, crushed
- salt and fresh-ground black pepper to taste
- 1/4 to 1/3 cup good tasting extra-virgin olive oil

Direction

- Rinse the fish and pat it dry.
- Examine the steaks for any bones and remove them.
- . Lightly film a slant-sided 12-inch skillet with the oil, and heat it over medium-high heat.
- Season the fish on both sides with the salt and pepper.
- Slip them into the skillet, and sear for 1 minute.
- Turn the fish with a metal spatula, taking care not to break it, and sear for 1 minute on the other side.
- . Sprinkle the garlic slices and orange zest around the fish.
- Turn the heat to medium low, cover the skillet and cook for 6 to 7 minutes, turning the steaks midway through cooking and bathing the pieces with the garlic and orange.
- Fish is done when the flesh is just firm when pressed.
- It should be barely opaque near the center.
- . Remove the fish to dinner plates, let stand about 5 minutes, scrape the pan juices over the pieces and set out the dipping oil in small bowls.
- 60-Second Thyme-Garlic Dipping Oil: Makes 1/4 cup to 1/3 cup, enough for 2
- . Put everything in a small, microwave-safe serving bowl.
- Cover with a paper towel and microwave on high 1 minute.
- Let cool for a moment, then set out on the table, or use the oil to sauce other dishes.
- Variations:
- Basil-Onion Dipping Oil
- Substitute 5 to 6 torn basil leaves for the thyme and a tablespoon of chopped onion for the garlic.
- Bay-Orange Dipping Oil
- Instead of the thyme, use 2 fresh bay leaves, the shredded zest of a quarter of an orange, and keep the garlic and oil.
- Oregano-Lemon-Garlic Dipping Oil
- Substitute 1/2 teaspoon dry oregano for the thyme, keep the garlic, and add a few strips of lemon peel.
- After cooking, squeeze a little lemon juice into the oil.
- Lamb, salads, feta cheese, and grilled vegetables marry beautifully with this oil.
- Black Pepper-Lemon Dipping Oil
- Let 1/4 teaspoon fresh-ground black pepper stand in for the thyme, along with the grated zest of 1/8 of a lemon.
- Cumin-Paprika Dipping Oil
- Let 1/2 to 1 teaspoon ground cumin and 1 teaspoon sweet or hot paprika stand in for the thyme and garlic

172.   Oriental Salmon Recipe

Serving: 2 | Prep: | Cook: 20mins | Ready in:

Ingredients

- 2 skinless salmon fillets
- 2 tablespoons sesame oil
- 2 tablespoons black sesame seeds
- 1 teaspoon salt
- 2 tablespoons minced garlic
- 2 tablespoons freshly minced ginger
- 1/2 cup sugar
- 1 cup soy sauce

- 2 tablespoons cornstarch mixed with 2 tablespoons water
- 1-1/2 cups fresh Asian vegetables of your choice
- 1-1/2 tablespoons vegetable oil to sauté vegetables
- Steamed white rice

Direction

- Preheat oven to 450.
- Season fillets by coating with 1 tablespoon sesame oil then the sesame seeds.
- Add salt to taste.
- Set in a baking pan or cookie sheet with sides and bake in preheated oven for 15 minutes.
- While fish is baking make sauce by combining garlic, ginger, sugar, remaining 1 tablespoon sesame oil and the soy sauce in a small saucepan.
- Bring to a boil then reduce heat to a simmer and cook 5 minutes.
- In small bowl mix cornstarch and water until smooth.
- Slowly add some of the mixture to the sauce and cook until thick enough to coat the back of a spoon.
- Add cornstarch mixture as needed.
- Sauté vegetables in the vegetable oil in a covered sauté pan until tender.
- When vegetables are tender add sauce and gently mix then spoon vegetables over baked fillets and serve immediately over steamed rice.

---

173.   Oven Slow Cook Salmon Recipe

Serving: 4 | Prep: | Cook: 30mins | Ready in:

Ingredients

- 4 (8 ounce) salmon fillets
- 1-2 tablespoons vegetable oil
- 3 navel oranges, cut into 1/4 inch slices

- 2 large onions, thinly sliced
- 1 large or 2 small fresh fennel bulbs, thinly sliced
- 3-4 sprigs fresh tarragon
- salt and pepper to taste
- Assorted garnishes such as crème fraiche, sliced oranges or fresh herbs

Direction

- Preheat to 250F. Lightly brush salmon with oil and season with salt and pepper. Let sit at room temperature for about 20 minutes.
- Grab a baking pan big enough to hold all fillets in single layer. Make a bed on the pan by layering the onions, fennel and two of the sliced oranges. Place the salmon fillets on the bed and tuck in the tarragon sprigs.
- Bake for 30 minutes. (If you're cooking more than 4 fillets, just add another 2 minutes per additional filet.) To test for doneness, stick a sharp paring knife in, if it goes in and out, it's done.
- Top with whatever finishing herbs, spices or ingredients you've chosen. After cooking, the salmon is going to look almost exactly the same as when you first put it in. Don't worry, after 30 minutes in the oven it will be cooked.
- Dress up your salmon however you like.

---

174.   PAN SEARED SALMON WITH SWEET AND SPICY ASIAN GLAZE Recipe

Serving: 4 | Prep: | Cook: 10mins | Ready in:

Ingredients

- MARINADE---
- juice of 1 orange
- 3 tbs rice wine vinegar
- 2 tbs reduced sodium soy sauce
- 2 tbs olive oil
- 1 small red or green chile pepper, thinly sliced

- 1 tbs grated ginger
- SALMON---
- 4 salmon fillets
- 1/8 tsp kosher salt
- 1/8 tsp pepper
- 2 tsp olive oil
- 2 tbs cilantro leaves

Direction

- In a shallow glass dish, combine all marinade ingredients. Add salmon and turn to coat. Cover and marinate in refrigerator 30 min. Remove salmon from marinade, reserve marinade. Sprinkle salmon with salt and pepper.
- Heat oil in a skillet. Add salmon skin side down and cook 4 min. Turn salmon and cook 4 min. or until just opaque in center. Transfer salmon to a platter. Cover loosely with foil and keep warm. Discard any drippings from skillet, add marinade and cook until thickened and syrupy. Drizzle glaze over salmon and sprinkle with cilantro.

---

175. Pacific Salmon With Ginger And Cilantro Recipe

Serving: 2 | Prep: | Cook: 30mins | Ready in:

Ingredients

- 1- Alaskan Pacific salmon fillet, approximately 1-1.5 lbs, skin still on. Suggested salmon varieties: Sockeye (red), Chinook (king) or Coho (silver).
- fine sea salt
- 1/2 cup low sodium soy sauce (omit sea salt above if using regular, higher sodium soy sauce)
- 2 Tablespoons freshly grated ginger root or pre-packaged minced ginger root
- 1 teaspoon crushed garlic
- 1 cup fresh cilantro leaves, some soft stems are ok.

- extra cilantro leaves for garnish

Direction

- Gently rinse salmon fillet in very cold water, about 10 seconds each side. Pat salmon dry with paper towel. Rub sea salt into salmon, flesh-side only, until most of exposed flesh is coated.
- In medium sized bowl, mix together soy sauce, ginger and garlic with a fork or whisk. Once well combined, briefly mix in cilantro, just enough to cause a little "bruising" of the leaves but not so much as to completely mash them to a pulp.
- Pour mixture into baking dish (preferably glass). If possible, try to match the size of the baking dish as closely as possible to the size of the salmon fillet.
- Place salmon fillet, skin side up, in the baking dish. If the fillet is a pretty uneven thickness (i.e. a difference of more than a 1 inch), I will sometimes choose to "tuck in" the thinnest parts and/or the edges, to keep those portions from being very overcooked when the thicker portion is just finished.
- Preheat oven to 375 degrees F.
- Cover baking dish, allow salmon to marinate for approximately 10 minutes.
- Baked covered salmon for 20 minutes, then remove from oven and turn fillet, if possible, to skin side down.
- At this point the majority of the salmon should flake easily with a fork and have changed color from a bright translucent reddish-pink to an opaque, bright orange-salmon color. Check the thickest part of the salmon with a fork, aligning tines along the natural grain of the fillet and pulling gently apart. The middle of the fillet should be opaque with a small amount of translucent portions.
- Return salmon to oven to bake for another 5-10 minutes, depending on how well cooked you wish it to be.
- Remove salmon from oven, transfer to serving plate and garnish with a few remaining cilantro leaves. Excellent served with rice,

vegetables or any other mildly flavored side dish (so as not to overpower).

176.   Pan Seared King Salmon And Diver Scallop With Sauce Piperade And A Horseradish Emulsion Recipe

Serving: 8 | Prep: | Cook: 6mins | Ready in:

Ingredients

- For the Piperade:
- 1 1/2 oz. spanish olive Oil
- 1 sweet onion, finely diced
- 1 Tbsp. garlic, finely minced
- 1 fennel bulb, finely diced
- 1 red bell pepper, finely diced
- 4-5 Vine Ripened tomatoes, seeds removed and finely diced
- 1 serrano chili, roasted and finely diced
- Sherry vinegar, to taste
- smoked paprika, to taste
- kosher salt, to taste
- Finely minced chives
- For the horseradish Emulsion:
- 2 cups water
- 2/3 cup prepared horseradish
- 4 oz. unsalted butter
- kosher salt to taste
- 2 tsp. Lecithin
- For the Seafood:
- 8 ea., 5 oz. fillets, fresh King salmon, rolled into a roulade and held with a wooden skewer to hold its shape (optional)
- 8 ea., U-10 Diver scallops, scored on one side
- kosher salt
- cooking oil

Direction

- For the Piperade:
- Pre-heat oven to 400 degrees F. Lightly coat the serrano chili with some oil, place on a pan,

and roast until all sides are charred and the skin is peeling away. This can also be done over a grill or open flame. Place the chili in a bowl and cover with plastic wrap for 5 minutes so that the steam will help the skin pull away. When cool, peel, remove seeds, and finely dice. Meanwhile, heat the olive oil in a large sauté pan on medium high. Add the onion and garlic, and cook until the onion is translucent and tender, but do not brown. Add the fennel and bell pepper, and cook until tender. Add the tomatoes and serrano chili, and cook until the tomatoes are soft but still have a little shape. Season to taste with the sherry vinegar, smoked paprika, and kosher salt. Reserve and re-heat when needed. Add chives just before plating.
- For the Horseradish Emulsion:
- Heat the water and butter until the butter is dissolved and the mixture is hot. Whisk in the horseradish, lecithin, and a fair amount of salt. Aerate the liquid with an immersion blender to form the foam. Taste the foam and adjust seasoning. Add more horseradish and salt if needed, add butter to balance if too bitter. The foam should be intensely flavored or else it won't stand up against the piperade. Keep warm, and heat to 120-130 degrees F to foam.
- For the Seafood:
- Pre-heat oven to 400 degrees F. Heat oil on high. Season the salmon and scallop with kosher salt. Sear both seafoods on one side (add scallop scored side down) until golden brown. Turn over, briefly sear on bottom and finish in oven until medium rare doneness, about 3 minutes. Serve with the piperade sauce and horseradish emulsion.

177.   Pan Seared Salmon And Scallops Umeboshi And Port Wine Reduction Sauce Plum Wine Emulsion Recipe

Serving: 6 | Prep: | Cook: 30mins | Ready in:

Ingredients

- 6 ea., 5 oz. Fresh King salmon fillets
- 12 ea., Atlantic Diver scallops, scored one one side and cleaned
- 1/2 bottle ruby port
- 1/3 lb. unsalted butter, cut into small cubes
- 2 tsp. Umeboshi paste
- 1 cup Japanese plum wine
- 1/4 cup Elderflower (sub. mirin or simple syrup)
- 2 tsp. Lecithin
- kosher salt to taste
- 1-2 tsp. Togarashi Shichimi
- canola oil

Direction

- In a sauce pan, reduce the port until the consistency of maple syrup. Remove from heat and whisk in the butter, a few cubes at a time until emulsified. Return to heat if the sauce gets cold, but do not boil. Whisk in the umeboshi paste and check for seasoning. Add more paste if needed. Reserve and keep warm.
- In a separate sauce pan, bring the plum wine to a boil and simmer for 3-4 minutes to cook off some of the alcohol and to take off the "bite" from it. Remove from heat and add the butter, elderflower, and lecithin. Season to taste and foam with an immersion blender (you'll need a good amount of salt to bring out the flavors).
- Heat enough oil in two large sauté pans on high until smoking. Score the skin side of the salmon and season with salt. Add skin side down and press down gently so that it sears evenly. Cook on high for 1 minute, then reduce heat to medium. Cook until the skin is golden brown and crispy, then flip and cook until medium doneness.
- Heat enough oil in two large sauté pans on high until smoking. Season the scallops with salt, and add the scored side down while pressing gently on each scallop so that it sears evenly. Cook until golden brown on each side, and until medium doneness.
- Serve the salmon and scallops with the two sauces layered, and a sprinkling of the togarashi on top.

---

178. Pan Seared Salmon With Caribe Rice Pilaf From Dick Clarks American Bandstand Grill Recipe

Serving: 2 | Prep: | Cook: 15mins | Ready in:

Ingredients

- Pan Seared salmon
- 8 ounces salmon
- oil to coat pan
- salt and pepper to taste
- 4 ounces baby spinach
- 2 ounces diced roma tomatoes
- 2 ounces sliced mushrooms
- 2 ounces white wine
- honey mustard Sauce
- 2 cups mayonnaise
- 1 teaspoon yellow mustard
- 1 teaspoon Dijon mustard
- 2 teaspoons honey
- 1/4 teaspoon cayenne pepper
- 1 teaspoon celery salt
- 1 teaspoon worcestershire sauce
- Caribe rice Pilaf
- 2 ounces butter
- 4 ounces yellow diced onions
- 1 pound white rice
- 1 quart water
- 1 teaspoon chicken base
- 1/4 teaspoon white pepper
- 1/4 teaspoon celery salt
- 1/4 teaspoon cumin
- 1/4 teaspoon chopped fresh garlic
- 1 cup black beans (canned, drained and rinsed)
- 1/4 cup diced green onions
- 1/4 pound shredded carrots

Direction

- Pan Seared Salmon:
- Heat oil in pan, dust salmon with salt and pepper.
- Place in hot pan, skin side down.
- Cook about 5-7 minutes.
- Add white wine and cook for additional time.
- Take out salmon and add spinach, mushrooms and tomatoes.
- Honey Mustard Sauce:
- In a mixing bowl, blend ingredients together.
- Caribe Rice Pilaf:
- Place butter in a rice pot, add diced yellow onions and cook until translucent.
- Add rice and mix together.
- Add water, white pepper, celery salt, chopped garlic, and cumin. Bring to a boil.
- Cover with foil, lower heat and stir rice occasionally until rice is tender.
- Remove from heat and fluff rice with a fork to release all steam to stop cooking.
- Mix in shredded carrots, diced green onions and washed and drained black beans.
- ***NOTE***
- I use Minute Rice, and have used both the white and the brown. Both are great

179.   Pan Seared Salmon With Chipotle Beurre Blanc Recipe

Serving: 8 | Prep: | Cook: 45mins | Ready in:

Ingredients

- Beurre blanc sauce
- 1/4 c finely diced red onion
- 2 cloves garlic minced
- 1/2 c whiskey
- 6 oz pineapple juice
- 3 T vinegar
- 3 T honey
- 2 teas paprika
- 2 T tomato paste
- 1 T Worchestershire
- 1 1/2 T chipotle and adobo sauce minced (more chipotle for hotter)
- 1 1/2 sticks chilled butter. cubed
- For the salmon
- 8   4-6 oz skinless salmon fillets
- 1/2 c brown sugar
- 1/4 c kosher salt
- 1 teas dried mustard
- 1 1/2 teas ground cumin
- 1/4 teas cinnamon
- 1/2 teas cayenne

Direction

- Combine all the ingredients except the butter for the beurre blanc sauce in a sauce pan. Bring to a boil and immediately reduce to a low simmer. Simmer until reduced by at least 1/3. Remove from heat. Whisk in the butter a couple of pieces at a time until all the butter in incorporated. The sauce will be about room temperature at this point and ready to use.
- Salmon
- Mix the sugar and all the spices together until well incorporated. Rub one side of the salmon fillet generously with the seasoning (don't put any on the other side). Preheat the oven to 400 F. Heat a frying pan to med high heat. Coat the bottom of the pan with a spray of Pam. Place the salmon seasoned side down and fry for 3-4 minutes. The sugar should start to caramelize around the edges. Place in an oil baking dish sugar side up. Bake for 10 minutes or until the salmon is just cooked through.
- Place 2 T of the beurre blanc sauce on a plate and place a salmon fillet on top with the pan crusted side up. Serve with pan crusted new potatoes.

180.   Pan Seared Salmon With A Ginger Scallion Cilantro Pesto Recipe

Serving: 8 | Prep: | Cook: 15mins |Ready in:

Ingredients

- For the salmon:
- 8 ea., 7-8 oz. salmon filets
- 6 Tbsp. olive oil
- kosher salt
- fresh cracked pepper
- For the Pesto:
- 3/4 to 1 c. macadamia nut oil
- 1 c. loosely packed fresh cilantro leaves (thin stems are ok)
- 1/2 c. chopped scallions
- 1/2 c. Unsalted macadamia nuts
- 3 Tbsp. fresh ginger, chopped
- 1 Tbsp. fresh garlic, chopped
- juice of 1 lemon + the zest
- kosher salt to taste

Direction

- In a food processor or blender, combine all of the ingredients for the pesto and blend until you get a medium-thick pesto consistency. Add more oil as needed. Season to taste with kosher salt and reserve.
- Heat 3 Tbsp. of oil in two large sauté pans until lightly smoking. Season both sides of the salmon with kosher salt and pepper, carefully lay the salmon into the pans, skins side down. Cook the salmon until about medium doneness, about 3-4 minutes per side. Serve with the pesto drizzled on top and around the salmon.

181.   Pan Seared Salmon With A Tomato Fennel Confit Recipe

Serving: 4 | Prep: | Cook: 60mins |Ready in:

Ingredients

- For the fish:
- 4 ea., 8 oz. Wild salmon fillets
- 1/4 c. all-purpose flour
- 3 Tbsp. oil for frying
- kosher salt and fresh cracked pepper
- For the confit:
- 2 lbs. roma tomatoes or equivalent
- 1 fennel bulb, cut into 1/4" julienne
- 1-2 c. extra-virgin olive oil
- 8-12 garlic cloves, whole
- 3 bay leaves
- 8-10 fresh thyme sprigs

Direction

- Prepare a pot of boiling water, and a large bowl or other vessel filled with iced water. On the bottom of each tomato, cut an X with the point of a paring or chef's knife. Each slit should be roughly an inch long, but try not to pierce too deep into the tomato's flesh. Place the tomatoes in the boiling water for about 1 minute, then immerse the tomatoes in the iced water to shock them and stop the cooking process. Remove them from the iced water and dry. Using a paring knife or vegetable peeler, skin the tomatoes starting at the of the X. The skin should come off fairly easily. Cut the tomatoes into quarters, and remove the seeds and excess juice, and drain the tomatoes in a colander or dry on paper towels.
- Pre-heat oven to 350 degrees. In a shallow baking dish, place the tomatoes, garlic, and fennel in one layer. Add the herbs, season with kosher salt and pepper, and pour enough of the oil in to just barely come to the top of the tomatoes and fennel. Cover with foil, and roast in the oven for 1 hour or until tender.
- Meanwhile, heat the frying oil in a sauté pan until lightly smoking. Lightly dust the salmon with flour, and season both sides with salt and pepper. Add the salmon to the pan and sauté until browned and crispy, about 3-4 minutes. Turn the fish over, and continue cooking until just barely cooked through, about 2-3 minutes.

Serve immediately with the confit and oil from the confit.

- Any extra confit can be stored in the fridge for up to 4-5 days. Any extra oil from the confit can be strained and stored for up to two weeks in the fridge.

182. Pan Seared White Wine Salmon Recipe

Serving: 4 | Prep: | Cook: 5mins | Ready in:

Ingredients

- 1 to 1 1/2 lbs fresh salmon
- 1/4 tsp salt
- 1/2 tsp course black pepper
- 1/2 tsp paprika
- 1/2 tsp basil
- 1/4 tsp dill weed
- 3/4 stick butter
- 1 Tblsp lemon juice
- 1/4 cup white wine
- 2 Tblsp olive oil
- (optinal for a sweeter tasting salmon, also add brown sugar to taste in sauce)

Direction

- Heat olive oil in skillet until almost smoking. Sprinkle salt and pepper on fillets and sear on both sides for 2 to 3 minutes until darkened.
- Melt butter in small sauce pan and add wine, lemon juice and remaining dry spices. Remove salmon from skillet and place on a plate and pour sauce over all. Enjoy!!
- This can also be done on the grill by coating the fillets with olive oil, sprinkling dry ingredients on fillets while on grill and use butter, wine and dry ingredients for sauce too. Takes 2 to 3 minutes per side.

183. Pan Roasted Salmon With Fresh Mint Sugar Snap Peas Recipe

Serving: 2 | Prep: | Cook: 15mins | Ready in:

Ingredients

- Salmon:
- 1 1/2 Tbsp dry white wine
- 1 1/2 Tbsp reduced-sodium soy sauce
- 1 1/2 Tbsp balsamic vinegar
- 1 tsp ground cumin
- 1 tsp ground ginger
- 2 salmon filets
- olive oil
- Peas:
- 3/4 lb sugar snap peas
- 1/4 cup chopped fresh mint
- 2 Tbsp lemon juice (or more to taste)
- splash olive oil
- 1 Tbsp reduced-sodium soy sauce
- 1/4 tsp salt + more to taste
- 1/4 tsp ground black pepper + more to taste

Direction

- To make marinade: In a medium bowl, whisk wine, soy sauce, vinegar, ginger, and cumin. Add salmon filets and turn to coat. Allow to sit, skin side up while peas are cooking.
- To make peas: In a saucepan, bring 4 cups water to a boil; add peas and cook 10 seconds. Drain in a colander and run under cold water to stop cooking. Dry on paper towels.
- In a bowl, whisk together mint, lemon juice, oil, soy sauce, salt, and pepper. Add to peas, tossing to coat. Adjust seasonings to taste.
- To make salmon: In a large nonstick skillet, heat oil and add salmon, skin side down. Partially cover and cook on medium-high heat until salmon is opaque and flakes easily with fork (3-5 minute per side, depending on thickness).
- Arrange salmon on plates and spoon sugar snap peas around and on top. Serve with Lemon Quinoa, Couscous, or Basmati Rice.

184. Pan Fried Salmon Burgers With Cabbage Slaw And Avocado Aioli Recipe

Serving: 6 | Prep: | Cook: 20mins | Ready in:

Ingredients

- 1 1/2 pounds skinless center-cut salmon fillet, finely chopped
- 1/2 cup mayonnaise
- 2 tablespoons Asian fish sauce
- 2 tablespoons sambal oelek (see Note) or hot sauce
- 2 garlic cloves, minced
- 1 medium shallot, minced
- 1 tablespoon minced fresh ginger
- 1/2 teaspoon finely grated lemon zest
- 1/2 cup plus 2 tablespoons chopped cilantro
- 1/2 cup plus 1 tablespoon chopped mint
- kosher salt and freshly ground pepper
- 1 1/2 cups Japanese panko or plain dry bread crumbs
- 2 tablespoons fresh lemon juice
- 2 tablespoons fresh lime juice
- 2 tablespoons unseasoned rice vinegar
- 1 teaspoon sugar
- 1/2 small green cabbage, shredded
- 1 small cucumber—peeled, halved lengthwise, seeded and julienned
- 1 small red onion, thinly sliced
- 1 small red bell pepper, thinly sliced
- 1/4 cup sesame seeds
- 1/4 cup vegetable oil
- avocado Aioli, for serving
- 6 onion rolls, split and toasted

Direction

- In a food processor, pulse the chopped salmon about 10 times, or until minced. Scrape the salmon into a bowl. Mix the mayonnaise with the fish sauce, sambal oelek, garlic, shallot, ginger, lemon zest, 2 tablespoons of the cilantro, 1 tablespoon of the mint, 1 teaspoon of salt and 1/2 teaspoon of pepper. Add the mixture to the salmon along with 1 cup of the panko. Fold the salmon mixture together with a rubber spatula. With lightly oiled hands, pat the mixture into 6 burgers. Cover with plastic wrap and refrigerate for 2 hours.
- Meanwhile, in a large bowl, combine the lemon and lime juice with the vinegar. Add the sugar; stir until dissolved. Add the cabbage, cucumber, onion, red pepper and the remaining 1/2 cup each of cilantro and mint and toss well.
- In a shallow bowl, mix the remaining 1/2 cup of panko with the sesame seeds. Pat the mixture onto the salmon burgers.
- In each of 2 large non-stick skillets, heat 2 tablespoons of the oil until shimmering. Add 3 salmon burgers to each skillet and cook over moderately high heat, turning once, until well browned but barely cooked in the center, about 7 minutes.
- Spread the Avocado Aioli on the rolls. Add the salmon burgers, top with the slaw, close the sandwiches and serve.
- MAKE AHEAD: The uncooked salmon burgers and the slaw can be refrigerated overnight.
- NOTES: Sambal is a condiment used in Indonesia, Malaysia, Singapore, the southern Philippines and Sri Lanka, as well as the Netherlands and in Suriname, made from a variety of peppers, although chili peppers are the most common. Sambal is used as a condiment or as a side dish, and is sometimes substituted for fresh chilies; it can be very hot for the uninitiated. It is available at exotic food markets or gourmet departments in supermarkets in numerous countries.

185. Pasta With Salmon Spinach And Sundried Tomatoes Recipe

Serving: 4 | Prep: | Cook: 15mins | Ready in:

Ingredients

- 1.5-1.75 pounds salmon fillet
- 16 oz penne pasta
- 1-2 T minced garlic
- 2 T olive oil(use oil from the tomatoes)
- 1/2 cup oil packed sundried julienned tomatoes
- 2-6 oz bags baby spinach
- 2 T chopped fresh basil
- 2 T chopped fresh parsley
- salt and pepper to taste
- 1/2 cup grated parmesan cheese

Direction

- Steam salmon, skin and flake and set aside.
- Cook pasta to your liking.
- While pasta is cooking sauté garlic in olive oil for a couple of minutes. Add spinach, cover and steam for about 5 minutes. Add sundried tomatoes, salt and pepper, salmon, basil and parsley. Turn heat off and keep covered until the pasta is done.
- Optional, when pasta is finished cooking add 2-3 T butter. Combine with the spinach/salmon mixture.
- Serve sprinkled with grated Parmesan.

186. Pastry Wrapped Salmon Ring Recipe

Serving: 6 | Prep: | Cook: 30mins | Ready in:

Ingredients

- 1, 15 oz can of slamon, drained and deboned
- 1 1/2 cups soft bread crumbs (2 slices white bread or as needed)
- 2 eggs, fork beaten
- 1/2 cup fine chopped celery
- 2 tbs fine chopped onion
- 1 Tbs fresh lemon juice
- 1, 8 oz pkg (8) refrigerated crescent rolls
- toppings:
- sour cream
- chopped chives
- finely diced tomatoes

Direction

- Generously butter a 5 cup oven safe ring mold.
- Mix salmon and remaining ingredients (except toppings) together to blend well.
- Separate crescent rolls into triangles.
- Arrange triangles in mold, alternating points and wide ends so dough drapes over center and outer edges of mold.
- Pat dough lightly to line mold.
- Pack salmon mixture into mold.
- Turn over ends of dough to cover salmon.
- Press to seal.
- Bake in a 375 oven for 30 minutes.
- Loosen edges.
- Invert carefully onto serving platter.
- Serve with sour cream mixed with chives and tomatoes, placing in small dish and place in center ring of mold

187. Pastry Wrapped Salmon The One That Got Away With A Side Of Green Beans And Shitake Mushrooms With Kalamata Dressing Recipe

Serving: 4 | Prep: | Cook: 30mins | Ready in:

Ingredients

- Two 8 oz piece of wild caught Sockeye salmon
- 2 cups flour
- 1 tsp. salt
- 3/4 c. butter

- ¼cup plus 3 tablespoons ice water
- Egg Wash:
- One egg slightly beaten and two tablespoons of water.
- For the green beans:
- 1/3 cup pitted kalamata olives
- 1/4 cup lightly packed fresh parsley leaves, plus 1 Tbs. roughly chopped
- 1/4 cup mayonnaise
- 3 medium cloves garlic, peeled
- kosher salt and freshly ground black pepper
- 4 oz of shitake mushrooms sliced into ¼-inch slices
- 1-tablespoon olive oil
- sea salt to taste
- ¼-teaspoon fresh ground black pepper.
- 2 lb. green beans trimmed

Direction

- Make the dough ahead and chill before rolling.
- Roll the dough as if making a piecrust. Roll around the clock. Start with the rolling pin in the center of your dough disk. Roll toward 12 o'clock, easing up on the pressure as you near the edge (this keeps the edge from getting too thin). Pick up the pin and return it to center. Roll toward 6 o'clock, as shown at right. Repeat this motion toward 3 and then 9 o'clock, always easing up the pressure near the edges and then picking up the pin rather than rolling it back to center. Continue to roll around the clock, aiming for different "times" (like 1, 7, 4, and 10) on each round
- Turn the dough and check often for sticking. After each round of the clock, run a bench knife underneath the dough (below left), to make sure it is not sticking, and reflour the surface if necessary. When you do this, give the dough a quarter turn — most people inevitably use uneven pressure when rolling in one direction versus another, so the occasional turn helps average it out for a more even thickness. Continue to turn and roll until the dough is the right width and thickness. For this, I rolled it out to about 1/8 inch "on the plus side"

- Trim off edges so you have a rectangle and use the scraps for your decorations.
- Place salmon onto dough with two inches of boarder and fold over dough tuck the dough with your hand around the salmon.
- Cut a tail shape and fin outline at the top and shape of a fish head with a sharp knife.
- Seal the edges by hand all around "lightly" pressing the edge with your fingers
- With a fork, seal the tail and top fin.
- Cut out the fins and make fork mark then attach to the body of the fish using a little water on the back of the fin.
- Make a small eye from the dough, wet it, and attach it to the dough.
- Cut a vent hole in the shape of a gill in the dough and lift slightly with the knife.
- Place on parchment paper lined cookie sheet and brush on egg wash.
- Bake for twenty minutes until lightly browned.
- In the meantime, make the green beans.
- Olive mixture:
- Put the olives, parsley leaves, mayonnaise, garlic, a pinch of sea salt and 1/4 tsp. pepper in a food processor and pulse into a coarse paste set aside the dressing.
- Green beans:
- Bring a large pot of well-salted water to a boil.
- Working in 3 batches, boil the green beans until tender, about 5 minutes per batch.
- Drain each batch well and keep warm in a large bowl covered with foil.
- In a small fry pan sauté the shitake mushrooms in one tablespoons of olive oil until tender add a pinch of salt and sauté a few minutes more add to the green beans and toss to combine.
- Dab the olive mixture over the green beans and toss well to combine.
- Season to taste with salt and pepper. Transfer to a platter, sprinkle with the chopped parsley, and serve.
- Make Ahead Tips
- The kalamata olive dressing can be made 1 day ahead and refrigerated until ready to use.

- Plate your pastry wrapped salmon and serve immediately.
- Serve with the green beans in a separate dish.

188.   Pecan Crusted Salmon With Sorrel Sauce Recipe

Serving: 4 | Prep: | Cook: 30mins | Ready in:

Ingredients

- 1/2 cup packed chopped fresh sorrel
- 2 tablespoons dry white wine
- 1-1/2 teaspoons minced shallots
- 1 cup whipping cream
- 1-1/2 teaspoons fresh lime juice
- 1/4 teaspoon ground white pepper
- 1/2 cup pecans
- 1-1/2 teaspoons chopped fresh tarragon
- 1-1/2 teaspoons chopped fresh basil
- 1 tablespoon butter at room temperature
- 4 salmon fillets

Direction

- Combine sorrel, wine and shallots in heavy small saucepan then stir over medium heat for 2 minutes.
- Add cream and lime juice then boil until reduced to sauce consistency.
- Transfer sauce to blender and purée until almost smooth.
- Return sauce to same saucepan and season with ground white pepper and salt.
- Finely grind pecans with tarragon and basil in processor then blend in butter and season with salt and pepper.
- Transfer to small bowl.
- Cover separately and chill.
- Let nut mixture stand at room temperature 30 minutes before using.
- Preheat oven to 350.
- Oil large baking sheet then arrange salmon on prepared sheet and sprinkle lightly with salt and pepper.

- Spoon equal amount of nut mixture over top of each fillet and bake salmon until cooked through about 20 minutes.
- Meanwhile bring sauce to simmer.
- Using spatula transfer salmon to plates and spoon sauce around fish.

189.   Pesto Crusted Salmon With Wilted Spinach Recipe

Serving: 6 | Prep: | Cook: 12mins | Ready in:

Ingredients

- 3 lbs. young spinach, large stems removed
- 1/3 cup fresh basil leaves
- 1/3 cup plain dry bread crumbs
- 2 strips lean bacon, coarsely chopped
- 3 Tablespoons pine nuts
- 3 Tablespoons freshly grated parmesan cheese
- 2 small garlic cloves
- 3 Tablespoons extra-virgin olive oil
- salt and freshly ground pepper
- 6 (7-oz.) skinless salmon fillets, about 1 inch thick
- 3 Tablespoons plus 2 teaspoons olive oil
- 1 medium shallot, finely chopped
- lemon wedges, for serving

Direction

- Bring 1 inch of water to a boil in a large saucepan.
- Add half of the spinach, cover and cook over moderately high heat, stirring until wilted, 2 or 3 minutes.
- Drain, rinse with cold water and squeeze to extract the excess liquid.
- Transfer to a plate and repeat with the remaining spinach.
- Preheat the oven to 400 degrees.
- In a food processor, combine the basil, bread crumbs, bacon, pine nuts, Parmesan cheese and garlic and finely chop.

- With the machine on, add the extra-virgin olive oil in a steady stream until smooth.
- Season with salt and pepper.
- Spread a rounded tablespoon of the pesto evenly on the skinned side of each salmon fillet.
- Heat 2 teaspoons of the olive oil in a large non-stick skillet.
- Add 3 of the salmon fillets, pesto side down, and cook over moderately high heat without turning until the pesto is browned, 1 to 2 minutes.
- Carefully invert the fillets into a large baking dish.
- Repeat with the remaining 3 salmon fillets
- Bake in the oven for about 10 minutes, or until the salmon is just cooked through.
- Meanwhile, wipe out the skillet and heat the remaining 3 Tablespoons olive oil.
- Add the shallot and cook over moderately high heat for 1 minute.
- Add the spinach, season with salt and pepper and toss until heated through, about 3 minutes.
- Set each salmon fillet in the center of a warmed plate, pesto side up. Arrange the spinach around the fish and serve with lemon wedges.

---

190.   Phyllo Wrapped Salmon With Gingered Spinach Filling Recipe

Serving: 4 | Prep: | Cook: 25mins | Ready in:

Ingredients

- 2   tablespoons vegetable oil
- 2   tablespoons shallot -- minced
- 1   tablespoon garlic -- minced
- 1   tablespoon fresh ginger -- minced
- 1/2   teaspoon crushed red pepper
- 1   cup baby spinach leaves -- coarsely chopped
- pinch salt
- pinch sugar
- 1/4   cup butter
- 1/4   cup olive oil
- 6   sheets phyllo pastry
- 1   tablespoon sesame seeds -- toasted
- 4   fillets salmon -- skin removed
- salt and pepper -- to taste
- herbed coconut Sauce
- 1   cup coconut milk -- unsweetened
- 1/2   cup water
- 1   tablespoon garlic -- minced
- 1   tablespoon fresh ginger -- minced
- 1   tablespoon shallots -- minced
- 1/2   teaspoon sugar
- 1/4   teaspoon crushed red pepper
- 1   teaspoon fresh lime juice
- 1/2   teaspoon cornstarch
- salt -- to taste
- 1/4   cup fresh cilantro -- chopped
- 1/4   cup fresh basil -- chopped
- 1   small red pepper -- sliced into rings

Direction

- Heat oil for the filling in a small sauté pan over medium-high heat. Add shallot, garlic, ginger, and pepper flakes. Cook just until fragrant, about 1 minute.
- Toss hot oil with spinach; season with salt and sugar. Remove from pan and set mixture aside until ready to assemble rolls.
- Combine 1/4 cup butter and olive oil and melt in microwave. Set aside to cool to room temperature.
- Lay out 3 of the Phyllo sheets on parchment paper per instructions on the box. Brush some of the butter-oil mixture on the Phyllo. Sprinkle half of sesame seeds on the buttered sheets.
- Season the salmon with salt and pepper to taste. To assemble, place fish fillet about 1" from the bottom of a short side of the Phyllo. Arrange half the spinach across the fillet. Top with a second fillet so the thick portion rests on top of the thin portion of the fillet below.

- To roll, lift the bottom edge of the Phyllo with thumbs and forefingers (using the parchment paper to help get started); keep top fillet in place with the tops of your other fingers and roll the fillets one half turn (the top fillet is now on the bottom). Brush the exposed Phyllo with butter, then fold the long sides in, all the way to the end of the sheet (as if folding a burrito). Brush these folds with butter-oil mixture, then roll to the end, brushing any uncoated Phyllo with a little butter. Transfer to a parchment-lined baking sheet (one with raised edges). Prepare remaining 3 sheets of Phyllo and assemble second roll as the first.
- Preheat oven to 425F. Bake wrapped fish until golden and crisp, about 20 minutes; remove from oven and let rest 5 minutes before slicing. To serve, slice off about 1/2" from the ends of each roll using a serrated slicing knife. Cut rolls in half, then cut each piece in half diagonally. To serve, stand two the pieces upright on each serving plate.
- Herbed Coconut Sauce:
- Combine and simmer unsweetened coconut milk, water, garlic, ginger, shallot, sugar, and red pepper flakes in a small saucepan over medium-high heat. Reduce to about 1 cup, about 15 minutes. Strain mixture through a fine mesh strainer and return liquid to a clean saucepan.
- Combine lime juice and cornstarch in a small bowl. Bring sauce to a boil again and whisk in cornstarch mixture. Simmer about 1 minute, then season with salt to taste.
- Makes 1 cup.
- To serve, spoon some of the sauce onto plates, then stand two pieces of the Phyllo-wrapped salmon in the sauce. Garnish with herb-chili mixture.
- You can wrap the fish in Phyllo and chill it 4 or 5 hours before baking; the sauce can be made ahead also and re-warmed while the fish is in the oven.
- Halibut or sea bass can be substituted, but increase cooking time 2 or 3 minutes.

---

191. Pineapple Bechamel With Bonito Poached Salmon And Spinach Recipe

Serving: 2 | Prep: | Cook: 25mins | Ready in:

Ingredients

- 2 Wild Caught salmon fillets
- 1 Package Organic baby spinach steamed lightly, just until it wilts
- 1/2 spanish onion chopped
- 1/2 cup Bonito Flakes
- 1 strip Dried Norri
- 1 tablespoon mushroom powder
- 1cup Nantucket Nector, pineapple, orange,Mango juice
- 1/2 cup vanilla soy milk
- 3 tablespoons sweet butter
- 3 Tablespoons flour
- 4 pineapple rings diced
- 1/4 cup pineapple juice
- 3 green onions sliced thin for garnish
- 2 Tablespoons sea salt
- 2 tablespoons Agave Nector
- 1 Tablespoon brown sugar
- 1 Tablespoon dark molasses
- 4 cups of water for poaching liquid

Direction

- In a pot, place the butter and the flour and turn to medium high.
- When the butter melts, add the onion and simmer until onions turn translucent.
- Add the Soy Milk and the Nantucket Nectar Juice the Pineapple juice while stirring with a rubber spatula until it is creamy.
- Adjust for seasoning; add pepper flakes or Fresh ground Black Pepper if desired.
- Add the steamed spinach and stir.
- Add the chopped Pineapple and set heat to low.

- In a second pot, place the water and then some sea salt along with the bonito flakes and the Nori strip.
- Poach the Salmon for 15 minutes.
- To Plate: place the Green onions around the perimeter, place a piece of Salmon on the plate.
- Spoon the Spinach and Pineapple Béchamel Sauce around and over the Salmon.
- Serve at once.

---

192.   Pineapple Teriyaki Salmon Recipe

Serving: 4 | Prep: | Cook: 20mins | Ready in:

Ingredients

- 2 tablespoons brown sugar
- 2 tablespoons low-sodium soy sauce
- 1 teaspoon finely grated orange zest
- 1 (6-ounce) can pineapple juice
- 1/2 teaspoon salt, divided
- 2 teaspoons canola oil
- 4 (6-ounce) salmon fillets (about 1 inch thick)
- 1/4 teaspoon freshly ground black pepper
- Grated orange rind (optional)

Direction

- Combine first 4 ingredients and 1/4 teaspoon salt in a small saucepan over high heat, and bring to a boil. Reduce heat, and simmer until reduced to 1/4 cup (about 15 minutes). Set aside.
- Preheat oven to 400 degrees F.
- Heat oil in a large non-stick skillet over medium-high heat. Sprinkle both sides of salmon with remaining 1/4 teaspoon salt and black pepper. Add fish to pan; cook 3 minutes. Turn fish over and place in oven; bake at 400 degrees F for 3 minutes. Remove from oven; brush 1 tablespoon sauce over each fillet. Return to oven, and cook 1 minute or until fish flakes easily when tested with a fork or until

desired degree of doneness. Sprinkle with orange rind, if desired.

---

193.   Pistachio And Sesame Encrusted Salmon With Roasted Garlic Teriyaki Sauce Recipe

Serving: 10 | Prep: | Cook: 15mins | Ready in:

Ingredients

- Ingredients:
- pistachio and Sesame Salmon:
- 5 pounds salmon fillet
- 1/2 cup pistachio nuts, roasted and salted
- 2 tablespoons yellow mustard seeds
- 2 tablespoons black sesame seeds
- 1/4 cup spicy honey mustard
- 1/4 cup honey
- 1/2 teaspoon salt
- 1/2 teaspoon black pepper, freshly ground
- roasted garlic-Teriyaki Sauce:
- 2/3 cup finely diced shallots
- 1 tablespoon finely chopped garlic (about 3 large cloves)
- 1 tablespoon mashed roasted garlic, about 4 to 6 cloves (recipe follows)
- 4 tablespoons Kikkoman® Teriyaki Baste and glaze
- 4 tablespoons low sodium soy sauce
- 1/2 cup orange juice, freshly squeezed
- 5 tablespoons unsulphured molasses
- 2 teaspoons toasted sesame oil

Direction

- Preparation:
- Salmon Preparation:
- Preheat oven to 350°F. Place one oven rack in the middle and one on top.
- Rinse fish in salted water, then pat dry and set aside. Discard the remaining salted water (as if you'd do anything else with it). Place

pistachios, mustard seeds and sesame seeds in a food processor and process until fine meal.

- In a small bowl, combine honey mustard with honey until well-blended. Spread alight coating of honey mustard mixture over top of salmon. Lightly season with salt and black pepper.
- Then, generously sprinkle with ground pistachio mixture to form an even coat. With your hands or back of spoon, pat the topping down so it adheres to salmon.
- Sauce and Bake:
- To make Roasted Garlic-Teriyaki Sauce, add all eight ingredients to small saucepan. Stir and place over low-medium heat to simmer for about 10 minutes. Meanwhile, bake salmon uncovered for 12 to 15 minutes or just until done (according to thickness).
- Once salmon is nearly cooked, remove from oven and turn setting to broil. Drizzle Roasted Garlic-Teriyaki sauce over entire salmon and broil for 3 minutes or until brown on edges. Remove from oven, and serve immediately.
- Presentation:
- Garnish with a sprig of fresh herbs. Serve with a little starch and something green.
- Variations:
- Substitute brown mustard seeds for yellow mustard seeds (if you must). If you can't find the Teriyaki Baste and Glaze, then use a teriyaki marinade.
- Tips:
- Don't place fish in oven until everything else is ready. Nothing's worse than overcooked fish (well, almost nothing). Keep a watchful eye while broiling. It only takes a distracted minute to ruin the entire meal and set off the smoke alarm.

---

194.   Planked Salmon With Cucumber Dill Sauce Recipe

Serving: 4 | Prep: | Cook: 20mins | Ready in:

Ingredients

- 1 /12 lbs salmon filets, skin on
- 2 Tbl olive oil
- 2 Tbl brown sugar
- 2 garlic cloves, minced
- 2 tsp dried dill, divided
- 1 medium cucumber, peeled, seede and thinly sliced
- 2 Tbl plain yougurt or sour cream
- 1 tsp white wine vinegar

Direction

- Submerge cedar plank in cold water at least an hour or overnight.
- Brush skin side of fillets and place in a large.
- In a small bowl, combine brown sugar, garlic and 1 tsp of the dill.
- Spread mixture over salmon, pressing to coat.
- Cover and refrigerate at least one hour.
- Preheat grill to medium low.
- Place plank on grill and heat until they begin to smoke, about 5 minutes.
- Season salmon with salt and pepper to taste and place skin side down on plank.
- Grill covered about 20 minutes or until fish slakes easily with a fork.
- Meanwhile, for sauce, in a small bowl combine remaining dill, cucumber, yogurt or sour cream, vinegar and salt and pepper to taste; stir, chill, serve with salmon.

---

195.   Poached Fingers Of Salmon And Turbot With Saffron And Julienne Of Vegetables Recipe

Serving: 10 | Prep: | Cook: 30mins | Ready in:

Ingredients

- 8 oz leeks
- 8 oz carrots

- 8 oz celery or celery root
- 8 oz onion sliced thin
- 2 1/2 qt water, cold
- to taste --- salt pepper
- 2 1/4 lb Turbot fillets
- 2 1/4 lb salmon fillets
- pinch --- saffron threads
- 1 oz Chopped chives

Direction

- Cut the leeks, carrots, and celery or celery root into julienne and keep the trimmings.
- Place the trimmings into a deep pan with the onion and cover with the water.
- Bring slowly to a boil and skim to remove any impurities.
- Simmer for 30 minutes, then strain into a shallow poaching pan and keep barely simmering to reduce to 1 1/2 of its original volume.
- Season to preference.
- Skin the fillets.
- Cut the fish into pieces, 1 × 4 in. and add to the cooking liquid with the vegetable strips and saffron.
- Simmer for 5 minutes.
- Check the seasoning.
- Serve in broad soup plates with the cooking liquid.
- Sprinkle with chopped chives.

196. Poached Salmon With Avocado Salsa Recipe

Serving: 4 | Prep: | Cook: 20mins | Ready in:

Ingredients

- 1 pound salmon filet
- 1/2 small white onion sliced
- 1 lemon sliced
- 3 whole black peppercorns
- 1 clove garlic cut in half

- Several sprigs fresh flat leaf parsley
- Several sprigs fresh dill
- 2 avocados diced
- 3 tomatillos diced
- 1 yellow bell pepper diced
- 1 red bell pepper diced
- 1 fresh jalapeno pepper
- 1 bunch scallions white and green parts sliced
- 1 bunch fresh cilantro chopped
- juice of 1 lime
- 1 teaspoon salt
- 1/2 teaspoon freshly ground black pepper

Direction

- Poach salmon strewed with the onion, lemon, peppercorns, garlic, parsley and dill.
- Toss together diced vegetables, cilantro, lime juice, salt and pepper.
- Arrange salsa on a platter with the salmon and serve.

197. Poached Salmon With Cucumber Lemon Sauce Recipe

Serving: 4 | Prep: | Cook: 10mins | Ready in:

Ingredients

- 1 quart water
- ½ cup white wine
- 1 small onion, quartered and sliced lengthwise
- 1 teaspoon salt
- 10 peppercorns
- 4 (6-oz) salmon steaks
- cucumber-Lemon Sauce:
- 1 large cucumber, peeled and seeded
- salt
- ¼ cup mayonnaise
- ¼ cup sour cream
- 1 teaspoon grated lemon peel
- 1 tablespoon lemon juice
- 1 teaspoon minced onion

Direction

- Combine water, wine, onion, salt and peppercorns in large skillet.
- Bring to boil.
- Add salmon steaks and return to boil.
- Reduce heat and simmer, covered, until salmon flakes easily when tested with fork, about 10 minutes.
- Remove steaks and drain.
- Serve with Cucumber-Lemon sauce.
- ****
- Cucumber-lemon Sauce:
- Shred cucumber and sprinkle lightly with salt.
- Let stand 30 minutes.
- Drain, squeezing to remove excess liquid.
- Place cucumber in bowl.
- Add mayonnaise, sour cream, lemon peel, lemon juice and onion and stir to blend.
- Taste and add more salt if needed.
- Makes 1 cup.

198. Poached Salmon With Sun Dried Tomatoes And Artichokes Recipe

Serving: 4 | Prep: | Cook: 20mins |Ready in:

Ingredients

- 4 salmon fillets, 4 to 6 ounces each
- 2 Tbs. olive oil
- 2 Tbs. finely chopped shallots
- 1 Cup white wine
- 2 Tbs. fresh lemon juice
- 2 Tbs. chopped fresh tarragon
- 1/2 Cup sun-dried tomatoes, rehydrated
- 1 jar (15 ounces) artichoke hearts, cut into quarters
- salt to taste
- Freshly ground black pepper
- 1 1/2 Cups of water or more to cook the salmon
- one bunch watercress, washed and stemmed

Direction

- Heat the olive oil in a large sauté pan over medium heat.
- Add the shallots and cook for 3 minutes.
- Increase the heat to high, add the wine, lemon juice, tarragon, sun-dried tomatoes and artichoke hearts, and simmer for 1 minute.
- Season the salmon fillets with salt and pepper and add them to the pan with enough water to cover.
- Bring the liquid to a boil and adjust the heat so mixture simmers.
- Cook 12 to 15 minutes, until salmon is just cooked through. (Thinner fillets will take less time, while thicker ones will take a little longer.)

199. Poached Salmon With Garden Harvest Sauce Recipe

Serving: 4 | Prep: | Cook: 8mins |Ready in:

Ingredients

- 1 cup cucumber, drained and finely diced
- ½ cup plain yogurt
- ¼ teaspoon celery salt
- ½ teaspoon ground black pepper
- ½ tsp dried dill
- 2 cups water, boiling
- 2 vegetable bouillon cubes
- 1 tablespoon white vinegar
- 1 small onion, sliced
- 1 ½ teaspoons dried dill
- 1 teaspoon ground black pepper
- 4 (4-ounce) salmon steaks

Direction

- To make the cucumber sauce, in a small bowl mix together the cucumber, yogurt, celery salt and pepper, and dill. Refrigerate until chilled before use.

- Over high heat combine the water, bouillon, vinegar, onion, dill weed, and black pepper.
- Reduce the heat to low, cover and simmer for 15 minutes.
- Add the salmon, cover and simmer for 8 minutes, or until the fish flakes easily.
- Plate the salmon steaks, and spoon the chilled cucumber sauce evenly over the salmon and serve immediately.

200. Poached Salmon With Lemon Mayonnaise Recipe

Serving: 4 | Prep: | Cook: 15mins | Ready in:

Ingredients

- 24 ounces bottled clam juice
- 3/4 cup dry white wine
- 3 lemon slices
- 3 fresh dill sprigs
- 4 whole peppercorns
- 4 salmon fillets
- Mayonnaise:
- 1 cup mayonnaise
- 2 tablespoons fresh lemon juice
- 2 teaspoons grated lemon peel
- 2 tablespoons chopped fresh chives
- 2 tablespoons chopped fresh parsley
- butter lettuce leaves
- 4 lemon slices
- 8 lemon wedges
- tomato wedges

Direction

- Combine clam juice, wine, lemon slices, dill sprigs and peppercorns in skillet.
- Simmer 10 minutes to blend flavors then add salmon and cover and simmer for 10 minutes.
- Transfer salmon to plate and reserve liquid in skillet.
- Cool salmon then cover and chill until cold.

- Boil salmon poaching liquid in skillet until reduced to 1/4 cup about 20 minutes.
- Combine mayonnaise, lemon juice, lemon peel, chives and parsley in medium bowl.
- Mix in 1 tablespoon poaching liquid.
- Season to taste with pepper.
- Line platter with lettuce then top with salmon.
- Make cut in each lemon slice from center to edge.
- Twist lemon slices and place atop salmon.
- Garnish with lemon wedges and tomatoes and serve with mayonnaise.

201. Poached Salmon With Melon Salsa Recipe

Serving: 6 | Prep: | Cook: 15mins | Ready in:

Ingredients

- 2 green onions, thinly sliced, including green portions
- 1 1/2 tsp. fresh mint, chopped
- 1 tsp. fresh ginger, grated
- 3 Tbsp. grated lime zest
- 1 1/2 lbs. salmon fillets, skinned and cut into 6 pieces
- melon salsa......
- 1 honeydew melon, about 3 lbs., peeled, seeded and cut into 1/2-inch cubes
- 1 yellow bell pepper, seeded, stemmed and cut into 1/2-inch squares
- 1/4 cup lime juice
- 1/2 red onion, chopped
- 1 jalapeno chili, minced
- 2 Tbsp. fresh mint, chopped

Direction

- Preheat oven at 450 F.
- In a small bowl, toss together onion, mint, ginger and lime zest.
- Place 6 pieces of aluminum foil, each 10 inches square, on a work surface. Place a piece of salmon in the center of each square.

- Top each with an equal amount of onion mixture.
- Fold in the edges of foil and crimp to seal.
- Place the packets in a single layer on a baking sheet and bake until opaque throughout, 12 to 15 minutes.
- Meanwhile, to make salsa, in a medium bowl, toss together the melon, pepper, lime juice, onion, jalapeno and mint.
- To serve, transfer the contents of each packet onto an individual plate.
- Top each with an equal amount of the salsa.

202. Poached Seafood Italiano Recipe

Serving: 4 | Prep: | Cook: 10mins | Ready in:

Ingredients

- 1 tablespoon olive oil
- 1 clove minced garlic
- 1/4 cup chicken broth
- 4(6ounce) salmon steaks
- 1 can diced tomatoes w/ Italian herbs
- 1/3 cup sliced olived (black or green)

Direction

- Heat oil in a large skillet. Add garlic; sauté 30 seconds.
- Add wine. Bring to a boil
- Add salmon. Cover. Reduce heat to a medium; simmer 6 minutes.
- Add undrained tomatoes and olives; simmer 2 minutes or until salmon flakes easily when tested with a fork.

203. Ponzu Style Salmon Pockets With Thai Pesto Recipe

Serving: 6 | Prep: | Cook: 30mins | Ready in:

Ingredients

- 6 6oz salmon fillets(or whole salmon, which you can later cut into serving size pieces), skin removed
- 6 flat breads or pita pockets
- For Ponzu Inspired sauce
- juice from 1 orange
- juice from 1 lime
- 2T rice vinegar
- 1T oyster sauce
- 1T Chinese hot mustard
- 2 green onions, sliced
- For Thai Pesto
- 3T fresh Thai basil leaves(can sub another basil, if desired)
- 3T fresh cilantro leaves
- 2T fresh mint leaves
- 2T fresh lemongrass OR 1T Thai seasoning blend with lemongrass
- 1 1-inch piece candied ginger
- 2 cloves garlic
- 1/4-1t red pepper flakes
- 3T peanut oil or olive oil
- fresh ground black pepper

Direction

- Combine all ingredients for Ponzu sauce and whisk well.
- Brush salmon (or pieces) with sauce on both sides. Make sure to toss a few of the onion bits on there, too. :) Reserve remaining sauce.
- Broil, grill or bake salmon as desired until just done. Do not overcook.
- Meanwhile, combine all ingredients for Thai pesto, other than olive oil, in food processor and process to finely chopped and well blended.
- Slowly add olive oil and continue processing until thickened and blended well.
- To plate, either place a piece of the salmon on, or in, the bread, whole, drizzle with a touch of the Ponzu sauce and top with a spoonful of the pesto OR, you can flake each pieces prior to putting it on/in the bread, drizzle with the sauce, then top with the pesto. Serve warm.

204. Quick Bake Salmon And Veggies Recipe

Serving: 2 | Prep: | Cook: 25mins | Ready in:

Ingredients

- 12 ounces of salmon, cut into two fillets
- 1 teaspoon of herb blend (thyme,citrus blend,cracked pepper)
- Half lemon
- 1 tbsp dark sesame oil
- 2 cloves garlic chopped
- 1 tbsp fresh ginger grated
- 1/4 cup onions chopped
- 2 cups mushrooms, sliced
- 2 cups cherry tomatoes, halved
- 5 oz can of water chestnuts, drained
- 3 cups baby spinach steamed

Direction

- Preheat oven to 350 degrees
- Rinse the salmon well and rub with lemon juice. Place the fillets on a cake rack, laid on a cookie sheet, on the middle rack of the oven. You can place the fillets directly on the cookie sheet, but raising them keeps the fish a little firmer. Bake for 20 minutes.
- While the salmon is cooking, heat the oil in a non-stick frying pan and add the garlic, onion and ginger. Stir fry for 2 minutes, then add the mushrooms and fry for 2 to 4 minutes more. Finally add the tomatoes and water chestnuts, fry until heated through and fold in the steamed spinach. Serve alongside the salmon.
- If you feel this dish needs additional flavoring, make a quick sauce by mixing 2 tbsp of low-sodium soy sauce with 2 tbsp of rice vinegar. Add to the stir-fry near the end of cooking.

205. Red Lobster Spicy Pineapple Glazed Salmon Recipe

Serving: 4 | Prep: | Cook: 20mins | Ready in:

Ingredients

- Spicy pineapple glaze Ingredients:
- 1/2 Cup sweet chili sauce
- 1 ea 8 oz can crushed pineapple in pineapple juice
- 1/2-1 Tsp cajun seasoning
- For theFish
- Ingredients:
- 4 ea 5-6 oz salmon fillets
- salt and pepper, to taste
- nonstick cooking spray

Direction

- Preparation:
- Preheat the oven to 400 degrees and place the Salmon in a 9X13 baking dish sprayed with Non-stick Cooking Spray. Season the Salmon with Salt and Pepper.
- In a small bowl, combine all the Glaze ingredients and mix well.
- Generously top each piece of Salmon with a scoop of the Spicy Pineapple Glaze.
- Bake the Salmon for 15-20 minutes or until the fish flakes easily with a fork.

206. Red Lobsters Maui Luau Shrimp Amp Salmon Recipe

Serving: 4 | Prep: | Cook: 15mins | Ready in:

Ingredients

- * 4 each 5-6 oz. skinned salmon fillet
- * 24 each 26-30 count peeled shrimp
- * 4 each bamboo skewers (soaked in water for 10-15 minutes)

- * 8 each fresh pineapple half moons (super sweet variety)
- * olive oil
- * salt, garlic powder and pepper to taste
- * sweet chili sauce (choose your favorite brand, but make sure it is sweet, this is by the asian sauces not the ketchup)

Direction

- 1. Brush both sides of salmon with olive oil and season with salt and pepper.
- 2. After soaking the skewers, slide 6 shrimp onto each skewer, leaving room on either end. Brush both sides with olive oil and season with salt and pepper.
- 3. Cut the fresh pineapple into slices approximately half inch in diameter and then cut in half. Brush both sides with olive oil.
- 4. On a medium heated grill, place the salmon flesh side down. Grill approximately 6–7 minutes per side or until the fish reaches 150 degrees.
- 5. Grill shrimp approximately 3–4 minutes per side or until 150 degrees.
- 6. Grill pineapple for 2–3 minutes per side or until there is good caramelization.
- 7. Brush all items generously with the sweet chili sauce.
- 8. To serve, place the pineapple at the top of each plate and crisscross. Top the pineapple with a scoop of your favorite rice. Crisscross the salmon and the shrimp skewer on top of the rice. Sprinkle with fresh parsley and serve with your favorite vegetable.

207.   Red Lobsters Salmon With Lobster Mashed Potatoes Recipe

Serving: 4 | Prep: | Cook: 45mins | Ready in:

Ingredients

- Ingredients:

- * 4 eight-to-ten ounce pieces of fresh salmon fillets, skinless
- * ½ cup canola oil
- * McCormick's season All
- * 4 heaping portions of your favorite mashed potato recipe
- * Fresh vegetables of your choice (asparagus is a nice touch)
- * 2 tbsp. chopped fresh parsley
- * 2 tbsp. chopped green onions
- * 4 lemon wedges
- lobster Sauce
- * 1 live Maine lobster, 1 ¼ pound
- * 1 quart heavy whipping cream
- * 1 medium onion, diced
- * 2 stalks celery, diced
- * 2 carrots, peeled and diced
- * 1 bay leaf
- * 1 tsp. black peppercorns, whole
- * ¼ cup flour, all purpose
- * ½ cup butter, salted
- * 2 tbsps. tomato paste
- * ½ cup cream sherry
- * 1 tsp. fresh thyme leaves, stem removed
- * salt and fresh-ground black pepper

Direction

- Lobster Sauce
- Prepare lobster by cutting in half lengthwise through the head and body first. Remove tail halves, and claw and knuckle sections. These are the sections with the meat for the sauce. Cut the body into two-inch pieces.
- In a two-quart stock pot heat the butter over medium heat. Add all diced vegetables, lobster, peppercorns, bay leaf, and thyme. Cook on medium to medium-high heat, stirring continually for ten minutes or until the lobster shells start to turn red. Remove just the lobster pieces that contain meat and let cool for ten minutes.
- Stir in flour and cook on medium heat, stirring continually for another 5 minutes.
- Deglaze pan with sherry, then add cream.
- Remove lobster meat from the shell, and set aside. Place leftover shells back into the lobster

cream. Let reduce on low heat to desired consistency. (We suggest thick enough to coat the back of a spoon.)

- Cut lobster meat into half-inch chunks.
- Strain lobster sauce into a smaller pot and discard shell/vegetable mixture.
- Stir in lobster meat and season sauce to taste with salt and pepper just before serving.
- Grilled Salmon
- Lightly brush both sides of fillets with olive oil and season with McCormick's Season All.
- Pre-heat grill on medium-high heat and place salmon on, skin-side up. Grill for 4-5 minutes until well-marked.
- Turn fish over and continue grilling another 5-6 minutes or until your fresh fish preference is reached.

208.   Red Pepper Salmon Pasta Recipe

Serving: 4 | Prep: | Cook: 14mins |Ready in:

Ingredients

- 4 (4 ounce) fillets salmon
- 2 tablespoons lemon juice
- 1/2 cup roasted red bell peppers
- 1/3 cup grated parmesan cheese
- 1 tablespoon cornstarch
- 2 teaspoons minced jalapeno peppers
- 1 clove garlic, minced
- 1/4 cup chopped fresh cilantro
- 1 cup chicken broth
- 1 (8 ounce) package angel hair pasta

Direction

- 1. In an 8 inch baking dish, arrange filets in a single layer. Sprinkle with lemon juice. Tightly cover dish with foil. Bake at 450 degrees F (230 degrees C). Cook until fish is opaque, but still moist looking in thickest part, 12 to 14 minutes.

- 2. Meanwhile, in a blender, smoothly puree red peppers, parmesan, cornstarch, chili, and garlic. Add cilantro and chicken broth; whirl to blend.
- 3. Pour pepper mixture into a 10 inch frying pan. Stir over high heat until boiling. Reduce heat to keep warm.
- 4. Cook pasta in 3 quarts boiling water until tender to bite, about 7 minutes. Drain, and return to pan.
- 5. Stir juices from the baked salmon into red pepper sauce. Mix 1 1/2 cups sauce with pasta. Spoon pasta onto plates. Top with fish, and drizzle with remaining sauce. Serve.

209.   Rice Stuffed Dijon Salmon Recipe

Serving: 8 | Prep: | Cook: 4hours |Ready in:

Ingredients

- ½ cup short-grain rice
- ½ cup vegetable broth
- 2 tbsp vinegar
- 2 tsp sugar
- 1 tbsp olive oil
- 2 thinly sliced leeks
- 1 medium chopped carrot
- 1 lb diced white mushrooms
- 1 cup packed baby spinach
- ¼ cup green peas
- salt and freshly ground pepper
- 4 lb piece of salmon, boned
- 1 tbsp Dijon mustard
- 1 tbsp soy sauce
- 1 tsp worcestershire sauce
- 2 tsp olive oil

Direction

- Cook rice in vegetable broth for 15-20 minutes or until done. Pour into a bowl.

- Add vinegar and sugar and mix gently with a wooden spoon, do not bruise or mash the grains.
- Heat oil in a frying pan and add leeks and carrots.
- Sauté for 2 minutes, or until slightly softened.
- Add mushrooms and sauté 6-7 minutes.
- Stir in spinach and peas and cook until spinach is wilted.
- Season well with salt and pepper. Stir into rice.
- Preheat oven to 450ºF and line a roasting pan with foil.
- Open up salmon to lay flat, and season the flesh side with pepper.
- Spread rice mixture over half of the fish, then fold over. It will self-seal.
- Place salmon in the roasting pan.
- Whisk together mustard, soy sauce, Worcestershire sauce and olive oil and brush over salmon skin.
- Bake, uncovered, for 35 minutes, basting with mustard mixture 2 more times as it bakes.

210.   Roasted Salmon James Bond Recipe

Serving: 6 | Prep: | Cook: 30mins | Ready in:

Ingredients

- The Fish:
- 1 large salmon filet (1 1/-2 lbs)
- The Martini:
- 1 t. dill weed
- juice of ½ lemon
- 1/3 cup vodka
- ¼ cup dry vermouth
- 4 T. melted butter (or more as required)
- 2 t. creamed horseradish
- 1 t. crushed garlic
- 1 t. Tabasco sauce

Direction

- 1 hour before cooking, take salmon from refrigerator. Rinse and pat dry. Remove any pin bones with a tweezers. Put the salmon on a double layer of large aluminum foil sheets. Close it on three sides. Add the "martini". Close the foil tightly. Let stand for 1 hour.
- Prepare a wood fire for indirect cooking.
- Cook the salmon for 30 minutes with foil closed. Carefully open the top. Let the salmon cook for 10-15 minutes longer until sauce reduces. Serve the salmon with the thickened sauce. If the sauce has become too thick, melt an additional tablespoon of butter over salmon.

211.   Romanos Macaroni Grill Grilled Salmon With Spinach Orzo Recipe

Serving: 4 | Prep: | Cook: 10mins | Ready in:

Ingredients

- 4 Bias Cut salmon Filets (2 lbs total)
- 1oz canola oil
- 1oz soy sauce
- 8oz Teriyaki glaze (posted below)
- 16oz garlic olive oil sauce
- 4oz Diced red bell peppers
- 24oz orzo pasta, precooked
- 8oz spinach, julienned
- TERIYAKI GLAZE:
- 2 cups soy sauce
- ¾ cups Italian dressing
- 4 cups honey
- ¾ cups lemon juice
- 2 TBSP red pepper, crushed
- 1/8 cup cayenne pepper

Direction

- Dip salmon in soy sauce then the oil.
- Place the salmon on hot grill silver side up.

- Grill salmon evenly until done, approximately 6-7 minutes or until the internal temperature reaches 145 F.
- Slowly ladle the teriyaki glaze over the salmon while still on the grill.
- In a hot sauté pan, add olive oil garlic mix, red bell peppers and orzo.
- At home, an ounce or two of chicken stock will help the orzo during this step.
- Sauté for approximately one minute until orzo is almost dry, stirring to prevent sticking.
- Remove pan from heat and add spinach.
- Toss for approximately three seconds until spinach is incorporated but is not wilted.
- Place spinach and orzo on a plate, then add salmon and additional honey teriyaki glaze if needed.
- TERIYAKI GLAZE
- Mix all ingredients together by hand whisk. Sauce will remain for 48 hours so it needs to be prepared fresh or the day before.

212.   SALMON PATTIES Recipe

Serving: 16 | Prep: | Cook: 10mins |Ready in:

Ingredients

- 1 can pink salmon,drained
- 2 eggs
- 1/2 C. chopped onion
- 1/4 to 1/2 C flour
- 2 Tbs. corn meal
- 1/2 tsp. salt

Direction

- Put all ingredients into large mixing bowl except flour.
- Use potato masher to mix to ensure it is mixed well and broken up good.
- While doing this add a little flour at a time until mixture has a good consistency to hold together good.

- Drop into skillet by tablespoon full and pat out with back of spoon.
- Cook over medium heat with plenty of oil until brown on bottom then flip and cook on other side until it is brown.
- Drain on paper towels.

213.   SMOKED SALMON ROTINI Recipe

Serving: 4 | Prep: | Cook: 21mins |Ready in:

Ingredients

- 1 pkg rotini
- 2 cups trimmed & halved fresh green beans
- 1 tsp butter
- 1 tsp minced garlic
- 1 cup chicken broth
- 1 cup cream
- 1 tbsp cornstarch
- 1 cup sliced red onion
- 5 oz smoked salmon, sliced in ribbons
- 2 tbsp fresh dill
- 1 tbsp capers
- 1 tsp grated lime zest
- Salt & pepper

Direction

- Prepare pasta according to package directions.
- Add green beans during the last 2 minutes of cooking.
- Heat butter in a large skillet set over medium heat.
- Add garlic; sauté for 1 minute or until fragrant.
- Whisk broth, cream & cornstarch until smooth.
- Add to skillet and bring to a boil.
- Reduce heat and simmer for 5-7 minutes or until thickened; stirring occasionally.
- Stir in onion and salmon.
- Toss hot rotini/beans with sauce, dill, capers and lime zest.

- Season with salt & pepper.
- Serve.

214. SPECIAL SALMON PATTIES Recipe

Serving: 4 | Prep: | Cook: 15mins | Ready in:

Ingredients

- 1 CAN pink salmon, 15OZ, CLEANED OF BONES
- 1 MED. onion, CHOPPED & DIVIDED
- 1 egg, BEATEN
- 1 tsp. LOUISIANNA hot sauce
- 1 TSP salt
- 1 TSP COURSE pepper
- 1/2 C. flour
- canola oil FOR FRYING
- 1 SLEEVE saltines
- 1 SMALL CONTAINER sour cream, [8OZ]
- 2 TBSP. butter OR margarine
- 1/2 tsp. red chili FLAKES
- 1TBSP FRESH dill [OR 1 tsp. DRY]
- salt AND pepper TO TASTE

Direction

- EMPTY SALMON INTO A BOWL AND REMOVE ANY SKIN AND BONES.
- USING A FORK, FLAKE SALMON.
- ADD 1/2 THE ONION, EGG, HOT SAUCE, SALT AND PEPPER. ADD FLOUR AND MIX WELL.
- FORM INTO 8 PATTIES AND SET ASIDE. PATTIES WILL BE MOIST.
- EMPTY SALTINES INTO FOOD PROCESSOR, AND PULSE UNTIL CRACKERS ARE REDUCED TO FINE CRUMBS.
- COAT EACH PATTY ON EACH SIDE WITH CRACKER CRUMBS AND FRY IN ABOUT 1/2 INCH OF OIL OVER MEDIUM, MEDIUM-HIGH HEAT UNTIL BROWNED ON BOTH SIDES. ABOUT 5 MINUTES PER SIDE.
- WHILE PATTIES ARE FRYING, SWEAT THE OTHER HALF OF THE ONION IN BUTTER OVER MEDIUM LOW HEAT. TRY NOT TO BROWN THEM.
- ADD CHILI FLAKES, SALT AND PEPPER.
- WHEN ONIONS ARE TENDER, ADD SOUR CREAM AND STIR WELL TO COMBINE. DO NOT BOIL.
- ADD DILL.
- TASTE FOR SEASONING.
- SERVE IMMEDIATELY OVER SALMON PATTIES.

215. Salmon Cedar Plank With Caper Sauce Recipe

Serving: 4 | Prep: | Cook: 30mins | Ready in:

Ingredients

- 1 to 1 1/2 lb salmon filet or steak
- 1 cedar plank soaked in water 30 minutes to 1 hour (we find them at hardware store)
- 1 tbsp extra virgin olive oil
- 1/2 tsp fresh ground pepper
- 1 tsp ground coriander
- kosher salt to taste
- 1/4 cup finely chopped chives (optional)
- caper Sauce:
- 3 tbsp butter
- juice from 1 large lemon
- 1/2 tbsp capers
- Charcoal grill
- Grill Master

Direction

- Prepare charcoal grill. (Coals should ash over and be spread)
- Place salmon skin side down on cedar plank. Brush with olive oil.
- Sprinkle coriander, pepper, salt, and chives (optional) over salmon.

- *Grill for 15 to 25 minutes or until fish flakes when pulled.
- Prepare caper sauce while fish is grilling:
- Melt butter in small saucepan over medium heat. Add capers and lemon juice. Bring to a boil and remove from heat. Serve while hot.
- Serving suggestions: Salmon is a rich, moist meat. Serve with a vegetable that is moderate flavored so your plate is not loaded with overpowering flavors. Allow the salmon to stand out! Dinner salad, steamed green vegetable, green beans, corn on the cob, etc.
- *Place plank directly on cooking grate over coals. Plank will smoke but should not flame up. Keep a spray bottle nearby in case of flare ups.
- Use mitts or oven tools to remove plank from grill.
- Save plank to use at a later date as flavor wood on coals.

---

216. Salmon And Broccoli Muffins Recipe

Serving: 2 | Prep: | Cook: 12mins | Ready in:

Ingredients

- 6 ounces salmon fillet
- 1/2 cup organic silken tofu medium firmness
- 1 teaspoon grated ginger root
- 1 teaspoon your favorite fresh herb dill, thyme, basil or a store bought citrus herb blend
- 1/4 cup fresh parsely very finely chopped
- 1/2 tsp lemon zest
- 1/2 tsp minced garlic
- 1/4 tsp red pepper flakes (optional)
- 1 teaspoon Dijon mustard
- 1 cup of steamed broccoli
- salt and pepper to taste

Direction

- Steam the broccoli to el dente fork touchable. Remove from heat and set aside.
- In your food processor combine your salmon cut into 3 inch cubes, tofu and remaining ingredients (except the broccoli). Blend till mixed not pureed (salmon should be recognizable but not in huge pieces). Remove from the processer and set in a bowl.
- Place the broccoli into the processer and give a few pluses, no large pieces should be remaining you want it to look like bread crumbs a little. Mix with your ingredients.
- Take your muffin tins and line with parchment paper or you can grease the sides and bottom (less calories with parchment paper), divide your salmon mixture into four of the muffin cups and bake at 350 for 12 minutes. Remove from oven and allow to rest for a few minutes before removing. There may be some liquids depending on the firmness of your tofu.
- May be served as a side dish or on top of a salad, or add some caramelized onions with a nice rice dish and you have a great dinner.

---

217. Salmon And Corn Casserole Recipe

Serving: 6 | Prep: | Cook: 45mins | Ready in:

Ingredients

- 1 can (14-3/4 ounces) salmon, boned and skin removed
- milk
- 3 Tbs of butter
- 1/2 cup chopped onion
- 1/2 cup chopped green bell pepper
- 2 eggs, beaten
- 2 cups shredded sharp cheddar cheese
- 1 can 15 ounces) creamed corn
- 1/4 tps. salt
- 1/2 tps. pepper
- 1-1/4 cups crushed crackers

Direction

- Preheat the oven to 350 F.
- Drain the salmon, pouring the liquid into a glass measuring cup. Flake the salmon and place in a large mixing bowl. Add enough milk to the measuring cup to make 1 cup of liquid. Add to the salmon.
- Melt 2 Tbs. of the butter in a small skillet over medium heat. Add the onion and green pepper and sauté until limp, about 4 minutes. Add to the salmon, along with the eggs, cheese, corn, salt and pepper. Mix well. Spoon into a 9-inch by 13- inch baking dish.
- Melt the remaining 1 Tbs. butter and combine with the crushed crackers. Sprinkle over the top of the casserole. Bake for 45 minutes, uncovered. Serve hot.

218. Salmon BLT Recipe

Serving: 2 | Prep: | Cook: 10mins | Ready in:

Ingredients

- 1/4 cup fat-free mayonnaise
- 1 teaspoon lemon zest
- 1 1/2 teaspoons lemon juice
- Pinch of cayenne pepper
- 4 slices center-cut bacon (turkey bacon)
- 2 teaspoons olive oil
- 10 ounces salmon, cut into 4 fillets, skin removed
- 8 slices country white (or whole-wheat) bread
- 4 lettuce leaves
- 8 slices tomato
- .

Direction

- Combine mayonnaise, lemon zest, juice and cayenne in a bowl; set aside.
- Cook bacon in a non-stick skillet over medium heat until crispy, about 6 to 8 minutes; remove

skillet from heat and transfer bacon to a plate lined with paper towels.
- Drain.
- Pour off all fat and wipe skillet clean; add oil.
- Return skillet to stove and heat to medium high; add salmon.
- Cook until fillets are no longer translucent in the center, 2 to 3 minutes per side.
- Toast bread and spread 4 slices with mayonnaise mix.
- Place 1 lettuce leaf, 2 slices tomato, 1 fillet and 1 piece bacon on top of each; close; cut in half; serve

219. Salmon Bake With Creamy Lemon Mustard Sauce Recipe

Serving: 4 | Prep: | Cook: 15mins | Ready in:

Ingredients

- 4 salmon Filets, about 5-6 oz each
- salt, to taste
- white pepper, to taste, (I substituted smoked paprika)
- 4 Tablespoons light sour cream
- 2 tablespoons white wine (don't use cooking wine)
- 1/2 tsp Tabasco, or other hot sauce
- 2 tablespoons lemon juice
- 2 tablespoons whole-grain or Dijon mustard

Direction

- PREHEAT oven to 450
- 1. Line baking sheet with aluminum foil or parchment
- 2. Season both sides of fish with salt and pepper
- 3. In a small bowl, whisk the sour cream, white wine, Tabasco, lemon juice and mustard. Spoon 2 tablespoons of the cream lemon-mustard sauce over each salmon filet.

4. Bake the salmon for 14 minutes (or until center is done)

---

220. Salmon Burger Steak With Tomato Sauce Recipe

Serving: 3 | Prep: | Cook: 20mins | Ready in:

Ingredients

- 2 (6 oz) caned salmon
- 1 cup chopped onion
- 1/2 cup chopped shitake mushrooms
- 2 Tbsp parsley, diced
- 1 tsp mix of dried herbs (rosemary, paprika, chili pepper, lemon peel)
- a pinch of salt & pepper
- 1/2 cup bread crumbs, or fresh whole wheat bread crumbs
- 2 Tbsp grated parmesan cheese
- 1 egg, lightly beaten
- 1 Tbsp milk
- Spray oil or melted butter
- FOR THE SAUCE
- 14 oz canned diced tomato
- 1/4 onion, diced
- 1 Tbsp minced garlic
- 2 Tbsp olive oil
- 1 bay leaf
- 2 Tbsp hot sauce
- 1 Tbsp parsley, diced
- 1 tsp sugar
- a pinch of salt & pepper

Direction

- Preheat the oven at 370 degree.
- Drain and flake Salmon, sauté onions & shitake mushrooms lightly.
- Combine salmon, onion, shitake mushrooms, parsley, bread crumbs, milk, egg, Parmesan cheese, and seasonings; mix well.
- Spray with non-stick oil or melted butter inside of muffin pan

- Form into 6 large muffin pan (silicon pan). Bake 15 minutes or more.
- In the meantime, prepare the mushrooms and sauce.
- Slice the mushrooms and stir fry in the pan; season with salt & pepper; remove from the heat; set aside.
- Preheat the saucepan; add olive oil; heat the oil
- Add onions & garlic; sauté slightly.
- Add tomato, bay leaf; boil-stir often
- Add hot sauce, parsley, salt & pepper, sugar; mix well; simmer about 3 to 4 minutes.
- Remove from the heat. Set aside.
- Remove the salmon from the muffin pan gently.
- Put some sautéed mushrooms on the plate, then salmon steak & top with tomato sauce.

---

221. Salmon Burgers With Miso Sesame Sauce Recipe

Serving: 4 | Prep: | Cook: 8mins | Ready in:

Ingredients

- 1 1/4 lb skinless salmon fillet
- 1 tbsp garlic, minced
- 2 tbsp Dijon mustard
- handful of chopped cilantro
- 2 tbsp hoisin sauce
- 1 green onion, finely chopped
- 1 tsp cayenne
- 1 egg
- 1/2 cup panko breadcrumbs
- 1 tbsp toasted sesame seeds
- 1 tbsp miso
- 2 tbsp rice wine vinegar
- 1 tbsp honey
- 1 tbsp soy sauce

Direction

- Finely dice salmon fillet and mix together well in large bowl with next 8 ingredients.
- Form burger mixture into 4 equal sized burgers and place on plate covered with plastic wrap. Cover burgers with more plastic wrap and refrigerate for 1 hour.
- While burgers are chilling make sauce by whisking remaining ingredients. Chill.
- Heat BBQ, Frying/Griddle pan or Broiler to high, spray with cooking spray and cook 4 minutes a side until just a touch of rare inside.
- Top with sauce and enjoy. Excellent on a bun with lettuce, tomato, pickled ginger and a side of crispy French fries.

222. Salmon Cakes Recipe

Serving: 4 | Prep: | Cook: 10mins | Ready in:

Ingredients

- vegetable oil for frying
- 18 ounces canned salmon drained well
- 1-1/2 cups cracker meal
- 2 large eggs beaten
- 2 rounded teaspoons Old Bay Seasoning blend
- 1/2 red bell pepper seeded and finely chopped
- 20 blades fresh chives snipped chopped
- 3 tablespoons fresh dill finely chopped
- 1 teaspoon cayenne pepper sauce
- 1 lemon zested and juiced
- salad greens
- coarse salt
- extra virgin olive oil for drizzling
- 1/2 cup mayonnaise
- 1/2 cup chili sauce
- 2 tablespoons dill pickle relish

Direction

- Heat large heavy skillet with 1 inch of oil over moderate heat. Flake the cooked cooled salmon with a fork. Add cracker meal to bowl and work through the fish with your hands. Add eggs, seasoning, pepper, chives, dill,

pepper sauce and the zest of one lemon to the bowl. Combine ingredients well with your hands. If the mixture is a little wet add a bit more cracker meal. Form salmon into 10 cakes then fry in a single layer for 4 minutes on each side. Drain well on paper towels. Toss salad greens with coarse salt and juice of the lemon you zested. Drizzle greens with a little extra virgin olive oil and re-toss salad to coat. Combine mayonnaise, chili sauce and relish in a small dish. Place salmon cakes on a bed of baby greens, 2 cakes per person and top with chili mayonnaise sauce.

223. Salmon Cakes With Spinach Salad Recipe

Serving: 4 | Prep: | Cook: 15mins | Ready in:

Ingredients

- salmon cakeS
- 8 oz salmon flaked and cooked
- 1 oz red onion minced
- 1 oz celery diced finely
- 1 oz red pepper diced finely
- 1 egg, beaten
- 1 oz bread crumbs
- salt - to taste
- pepper - to taste
- garlic pepper - to taste
- spinach SALAD
- 1 bag baby spinach
- lemon juice
- 1 red pepper, diced
- 1 yelllow pepper, diced
- 4 oz Peccorine Ramono cheese
- GARNISH
- 1/2 c pecans
- canola oil
- PInch cayenne pepper
- Pinch sugar

Direction

- SALMON CAKES
- Combine all ingredients
- Form into patties
- Sear in a sauté pan
- SPINACH SALAD
- Wilt spinach in small amount of olive oil in sauté pan
- Sprinkle with lemon juice
- Dice red pepper and yellow pepper
- GARNISH
- Place pecans on baking sheet
- Lightly sprinkle with oil, cayenne and sugar
- Toast at 350 8-12 minutes
- PUTTING IT TOGETHER
- Top salmon cakes with spinach, pepper dice, and cheese
- Garnish with toasted pecans

---

224. Salmon Cakes With Lemon Dill Dip Recipe

Serving: 4 | Prep: | Cook: 5mins | Ready in:

Ingredients

- 1 can salmon (14-15 oz.)
- 2 tsp mayo
- 1/2 red bell pepper ~ diced very fine
- 1 egg
- 1 tsp dill
- zest of half a lemon
- 1 tsp lemon juice
- a pinch of salt and a shake of pepper.
- 1 c bread crumbs or cracker meal + 1 tsp garlic powder and 1/2 tsp dill
- The Dip...
- 1/4 c mayo
- 1/4 c plain yogurt
- 1 clove garlic ~ chopped super fine (I use a microplane)
- 1 tsp dill
- zest of the rest of your lemon
- salt

Direction

- If you are using canned salmon, you want to sift through and remove all of the big bones and chunks of skin. Set aside.
- In a medium bowl, mix your mayo, egg, dill, lemon zest and juice, and bell pepper.
- Gently fold the salmon into the mix, careful not to break it up into too many chunks.
- Cover and stick it in the fridge for a few hours if you can. (I think this is more important for the dip.)
- Shape into 8 even cakes and cover with bread crumbs or cracker meal mix.
- Fry in half butter/half olive oil for about 2 minutes on either side over medium heat.
- The dip....
- Mix all that stuff and keep it in the fridge until ready to eat.
- Enjoy!

---

225. Salmon Cannelloni With Lemon Cream Sauce Recipe

Serving: 6 | Prep: | Cook: 30mins | Ready in:

Ingredients

- For crespelle
- 2 large eggs
- 2/3 cup water
- 1/2 cup all-purpose flour
- 1/4 teaspoon salt
- 1 tablespoon finely chopped fresh tarragon
- 3 tablespoons unsalted butter, melted
- For sauce
- 2 tablespoons unsalted butter, cut into pieces
- 2 tablespoons all-purpose flour
- 1 (8-oz) bottle clam juice
- 1/3 cup water
- 1/4 cup heavy cream
- 2 teaspoons finely grated fresh lemon zest
- 1/4 teaspoon black pepper
- For salmon cannelloni

- 2 tablespoons unsalted butter, softened
- 1 shallot, finely chopped
- 1 teaspoon salt
- 1/2 teaspoon black pepper
- 6 (5-oz) center-cut pieces salmon fillet (preferably wild; 1 inch thick), skin and little bones discarded

Direction

- Make crespelle:
- Blend together eggs, water, flour, and salt in a blender until smooth. Transfer to a bowl and stir in tarragon.
- Lightly brush a 10-inch non-stick skillet with melted butter and heat over moderate heat until hot but not smoking. Ladle about 1/4 cup batter into skillet, tilting and rotating skillet to coat bottom, then pour excess batter back into bowl. (If batter sets before skillet is coated, reduce heat slightly for next crespella.) Cook until just set and underside is lightly browned, about 30 seconds, then invert crespella onto a clean kitchen towel in one layer to cool. (It will be cooked on one side only.) Make 5 more crespelle with remaining batter in same manner, brushing skillet with butter as needed and transferring to towel as cooked, arranging them in one layer.
- Make sauce:
- Heat butter in a 1- to 2-quart heavy saucepan over moderately low heat until foam subsides. Add flour and cook, whisking, 2 minutes. Add clam juice and water in a slow stream, whisking, then bring to a boil, whisking. Reduce heat and simmer, whisking occasionally, 5 minutes. Stir in cream, zest, and pepper, then remove from heat.
- Assemble cannelloni:
- Put oven rack in middle position and preheat oven to 425°F. Butter a 13- by 9-inch or other 3-quart glass or ceramic baking dish and spread half of sauce in dish.
- Stir together butter (2 tablespoons), shallot, salt, and pepper and spread 1 teaspoon on top of each fillet.

- Put 1 crespella, pale side down, on a work surface, then place 1 salmon fillet, buttered side down, in center of crespella and fold crespella around salmon, leaving ends open. Transfer to baking dish, arranging, seam side down, in sauce. Make 5 more cannelloni with remaining salmon and crespelle in same manner, arranging in baking dish. Spoon remaining sauce over cannelloni.
- Bake until salmon is just cooked through and sauce is bubbling, 15 to 20 minutes.
- Notes:
- • Sauce can be made 1 day ahead and cooled, uncovered, then chilled, covered. Thin with water if necessary.
- • Cannelloni can be assembled and covered with sauce (but not baked) 1 day ahead and chilled, wrapped tightly in plastic wrap. Bring to room temperature before baking.
- • Crespelle can be made 3 days ahead and chilled, wrapped tightly in plastic wrap.

226.   Salmon Casserole Recipe

Serving: 4 | Prep: | Cook: 35mins | Ready in:

Ingredients

- 7-3/4 ounce can salmon
- 3 cups cooked egg noodles
- 1 cup grated cheddar cheese
- 1 cup frozen peas thawed
- 1/4 cup sliced green onions
- 2 tablespoons minced parsley
- 1 can cream of celery soup
- 1/2 cup sour cream
- 1 tablespoon lemon juice
- 1/2 teaspoon dry mustard
- 1/2 teaspoon salt
- 1 teaspoon freshly ground black pepper
- Grated parmesan cheese

Direction

- Drain and flake salmon reserving liquid.

- Combine salmon and liquid with remaining ingredients except Parmesan cheese.
- Place in buttered casserole and sprinkle with grated Parmesan cheese.
- Bake at 375 for 35 minutes then garnish with parsley and serve.

---

227. Salmon Cheese Casserole Recipe

Serving: 6 | Prep: | Cook: 25mins | Ready in:

Ingredients

- 1 can salmon , drained, skinned and boned
- 1 envelop (1.5 oz 4-cheese pasta sauce mix
- 1 cup milk
- 1 cup frozen pearl onions
- 1 10 oz package frozen peas and carrots
- 1 box corn bread muffin mix (8 1/2 oz)

Direction

- Preheat oven to 375 degrees.
- Spray an 11 x 7 x 2 inch baking dish with cooking spray.
- Flake the salmon into the prepared dish.
- Wisk sauce mix and milk in saucepan; add onions.
- Simmer 5 minutes; stir in peas and carrots.
- Return to simmer; spoon over salmon.
- Prepare corn bread mix according to package directions.
- Spoon around outer edge of baking dish.
- Bake 375 degrees for 25 minutes or until heated through.

---

228. Salmon Croquettes Recipe

Serving: 4 | Prep: | Cook: 5mins | Ready in:

Ingredients

- 1 7 1/4 oz can of salmon
- 2 eggs, beaten
- 1 tsp oil
- 1/3 cup crushed corn flakes or saltine crackers (for mixing)
- 1/4 cup crushed corn flakes or saltine crackers (for coating)
- 1 tsp baking powder
- oil for frying

Direction

- Drain salmon and reserve the liquid
- In a large bowl mix the salmon, liquid, eggs, salt, 1/3 cup crushed corn flakes (or saltines) and baking powder
- Shape into patties or croquets
- Coat the patties by rolling them in the remaining 1/4 cup crushed corn flakes (or saltines)
- Heat the oil for frying in a skillet or frying pan and fry the croquettes until golden brown
- Serve with a light white sauce or hollandaise or lemon wedges

---

229. Salmon Croquettes With Remoulade Sauce Recipe

Serving: 8 | Prep: | Cook: 3mins | Ready in:

Ingredients

- 2 tablespoons butter
- 1/2 medium-size red bell pepper, diced
- 4 green onions, thinly sliced
- About 3 cups canned salmon, drained, flaked
- 1 cup soft breadcrumbs (fresh, make my own)
- 1 large egg, lightly beaten
- 2 tablespoons mayonnaise *
- 1 tablespoon creole mustard
- 2 teaspoons creole seasoning
- 1/4 cup vegetable oil

- *NOTE: Can add a little more mayonnaise for binder if you have to
- REMOULADE SAUCE
- 1 cup mayonnaise
- 3 green onions, sliced
- 2 tablespoons creole mustard
- 2 garlic cloves, pressed
- 1 tablespoon chopped fresh parsley
- 1/4 teaspoon ground red pepper
- Serve on side of croquette, or dollop on top

Direction

- In large skillet, melt butter
- Add bell pepper, green onions, sauté until tender
- In large bowl mix bell pepper mixture with salmon, and next 5 ingredients
- Shape into patties, about 8??
- Fry 4 patties in about 2 tablespoons hot oil over medium heat, about 3 minutes on each side until golden brown
- Repeat with 2 more tablespoons oil and other patties
- REMOULADE SAUCE
- In large bowl, stir together all ingredients
- Garnish with sliced green onions, if desired
- This makes about 1-1/4 cups

---

230. Salmon Donburi Dated 1962 Recipe

Serving: 4 | Prep: | Cook: 20mins | Ready in:

Ingredients

- 4 cups cooked white rice
- 16 ounce can salmon
- 4 tablespoons soy sauce
- 4 tablespoons dry sherry
- 2 tablespoons vegetable oil
- 6 tablespoons white sesame seeds

Direction

- Simmer salmon in soy sauce and sherry until liquid is gone.
- Heat oil and sesame seeds until light golden color then immediately remove from heat.
- Put hot rice in 4 bowls then top with salmon and sprinkle sesame over all and serve hot.

---

231. Salmon En Croute Recipe

Serving: 6 | Prep: | Cook: 45mins | Ready in:

Ingredients

- basil cream cheese:
- handful of fresh basil leaves
- 1-2 cloves garlic
- 1/4 cup grated parmigiano Reggiano
- 1/4 extra virgin olive oil (good quality)
- 12 oz cream cheese
- sea salt & fresh ground black pepper (to taste)
- ~
- for spinach layer:
- 2 lbs fresh spinach, cooked, excess water squeezed out, chopped
- 2 tablespoons olive oil
- 2 cloves garlic, minced
- 1 medium shallot, minced
- sea salt & fresh ground black pepper (to taste)
- ~
- 6 (6 oz) wild salmon filet (skinless)
- 4 sheets frozen puff pastry, thawed
- 1 beaten egg

Direction

- Preheat oven to 400°.
- Heat olive oil in a large sauté pan over medium heat. Add the shallot and sauté until softened but not browned, about 5 minutes. Add the spinach and garlic, season with salt and pepper.
- In a food processor or with a hand blender, pulse 1st 4 ingredients for basil cream cheese until pesto like consistency.

- Place cream cheese in a bowl and stir to make creamy. Add the basil sauce and stir to evenly incorporate.
- Lay out the puff pastry on lightly floured surface, roll out a little bit, cut into 6 equal squares. Season salmon fillets with salt and place a thick layer of cream cheese mixture on one side of the puff pastry squares. Place each salmon fillet in the middle of each pastry square. Top salmon with spinach mixture. Brush edges with egg wash, fold edges over and press to seal. Flip packets over, place on baking sheet, shaping it nicely and lightly score tops with a sharp paring knife. Brush with beaten egg.
- Bake for 30 minutes or until the pastry is crisp and browned. Remove from oven and let cool 10 minutes. Cut in half on the diagonal. Serve with pan fried potatoes and drizzle with any extra basil sauce.

232. Salmon Fillet With Papaya Avocado Salsa Recipe

Serving: 2 | Prep: | Cook: 20mins | Ready in:

Ingredients

- 1 medium ripe papaya cut into 1/2" pieces
- 1 large ripe avocado cut into 1/2" pieces
- 6 tablespoons fresh lime juice
- 2 serrano chili peppers shredded and finely chopped
- 1/2 cup fresh cilantro leaves
- 5 scallions finely chopped
- 1 medium red bell pepper seeded and chopped
- 1/4 teaspoon salt
- 1/2 pound salmon fillet
- olive oil

Direction

- Prepare salsa in a medium bowl by combining papaya and avocado.

- Add lime juice and toss gently to coat then add chilies, cilantro, scallions and bell pepper.
- Toss gently then season to taste with salt and set aside.
- In large non-stick skillet heat oil over high heat.
- Add salmon slices and cook over medium high heat 30 seconds on each side.
- To serve arrange salmon slices on individual serving plates.
- Garnish with slices of papaya and avocado then serve salsa on the side.

233. Salmon Fillets With Mustard Sauce Recipe

Serving: 4 | Prep: | Cook: 20mins | Ready in:

Ingredients

- 1 Tbs. olive oil
- 4 salmon fillets, 3/4" thick each
- 1 C.chicken broth)
- 2 Tbs. balsamic vinegar
- 1 Tbs. Dijon mustard
- 2 tsp. packed brown sugar

Direction

- Heat oil in medium skillet over medium-high heat.
- Add salmon, skin-side up, and cook for about 5 min. or until browned.
- Turn salmon and season with black pepper.
- Add 1/2 cup broth.
- Heat to a boil.
- Cover and cook over low heat 5 min. or until fish flakes easily when tested with a fork.
- Remove salmon and keep warm.
- Add remaining broth, vinegar, mustard and brown sugar.
- Heat to a boil.
- Cook over medium heat 10 min. or until mixture is slightly thickened and reduced to 1/4 cup.

- Serve over salmon..

234. Salmon Herb Pie Recipe

Serving: 4 | Prep: | Cook: 10mins | Ready in:

Ingredients

- 1 cup whole wheat couscous
- 1 package (5.2 oz) herbed cream cheese, such as Boursin, room temperature
- 1 can (14.5 oz) spinach drained
- 1 can (14.75 oz) pink salmon, drained
- 1/4 cup shredded part-skim mozzarella cheese

Direction

- Preheat oven to 450°F. Coat a 9 1/2-inch pie plate with a little vegetable oil (about 1 teaspoon).
- Spread the couscous over the bottom of the dish and pour 1 cup boiling water over top. Stir to moisten and spread in an even layer.
- Spoon the herbed cream cheese in small spoonfuls over the couscous, leaving 1/4 inch border all around.
- Scatter the spinach and salmon over top of the cream cheese, and top with mozzarella cheese.
- Bake for 10 minutes until cheese is melted and the pie is hot through. Cut in wedges and serve.
- Total cost: $9.98
- Nutritional Information per Serving:
- (including 1 teaspoon oil for pie plate): Calories 430; Total fat 20g; Saturated fat 10g; Cholesterol 125mg; Sodium 650mg; Carbohydrate 29g; Fiber 6g; Protein 34g; Vitamin A 210%DV*; Vitamin C 25%DV; Calcium 50%DV; Iron 25%DV
- *Daily Value
- COURTESY OF MEALTIME.ORG

235. Salmon Hobo Packs Recipe

Serving: 4 | Prep: | Cook: 12mins | Ready in:

Ingredients

- 2 lb. skinless salmon fillets, about 1-inch thick
- salt and freshly ground pepper
- 1/2 cup light-colored molasses
- 1/4 cup packed brown sugar
- 1 Tbsp. soy sauce
- 12 oz. green beans, or haricot verts (tender young green beans), ends trimmed
- 2 small yellow summer squash, halved lengthwise and cut into 1/2-inch slices
- 2 Tbsp. coarse grain mustard
- 2 Tbsp. snipped fresh parsley, optional
- 2 tsp. finely shredded lemon peel, optional
- 1/4 tsp. freshly ground pepper, optional

Direction

- Sprinkle salmon lightly with salt and pepper; set aside. For glaze, in a small saucepan stir together molasses, brown sugar, and soy sauce*; heat just until sugar is dissolved, stirring occasionally. Set aside.
- Grill salmon directly over medium coals for 6 minutes; turn. Grill for 4 minutes; brush with molasses mixture. Grill for 2 to 4 minutes more or until fish flakes easily with fork, brushing occasionally with glaze. Remove from grill. Cut salmon into 8 pieces. Cover and refrigerate 4 of the portions.
- Tear off four 36x18-inch sheets of heavy foil; fold in half to make 18-inch squares. In a bowl combine beans and squash; toss with mustard. Sprinkle lightly with salt and pepper. Divide evenly among foil sheets, placing vegetable mixture in the center. Place a salmon portion on each; spoon on any remaining glaze. Bring up two opposite edges of foil and seal with a double fold. Fold remaining edges together to completely enclose, leaving space for steam to build.

- Grill foil packets directly over medium coals for 20 minutes.
- To serve, transfer salmon and vegetables from packets to dinner plates. Combine parsley, lemon peel, and the 1/4 teaspoon pepper; sprinkle on salmon.

---

236.   Salmon Leek And Potato Gratin Recipe

Serving: 6 | Prep: | Cook: 50mins | Ready in:

Ingredients

- 1 3/4 lbs potatoes
- 3/4 cup unsalted butter, softened
- 3 small leeks, thinly sliced
- 5 oz fresh salmon fillet, skin removed
- 6 oz smoked salmon, diced
- 1 1/4 cups whipping cream
- 3/4 cup shredded gruyere cheese
- 3 tbs unsalted butter, chopped
- Sprigs of fresh dill, to garnish

Direction

- Peel the potatoes and place them in a large saucepan of salted water. Bring to a boil, then reduce the heat and simmer for 20 to 25 minutes, or until the potatoes are tender to the point of a knife. Drain and finely mash the potatoes, or puree them using a food mill or ricer. Mix in half the softened butter, then set them aside and keep warm.
- Melt the remaining softened butter in a skillet over low heat. Gently cook the leeks for 2 to 3 minutes without coloring. Drain the excess butter and spread the leeks evenly in an oval gratin dish. Set aside.
- If necessary, remove any fine bones from the salmon using a pair of tweezers. Place the fillet in a steamer basket, then cover and steam for 5 to 10 minutes, or until the fish changes color and begins to break apart when pressed with a

fork. Break the fish into pieces and mix into the potatoes with the smoked salmon.
- Preheat the broiler to hot. Bring the cream to a boil in a small saucepan, then stir into the salmon and potato mixture. Mix well and season to taste with salt and pepper. Transfer to the gratin dish and sprinkle with the shredded cheese. Dot with the butter and brown under the broiler for 2 to 3 minutes, or until golden. Before serving, garnish with sprigs of dill.
- Note: You can also use smoked haddock or cod.

---

237.   Salmon Lime Light Recipe

Serving: 2 | Prep: | Cook: 30mins | Ready in:

Ingredients

- 1 Tbl butter, not margerine
- 2 4 oz salmon fillets, skin removed
- 2 Tbl lime juice
- 1 Tbl teriyaki sauce
- 2 green onions, sliced (white part only)
- ½ tsp herbs de Provence
- 1 lime, cut into wedges (optional)

Direction

- 450 oven.
- Add butter to baking dish, melt, turn dish to coat.
- Place fillets in baking dish, unskinned side up.
- Stir together all ingredients except lime wedges.
- Drizzle over salmon.
- Bake until fish flakes easily with fork, about 25-30 minutes.
- Serve with lime wedges, if desired.

238. Salmon Loaf Recipe

Serving: 8 | Prep: | Cook: 1mins | Ready in:

Ingredients

- 1 15oz can of salmon (pink or red) remove bone and skin
- 1 10oz can cream of celery soup or any cream of soup
- 1 ½ cups seasoned bread crumbs
- 2 eggs or substitute
- ½ cup chopped onion
- 1 Tbs lemon juice
- 2/4 cup milk (any type)
- ¼ cup water
- I cup grated parmesan cheese

Direction

- Preheat oven 375°
- Mix all ingredients thoroughly.
- Pour into Pam sprayed loaf pan 5" x 9"
- Bake at 375° for 1 hour or till golden brown.

239. Salmon Miso Yaki Sake No Miso Yaki Recipe

Serving: 4 | Prep: | Cook: 12mins | Ready in:

Ingredients

- 1- 1 1/2 lbs fresh wild salmon
- 1/4 cup white soybean paste (shiromiso)
- 1/2 tbl sugar
- 3-4 1/2 tbl soy sauce
- 2 cloves crushed garlic
- 2 x green onions chopped

Direction

- Mix the marinade paste. Brush fish on all sides with paste. Can be done ahead and refrigerated.

- Broil 6 min per side until fish is brown and somewhat charred.
- Note: Shiromiso can be purchased in plastic tubs at Asian markets. Made from fermented tofu, it is the same paste used in miso soup and miso dressing.

240. Salmon Patties Recipe

Serving: 6 | Prep: | Cook: 15mins | Ready in:

Ingredients

- 1 can of salmon
- saltine crackers (about 1 sleeve or so)
- 3 T of water or milk
- 1 onion, diced
- 1 egg
- 2 T ketchup
- Salt
- pepper
- *update-recently discovered this, I had no eggs so added some flour to the mixture and it still tasted good, just used as stick together agent*

Direction

- Combine all ingredients above together then form into patties. I cook mine on my griddle. Cook on medium heat until well browned on both sides!

241. Salmon Patties Smothered In Creamed Peas Recipe

Serving: 2 | Prep: | Cook: 10mins | Ready in:

Ingredients

- salmon Patties

- 7 ounce can red salmon, drained, skin and bones removed (I know, I know…the bones are actually good for you, but I still like to pick out the big pieces!)
- ¼ cup diced onion
- 8 saltine crackers, finely crushed (I've also used finely crushed garlic croutons for a nice flavor enhancer)
- 1 egg, beaten
- ¼ teaspoon garlic salt
- 1/8 teaspoon Emeril's fish Rub (optional, but it's good stuff)
- 1/8 teaspoon pepper
- flour for coating salmon patties
- 2 tablespoons butter for frying pan
- Creamed peas
- 2 tablespoons butter (no margarine, please)
- 2 tablespoons flour
- ¼ teaspoon salt (I like to use sea salt, if I've got it on hand)
- 1/8 teaspoon Jane's Crazy Mixed Up Salt (optional, but pick some up if you've never tired it – it's a great seasoning, and I'm pretty sure it's available online, too)
- 1/8 teaspoon pepper
- 1 cup half-and-half (of course you can use milk, but I'm going for a richer sauce here!)
- 8.5 ounce can Le Sueur Very Young Small sweet peas (these make THE best creamed peas, but use whatever is available in your area), drained well

Direction

- It's best to make the creamed peas first, so it's ready to pour over the salmon patties when they are done – the patties take very little time to fry up.
- For the creamed peas, melt the butter in a small pan and stir in the flour and seasonings.
- Gradually stir in the half-and-half, using a whisk to help prevent lumps.
- Heat, whisking often, until sauce begins to thicken.
- Add drained peas and gently stir with a spoon (a whisk may break up the peas too much).
- Stir often as it continues to heat and thicken.

- To prepare the salmon patties, break up the salmon in a shallow bowl and mix with remaining patty ingredients.
- Sprinkle a piece of waxed paper generously with some flour.
- Shape salmon into 3 or 4 patties, and place them in the flour.
- Carefully flip the patties over so both sides are coated with the flour.
- Preheat skillet until hot (but not hot enough to burn the butter when added) and add butter to pan – as soon as it's melted, place the salmon patties into the hot, melted butter.
- Fry until golden on bottom, then carefully flip and continue to fry until brown on bottom.
- Serve immediately with creamed peas poured over each patty.

242.   Salmon Patties With Lemon Sauce Recipe

Serving: 6 | Prep: | Cook: 15mins | Ready in:

Ingredients

- 1 (14.75 oz) can good quality pink salmon
- 2 tablespoons butter
- 1 medium onion, chopped
- 2 cloves garlic, minced
- 2/3 cup cracker or panko crumbs
- 2 teaspoons Old Bay Seasoning
- 2 eggs, beaten
- 1/4 cup chopped fresh parsley
- 1 teaspoon dry mustard
- olive oil and butter for frying
- SAUCE
- 2 tablespoons butter
- 4 teaspoons flour
- 3/4 cup milk
- 2 tablespoons lemon juice
- 1/4 teaspoon salt
- 1/8 or more cayenne pepper

Direction

- PATTIES
- Drain the salmon, reserving 3/4 cup of the liquid
- Flake the meat
- Melt butter in a large skillet over medium high heat and sauté the onions and garlic until tender
- In a medium bowl, combine the onion and garlic mixture with the reserved salmon liquid, 1/3 of the cracker crumbs, eggs, parsley, mustard, Old Bay, and salmon
- Mix until well blended, then shape into 6 patties
- Coat patties with remaining crumbs
- Melt butter in a large skillet and add olive oil over medium heat
- Cook patties until browned, turn and brown other side
- SAUCE
- Melt butter in a saucepan over medium heat
- Stir in the flour to form a smooth paste
- Gradually stir in the milk and bring to a boil, stirring constantly
- Cook for 2 minutes or until thickened
- Remove from heat and stir in lemon juice, salt and cayenne pepper
- Serve over Salmon patties

243. Salmon Pot Pie Recipe

Serving: 6 | Prep: | Cook: 40mins | Ready in:

Ingredients

- 15 oz. cooked salmon
- 4 tbsp. butter
- 4 tbsp. flour
- salt and pepper to taste
- 1/2 cups milk
- 2 cups grated cheddar cheese
- 1/2 cup chopped celery
- 2 medium carrots, grated
- 1 medium onion, chopped finely
- 3 cups prepared mashed potatoes

Direction

- Flake salmon. Make a white sauce from butter, flour, seasonings and milk. When it's thick, remove from heat; add grated cheese; stir to combine until cheese is melted. Add flaked salmon, celery, carrot and onion. Pour mixture into buttered shallow 2 quart casserole dish. Pipe potatoes around edge. (I simply cover the salmon mixture with potatoes.) Bake at 450 F for 30 to 40 minutes, until bubbly and potatoes are nicely browned.

244. Salmon Roulade With Garlic Potatoes Morels And Fresh Peas Recipe

Serving: 6 | Prep: | Cook: 20mins | Ready in:

Ingredients

- 3 large yukon gold potatoes, peeled and quartered
- 2 teaspoons minced garlic
- 1/4 cup unsalted butter
- Six 7-ounce pieces of salmon fillet, each about 1 inch wide, skin removed
- basil infused extra virgin olive oil, to brush salmon
- English peas and Morels:
- 2 TB butter
- 6 or so morel mushrooms, halved
- splash of dry white wine
- splash of cream
- 2 cups fresh English peas, shelled and steamed
- a couple sprigs of fresh thyme leaves
- chopped chives, for garnish
- kosher salt and white pepper, to taste

Direction

- Preheat the oven to 375 degrees F. Line a 9 x 13-inch baking dish with foil.
- Place the potatoes in a medium saucepan, and add lightly salted water to cover. Bring to a

boil, and cook until soft, about 20 minutes. Drain the potatoes and put them in a mixing bowl. Mash with garlic and 1/4 cup of the butter. Pass the potatoes through a food mill or ricer, then whip until smooth and fluffy.

- Brush the salmon with basil oil and season with salt and pepper. Roll each salmon fillet into the shape of a donut, and affix the ends with a toothpicks. Place them in the baking dish. With a piping bag (or zip lock with one end snipped off) fill the center of each piece with the potatoes. Lightly cover with foil (as to not squish down the filling) and bake for about 15 minutes. Remove the foil and bake until the potatoes are golden brown, about 5-8 minutes longer.
- In the meantime, sauté the morels in butter. Add the wine and slightly reduce. Add the peas, thyme and cream, season with salt and pepper; keep warm.
- Using a spatula, transfer the salmon fillets to warmed plates. Carefully twist out the toothpick, leaving the roll intact. Spoon peas and mushrooms on side, drizzle with sauce, sprinkle with the chives, and serve.
- Note: The potatoes may be made up to 8 hours in advance and refrigerated until ready to use.

---

245. Salmon Salad Recipe

Serving: 4 | Prep: | Cook: 15mins | Ready in:

Ingredients

- 1 14.75 ounce can alaskan salmon, deboned and skin removed
- 5 cups diced potatoes (6-8 medium thin-skinned red potatoes)
- 2 tablespoons diced sweet gerkins
- 1/2 cup diced onion bermuda or green onions (white or yellow can be used but add no color)
- 1 to 1 1/2 cup mayo
- 1/4 cup sour cream
- juice of half a lemon
- juice of half a lime

- 1/4 tsp. lemon zest
- 1/4 tsp. garlic powder or very finely minced fresh garlic
- 1 teaspoon dried dill OR 1 tablespoon fresh chopped dill leaves
- 1/4 tsp. paprika
- 2-3 ripe tomatoes

Direction

- Scrub potatoes and cut into cubes of equal size, about 1 inch squares
- Place in pot of salted (about 1 tablespoon) cold water and bring to boil, cooking until just tender (about 15 minutes)
- Remove from heat, drain and place in bowl of cold water to stop cooking and cool the potatoes
- Drain VERY well after they have cooled
- Clean the salmon and crumble into a large bowl (this is a personal preference of mine, many don't mind the bones)
- In a small bowl, mix the mayonnaise, sour cream, lemon juice and zest, lime juice, dill, garlic and paprika together well. Add salt and pepper to taste and set aside
- Add the onions and pickles to the salmon and toss lightly
- Gradually add the drained potatoes to the salmon mixture, stirring gently to keep the potatoes from becoming too mashed.
- Fold in the mayo mixture, chill at least 15-20 minutes before serving.
- Place lettuce in the center of the plates, circling with the tomato wedges and crackers.
- Spoon the chilled salad into the center of the lettuce and serve.
- Garnish with some added dill, a green onion, and/or paprika if desired
- *OPTIONS:
- Any type of potato may be used with good results, but I do peel anything other than red ones.
- If you like celery, which no one in my family does, you may add 1/4 cup diced celery when you add the pickles and onions for some extra crunch and flavor.

- Fat free or reduced fat mayo and sour cream work great in this recipe!

246. Salmon Seared On Bacon With Balsamic Vinegar Honey And Rosemary Recipe

Serving: 4 | Prep: | Cook: 15mins | Ready in:

Ingredients

- 1/4 cup balsamic vinegar
- 1 Tbs. honey
- 1/2 tsp. finely chopped fresh rosemary (I used 1 tsp.)
- 2 Tbs. water
- 2 slices bacon
- 4 - 6 oz. skin on, scaled, center-cut salmon fillets
- kosher salt and freshly ground pepper

Direction

- In a measuring cup, combine the vinegar, honey, rosemary and water.
- Cut the bacon in half crosswise. Lay a slice (I used two due to the size of my salmon) on the flesh side of each piece of salmon and arrange the salmon, bacon side down, in a 12 inch heavy duty, non-stick skillet. Sprinkle the salmon skin with salt and pepper. (I sprinkle the flesh side - I don't eat the skin.)
- Set the skillet over medium-high heat and cook until the bacon is golden and crisp, 4 to 5 minutes from when it begins to sizzle. Turn the salmon and continue to cook until the skin is crisp and the salmon is just cooked through, 4 to 5 minutes more.
- Take the skillet off the heat and transfer the salmon to a platter. Pour off the fat and return the skillet to medium-high heat. Stir the vinegar mixture well and add to the skillet. Simmer until slightly thickened, 1 to 2 minutes. Pour over the salmon and serve.

- Note: If your pan is super hot, which it probably will be if you use cast iron, you may want to let the pan cool for a bit before you pour the vinegar mixture in.

247. Salmon Shawarma Recipe

Serving: 8 | Prep: | Cook: 45mins | Ready in:

Ingredients

- - 8 pieces of thawed salmon fillets (drained well and cut into strips)
- - 2 cups plain yogurt
- - 1 onion, 4 cloves of garlic finely minced in food processor
- - 1/2 cup olive oil
- - 2 tbsp white vinegar
- spices
- - 1 tbsp curry powder
- - 1 tbsp ground cinnamon
- - 1/2 tsp ground cloves
- - 1 tbsp dry ginger or fresh paste
- - 1/2 tsp dried mint
- -salt
- - black pepper

Direction

- -In a large bowl mix together all the above ingredients and let them marinade well, could go in the fridge overnight.
- -Do NOT add salt to the mixture just yet, as that will cause more water to come out.
- -When it's time to cook, heat oven to 400 F and pour mixture into a baking dish/lasagne pan,
- -spread it all out nicely until it's about 1 inch thickness in the pan.
- -Bake for 45 or so, every now and then checking on it, taking it out and stirring until it's all dried and coated well.
- -Once the mixture comes together well sprinkle it generously with salt and bake until it's dried up well, taste and add more salt if needed.

- -Let it cool completely for spices to settle and flavours to come out.
- Meanwhile prepare pita bread, chop veggies (tomato, lettuce, pickles, cucumbers, etc.) for sandwiches and make the dip by mixing:
- - 1/2 cup tahini
- - Salt
- - Sumac (can be found in Middle Eastern shops, leave out if not available)
- - pickle juice or water
- - Fresh lemon juice or citric acid crystals
- - 2 tbsp. mayonnaise
- Whisk together the tahini with the spices and add the water/pickle juice mixture gradually until it thickens, it may separate at first but keep whisking and the mixture should come together and form a creamy dressing like consistency.

248. Salmon Souffle Recipe

Serving: 4 | Prep: | Cook: 45mins |Ready in:

Ingredients

- 1 small green bell pepper coarsely chopped
- 1 small red bell pepper coarsely chopped
- 1 tablespoon margarine
- 1/4 cup all purpose flour
- 1-1/2 cups milk
- 10 ounces frozen whole kernel corn
- 3/4 teaspoon dried dill weed
- 1/4 teaspoon salt
- 1/8 teaspoon white pepper
- 3 egg yolks lightly beaten
- 6-1/2 ounce can salmon drained flaked and bones removed
- 5 egg whites
- 1/8 teaspoon cream of tartar

Direction

- Sauté bell peppers in margarine for 5 minutes then stir in flour and cook 2 minutes.

- Gradually blend in milk, corn, dill weed, salt and pepper then heat to boiling over medium heat.
- Remove from heat.
- Gradually stir in small amount of vegetables into egg yolks then stir yolks into vegetables.
- Mix in salmon then beat egg whites and cream of tartar in large bowl to stiff peaks.
- Fold into salmon mixture then pour into lightly greased soufflé dish.
- Bake uncovered at 350 for 45 minutes then serve immediately.

249. Salmon Steaks With Cucumber Dill Sauce Recipe

Serving: 2 | Prep: | Cook: 6mins |Ready in:

Ingredients

- 2 salmon steaks
- 1/4 cup dry white wine
- 1 Bay Leaf
- 2 Tbsp fresh dill
- 1 stalk celery, cut up
- cucumber dill Sauce:
- 1/4 cup plain low-fat yogurt
- 1/4 cup lite Mayonaise
- 1 small seeded grated cucumber
- 1 small onion, peeled & grated
- 1/8 tsp dry mustard
- 1/4 cup freshly chopped dill
- salt & pepper, to taste

Direction

- Place steaks in microwave dish w/ thick end to outside. Add remaining ingredients on top of steaks. Cover and microwave on high for 4-6 minutes.
- Cucumber Dill Sauce Directions:
- Combine all ingredients in a food processor. Process until blended. Pour into bowl and refrigerate 1-2 hours before serving. Pour small amount of dill sauce across salmon

steaks and sprinkle with small amount of fresh dill. Serve remaining sauce in serving dish.

---

250. Salmon Stuffed Shells Recipe

Serving: 0 | Prep: | Cook: | Ready in:

Ingredients

- 1 Large salmon fillet
- Grated zest of 1 lemon, juice of 1/2
- 1/3 Cup Chopped fresh dill
- 1 leek, rinsed well and diced
- 1/2 Cup white wine
- 1/2 Cup Grated parmesan cheese
- 1 Tbspn parsley, Separated
- About 1 tspn each garlic and onion powder, separated
- 1 Large egg
- plain breadcrumbs
- Jumbo Stuffing Shells (I used a little more than half the box)
- salt and pepper to taste
- Your favorite alfredo sauce, fresh or jarred. If you don't have a good alfredo sauce recipe, this site has tons. A good example is this one: alfredo sauce

Direction

- Preheat oven to 350 F.
- Rinse the salmon fillet under cool water. Make shallow slices in the flesh and skin, then set it in a roasting pan.
- Add lemon juice, wine, 1/2 teaspoon of garlic and onion powder, and a few sprinkles of the dill and parsley. Bake at 350 for 20-25 minutes until cooked through. When the fish flakes off with a fork, it's done. Set aside and allow the fish to cool a bit.
- In the meantime, boil water and cook the stuffing shells to al dente'. When they're done, drain them and set aside.

- When it's cool enough to handle, flake off all the meat from the skin and put it into a large mixing bowl. Add the lemon zest, cheese, diced leeks, chopped dill, the rest of the parsley, garlic and onion powder, salt, pepper and enough breadcrumbs to coat. Mix well.
- Only add the egg when the fish has cooled down to room temperature, or you'll risk the egg cooking right in the mixing bowl. That would be gross.
- If you need more breadcrumbs to make the consistency of the mix better, by all means, do so.
- In a large baking dish, spread a thin layer of the Alfredo sauce on the bottom as a bed for the shells, to prevent them from burning.
- Take a large fistful of the mixture and stuff the shells, lining them in a single layer inside the dish. You can keep them as close together as you want.
- Drizzle the Alfredo sauce over the shells liberally, filling in the spaces between them if you have enough.
- Bake at 350 for 30-40 minutes. Remove from heat and let it cool for 2-3 minutes before serving.
- Garnish the shells with extra parmesan, parsley and/or dill for color if you feel like it. Not only is it pretty, goes great with Chardonnay, but it will totally get you laid.

---

251. Salmon Tostadas Recipe

Serving: 4 | Prep: | Cook: 10mins | Ready in:

Ingredients

- 4 pieces of skinless salmon fillets
- 3 tablespoons blackening spice
- olive oil cooking spray
- 2 tablespoons canola oil
- 1 cup mayonnaise
- 1 cup sour cream
- 1 package dry taco seasoning mix

- 4 tortillas
- 2 cups canola oil
- 1 large lime
- 7 ounce can whole kernel corn drained
- 1 cup diced red onion
- 2 cups shredded red cabbage
- 2 ripe avocadoes sliced into wedges
- 2 cups grape or cherry tomatoes sliced in half
- 1/4 cup fresh cilantro chopped

Direction

- Mix mayonnaise, sour cream and taco seasoning in a small bowl then set aside.
- Spray salmon pieces with olive oil and coat them in spice mixture then set aside.
- Heat oil in a large sauté pan then fry tortillas until crispy shells are formed.
- Fry them one at a time until brown turning over halfway through the frying process.
- Drain well on paper towels and keep warm.
- Heat cooking spray in pan and place salmon fillets in the pan and lightly brown on both sides.
- Coat one side of tortillas with mayonnaise mixture then place tortillas sauce side up on plates.
- Place some of the cabbage and red onion on top then sprinkle on some corn.
- Top with salmon and drizzle salmon with lime juice.
- Top with avocado slices, tomatoes, remaining corn and cilantro.

252. Salmon Tuna Patties Recipe

Serving: 6 | Prep: | Cook: 30mins | Ready in:

Ingredients

- 2 (15-16oz) cans salmon
- 2 (5 oz) cans oil-packed tuna, well drained
- 2 eggs
- 1 medium onion, minced

- 1 medium sweet green bell pepper, minced
- 1 cup flour
- 1 tsp salt
- 1/2 tsp Mrs Dash Original seasoning
- 2 tsps baking powder
- cornmeal (optional)
- 1 1/2 cups vegetable oil
- creamed peas

Direction

- Drain salmon and set aside 6 tbsps. of the broth; debone and flake the meat.
- In a medium mixing bowl, mix salmon, tuna, eggs, onion and bell pepper until sticky. Stir in flour. Add salt, Mrs Dash, and baking powder to salmon broth; stir into fish/veggie mixture.
- Form into small patties, and dredge in cornmeal if desired. Refrigerate on a platter in a single layer for an hour or two to facilitate easier handling.
- When ready, fry patties four at a time in hot cooking oil until golden, about 5 minutes per side.
- Serve topped with tartar sauce or creamed peas.
- These can also be served on burger buns with tartar sauce.

253. Salmon Wellington Recipe

Serving: 6 | Prep: | Cook: 30mins | Ready in:

Ingredients

- 6 salmon fillets, 4 oz. each
- 6 oz. cream cheese & chives, room temperature
- 1/2 c. sliced almonds (optional)
- 1/2 pkg. puff pastry

Direction

- Preheat the oven to 400 degrees. Slice the salmon fillets lengthwise to make a pocket for

132

stuffing if they're thick enough. If the fillets are thin, just leave them flat. Mix the cream cheese with the almonds. Gently work the stuffing into the pocket of the salmon fillet. For thin fillets, spread the cream cheese-almond mixture on half of the fillet and fold the other half over it. Divide the puff pastry sheet into 6 portions. Roll out to 1/8 inch thickness. Working quickly, wrap each fillet completely in pastry dough. Seal the edges with water. Bake until the dough is browned, approximately 25 to 30 minutes.

---

254.   Salmon Wellington With Dilled Cream Sauce Recipe

Serving: 4 | Prep: | Cook: 25mins | Ready in:

Ingredients

- 1 pound salmon fillet, cut into 4 pieces
- 2 teaspoons lemon juice
- 2 tablespoons butter OR margarine
- 2 cups sliced mushrooms
- 2 green onions, chopped
- 1/2 package puff pastry sheets (1 sheet)
- 1 egg
- 1 tablespoon water
- dilled Cream Sauce
- 3/4 cup sour cream
- 1 tbsp. Dijon mustard
- 1 tbsp. chopped fresh dill weed or 1 tsp. dried dill weed (crushed).

Direction

- Season salmon with salt and pepper if desired.
- Sprinkle with lemon juice.
- Melt butter in skillet.
- Add salmon and cook 5 min. or until it just flakes.
- Remove salmon.
- Add mushrooms and onions and cook until tender and liquid evaporates.

- Cover and refrigerate salmon and mushroom mixture at least 1 hr. or until cooled (can be refrigerated up to 24 hrs.).
- Thaw pastry sheet at room temperature 30 mins.
- Mix egg and water.
- Preheat oven to 400°F.
- Unfold pastry on lightly floured surface.
- Roll into 14" square and cut into 4 (7") squares.
- Spoon mushroom mixture in center of each.
- Remove skin from salmon and place on top.
- Brush edges of pastry sheets with egg mixture.
- Fold each corner to center on top of salmon and seal edges.
- Place seam-side down on baking sheet. Brush with egg mixture.
- BAKE 25 min. or until golden.
- While baking, prepare sauce by mixing all ingredients.
- Serve after setting 5 minutes.

---

255.   Salmon With Avocado Mango Salsa Recipe

Serving: 2 | Prep: | Cook: 15mins | Ready in:

Ingredients

- 2 tsp paprika
- 2 tsp ground coriander or cumin
- ¾ tsp salt
- 2 salmon fillets
- 1 mango, peeled and cubed
- 1 avocado, peeled, pitted, cubed
- 1/3 c. chopped cilantro
- 1 tsp grated lemon zest
- 2 T lemon juice
- 2 tsp olive oil

Direction

- In large bowl, stir paprika, coriander or cumin, salt.

- Measure out spice mixture and sprinkle over salmon, rubbing it into the fish. Place salmon, skin-side down, in broiler-pan. Put the rack on the high ridge and preheat the oven broiler on high.
- Blend mango, avocado, cilantro, lemon zest, lemon juice, olive oil.
- Broil salmon 5-6 minutes for medium doneness. Peel off the skin, then garnish with salsa.

256. Salmon With Avocado Lime Salsa Recipe

Serving: 2 | Prep: | Cook: 30mins | Ready in:

Ingredients

- 2 salmon steaks or fillets
- 1/2 tbsp. olive oil
- 1/4 tsp. salt
- 1/2 tsp. ground cumin
- 1/2 tsp. paprika
- 1/2 tsp. onion powder
- 1/4 tsp. ancho chili powder
- 1/2 tsp. fresh ground pepper
- For the salsa:
- 1 avocado,sliced
- 2 heaping tbsp. red onion
- juice from 1/2 lime
- 2 tbsp. chopped cilantro
- salt to taste

Direction

- Mix the salt, chili powder, cumin, paprika, onion powder, and black pepper together.
- Rub the salmon with olive oil and then sprinkle both sides with the rub mixture. Place on a small greased baking tray and set aside.
- Combine the avocado, onion, cilantro, lime juice and salt in a bowl, and mix well. Chill until ready to use. I set the avocado pit in the salsa mixture until serving time so it doesn't turn brown.

- Bake fillets in 350F oven for about 20 minutes, depending hoe thick your salmon is, or until cooked through and flakes easily.
- Top with salsa. Enjoy!

257. Salmon With Basil Pesto And Polenta Crust Recipe

Serving: 6 | Prep: | Cook: 15mins | Ready in:

Ingredients

- 2 cups half-and-half
- 1/2 cup polenta (a.k.a. corn grits. I like Bob's Red Mill brand)
- 2 tablespoons mascarpone
- 1/4 tsp kosher salt
- 1/4 cup white wine
- 3 tablespoons unsalted butter
- Six 6-oz pieces of fresh salmon filet, each about 2 inches wide, seasoned on each side with kosher salt and pepper, skin on or off (I leave it on because it helps keep the salmon in one piece)
- 1/4 cup fresh basil pesto (recipe below)
- 2 tablespoons chopped Italian parsley
- ~~~~~~~~~~~~~~~~~~~~~~~~~~~~~~~~~~ ~~~~~~~~~~~~~~~~~~~
- Fresh basil pesto Recipe:
- 2 cups fresh basil leaves, packed
- 1/2 cup freshly grated parmigiano-reggiano cheese (tip: grate it in your food processor before you start the pesto)
- 1/2 cup extra virgin olive oil
- 1/3 cup pine nuts
- 3 medium sized garlic cloves, minced
- salt and freshly ground black pepper to taste
- Combine the basil in with the pine nuts, pulse a few times in a food processor. Add the garlic, pulse a few times more.
- Slowly add the olive oil in a constant stream while the food processor is on. Stop to scrape down the sides of the food processor with a rubber spatula. Add the grated cheese and

pulse again until blended. Add a pinch of salt and freshly ground black pepper to taste. Makes 1 cup.

Direction

- Preheat broiler. Bring the half-n-half to a boil in medium saucepan, and lower the heat to a simmer. Add salt and gradually add the polenta, whisking constantly until it is incorporated. Using a wooden spoon, continue cooking and string until mixture thickens, 3-4 minutes. Remove from heat and stir in mascarpone.
- Simmer the white wine in a small saucepan until reduced to about 3 tablespoons. Remove from heat, stir in lemon juice and butter, and keep warm.
- Broil salmon filets until cooked through, about 4 minutes per side (less if you like the center rare). Remove the salmon from the broiler and spread basil pesto over the tops. Spread the polenta evenly over the pesto and return to broiler to brown, 3-4 minutes.
- Stir fresh parsley into the lemon butter sauce and drizzle it around the fillets.
- Note: the polenta may be made up to 8 hours in advance and refrigerated until ready to use. Bring to room temp to make more malleable.

---

258.   Salmon With Blackberry Hollandaise Recipe

Serving: 4 | Prep: | Cook: 20mins | Ready in:

Ingredients

- 4 egg yolks
- 2 tablespoons fresh lemon juice
- 1-1/2 sticks sweet butter
- 1/2 teaspoon salt
- 1/2 teaspoon white pepper
- 2 cups blackberries
- 1 teaspoon Dijon mustard
- 1/2 teaspoon garlic minced
- 1/2 teaspoon shallot minced
- 1 lemon, juiced
- 3 tablespoons madeira wine
- 1 lemon quartered
- fresh mint
- 2 cups white wine
- 3 cups fish stock
- 4 salmon fillets

Direction

- Whisk egg yolks and lemon juice in top pan of double boiler.
- Place pan onto double boiler with water.
- Whisk continuously until sauce just begins to thicken.
- Remove from heat and slowly pour melted butter in steady stream.
- Continue to whisk until all butter is incorporated then add salt and white pepper.
- Reserve 2 tablespoons blackberries for garnish.
- Combine blackberries, mustard, garlic, shallot, lemon juice and wine in saucepan.
- Reduce by one-fourth stirring often to keep from scorching.
- Puree in a food processor then pass through a fine sieve.
- Set aside one quarter of the reduction for garnish.
- Fold remaining portion into the hollandaise.
- Combine quartered lemon and one sprig of mint with white wine and fish stock.
- Bring to a boil then reduce to simmer.
- Using a spatula carefully place salmon fillets in saucepan and poach for 10 minutes.
- Remove fillets with spatula so they retain their shape.
- Spoon hollandaise into center of each serving plate then drizzle thin line of puree.
- Lightly draw back of a spoon across it making a scallop effect toward outside of plate.
- Place a salmon fillet in the circle and garnish with whole blackberries.

259. Salmon With Bourbon And Brown Sugar Glaze Recipe

Serving: 4 | Prep: | Cook: 15mins | Ready in:

Ingredients

- 4 TBS. butter
- 1/2 cup dark brown sugar
- 1 1/2 LBS. salmon steaks (4)
- 1/3 cup bourbon

Direction

- 1. Melt butter in a large skillet over medium heat.
- 2. Stir in brown sugar.
- 3. Place salmon steaks on top of mixture and cook for 5 minutes.
- 4. Turn salmon, and pour bourbon around the steaks.
- 5. Continue cooking for 5 minutes or until fish tests done with a fork.
- 6. Serve salmon with the glaze spooned on top.

260. Salmon With Bow Ties And Tarragon Mustard Sauce Recipe

Serving: 3 | Prep: | Cook: 30mins | Ready in:

Ingredients

- 8 ounces fresh pasta such as bowtie or linguine,
- 1 tablepoon olive oil
- ½ cup onion, chopped
- 1 tablespoon chopped fresh tarragon or 1 teaspoon dried tarragon
- 1 tablespoon chopped fresh parsley or 1 teaspoon dried parsley
- ¼ cup dry chardonnay
- 1 cup whipping cream or half and half

- 2 tablespoons stone ground, whole grain or Dijon mustard
- 1/3 to 1/2 cup cooked peas, diced broccoli, or chopped spinach
- 3 to 6 ounces cooked lightly seasoned salmon or smoked salmon
- 1/3 cup freshly grated or shredded Parmesan cheese, plus extra for garnish

Direction

- 1. Cook pasta and drain.
- 2. While pasta is cooking, heat oil in 10 inch skillet over medium heat. Cook onion, tarragon and parsley in oil about 5 minutes, stirring frequently, until onion is tender. Stir in wine. Cook; uncovered about 4 minutes or until wine is gone. Stir in whipping cream and mustard. Heat to boiling; reduce heat. Simmer uncovered 5 to 10 minutes or until sauce is slightly thickened.
- 3. Add pasta, salmon and ¼ cup of the cheese to sauce in skillet; toss gently until pasta is evenly coated. Remove from heat. Sprinkle with extra cheese to serve.
- Note: I added an extra tablespoon of Dijon mustard and used peas.

261. Salmon With Dilled Creamy Pasta Dated 1984 Recipe

Serving: 4 | Prep: | Cook: 20mins | Ready in:

Ingredients

- 2 salmon filets approximately 6 ounces each cut in thin long strips
- 1 teaspoon cajun seasoning
- 4 tablespoons olive oil
- 3/4 cup breadcrumbs
- 1/4 cup parmesan cheese
- 2 tablespoons fresh chopped dill
- 1 teaspoon salt
- 1/2 teaspoon freshly ground white pepper

- Pasta:
- 1 tablespoon heavy cream
- 1 tablespoon butter
- 2 cups fully cooked egg noodles
- 1/4 teaspoon salt
- 1/4 teaspoon freshly ground black pepper
- 1 tablespoon chopped fresh dill

Direction

- Sprinkle both sides of filets with Cajun seasoning then rub in 1 tablespoon olive oil.
- Combine breadcrumbs, parmesan, dill, salt, pepper and 1 tablespoon olive oil.
- Dredge filets in breadcrumb mixture pressing firmly to make crumbs adhere.
- In medium sauté pan heat remaining oil over medium high heat and carefully add salmon.
- When first side has formed a golden crust turn carefully then reduce heat to low.
- Cook 3 minutes more then serve salmon on bed of pasta.
- To make pasta heat cream and butter over low heat then add noodles.
- Season with salt and pepper then toss until well mixed and heated through.
- Remove from heat and toss in dill then serve immediately.

262. Salmon With Fried Capers Recipe

Serving: 4 | Prep: | Cook: 20mins | Ready in:

Ingredients

- 4 salmon steaks
- 1/2 teaspoon salt
- 1 teaspoon freshly ground black pepper
- 2 tablespoons grated lemon peel
- 3 tablespoons minced chives
- 5 tablespoons butter
- vegetable oil
- 2 tablespoons capers

Direction

- Preheat oven to 350.
- Pat fish dry with paper towels then sprinkle with salt and pepper and place in baking dish.
- Sprinkle with lemon peel and chives then dot with butter.
- Bake 12 minutes.
- While fish bakes put 1/2" oil in small saucepan set over high heat.
- Pat capers dry with paper towels.
- Add capers to hot oil and cook 2 minutes.
- Immediately remove with a slotted spoon to paper towels.
- Place fish on warm plates then divide cooking juices among them.
- Sprinkle with capers then serve immediately.

263. Salmon With Ginger Scallion Sauce Recipe

Serving: 2 | Prep: | Cook: 10mins | Ready in:

Ingredients

- 2 salmon fillets, Skin On thoroughly scaled, (Approx. 1 inch Thick)
- 1/4 Cup Fresh ginger (I/4 inch Dice)
- 4 scallions (Sliced on a bias 1 1/2 Inch Long)
- 3/4 Cup dry white wine
- 2 Tbls soy sauce
- 1/2 Cup water
- 1 Tsp sugar
- 1 - 2 Tables olive oil
- toasted sesame oil (Garnish)
- salt & pepper

Direction

- Place Fillets on paper towels and pat dry. Make sure both skin and flesh sides are very dry. Salt & Pepper both sides.
- Place a heavy 10 - 12 inch skillet on high heat. When hot, add Olive Oil to barely coat bottom.

- When oil smokes, place Salmon Fillets skin side down in skillet. Sear on high 1 min. Turn heat to Med High and cook 2 mins longer. (Do not move or touch the Fillets until you flip them)
- Flip Fillets and cook 2 mins. Remove to a rack and place flesh side down. Remove crispy skin (It will pull off easily) set aside for garnish.
- Turn heat back to high. Add Ginger. Cook 1 min. Add Scallions. Cook 30 sec. Add wine. Deglaze until the Wine reduces to 1/2 cup or less.
- Add Water, Soy Sauce, and Sugar. Bring to a simmer and reduce heat to med. Simmer approx. 1 - 2 Mins.
- Place Fillets back in the pan with the now skinned side down. Simmer for approx. 1 min. or to desired doneness.
- To Serve: Remove Salmon Fillets to a serving plate. Spoon the Ginger/Scallion sauce over the Salmon and drizzle with toasted Sesame Oil, Garnish with rolled up crispy skin and some chopped Scallion.
- This dish goes very well with Lemon or Orange-zested Jasmine Rice.

264. Salmon With Ginger And Garlic Recipe

Serving: 4 | Prep: | Cook: 30mins | Ready in:

Ingredients

- 1 Large salmon fillet (Chopped into large cubes)
- 2 x Pak Choi - Sliced
- 2 x Large carrots -Sliced thinly
- 1 x Large green bell pepper - Sliced into sticks
- Several mushrooms - sliced
- 600ml chicken stock
- 3 tbsn soy sauce
- 3cm Fresh ginger - Finely Chopped
- 4 cloves garlic - Finely Chopped
- 2 tsp fish sauce

- 1 tbsp Mirim (Sweet Chinese wine)
- 2 tbsn Saki (or Shinese cooking wine)
- Large Portion of Thin egg noodles

Direction

- MARINADE
- Mix the Garlic, Ginger, 2 tbsp Soy Sauce, Mirin, Fish Sauce and Saki in a container and add the Salmon.
- Cover and leave for a few hours, or overnight would be perfect.
- MAIN COURSE
- Add the stock to a large wok and bring to the boil. Add all the vegetables plus 2 tbsp of Soy Sauce.
- Simmer for 5 mins
- Add the Salmon and the marinade to the vegetables
- Simmer gently for 10 mins or until the Salmon is cooked
- Prepare the noodles according to the instructions and add to the wok and stir for 1 min
- Serve with Crusty Bread

265. Salmon With Red Pepper And Corn Salsa Recipe

Serving: 4 | Prep: | Cook: 15mins | Ready in:

Ingredients

- 4 salmon steaks
- 1 large red pepper, cut into 1/2" chunks
- 1 cup of fresh or frozen corn, cooked and cooled
- 1/4 cup of red onion, minced
- 1 Tbsp cajun spice
- 1 Tbsp Grilling Spice- I use something with lots of pepper in it
- 2 Tbsp lemon juice
- 1 Tbsp honey
- 1 Tbsp olive oil
- 1/4 cup of chopped cilantro

Direction

- Preheat oven to 400 degrees
- Combine red pepper, corn, onion, the Cajun spice, lemon juice, olive oil, and honey.
- Mix well and refrigerate
- Spray salmon with olive oil and sprinkle with the Grilling spice.
- Place steaks on foil lined baking sheet and roast in oven for 10-12 minutes or grill each steak 5-6 minutes per side on a medium high grill.
- Finely chop the cilantro and add to corn mixture and serve over cooked salmon.

---

266. Salmon With Spaghetti Noodles Recipe

Serving: 4 | Prep: | Cook: 10mins | Ready in:

Ingredients

- 8 oz. spaghetti
- 1 Tbl. minced garlic
- 1/3 cup olive oil
- 1 can (14 3/4 oz.) boneless, skinless salmon
- 3/4 cup chicken broth
- 1/4 cup minced parsley
- 4 oz. cream cheese, cut into pieces
- 1/4 cup evaporated milk
- 1/4 cup sliced black olives
- salt to taste

Direction

- Boil spaghetti according to package.
- In a large skillet heat oil.
- Add garlic and sauté.
- Add salmon, broth, parsley, cream cheese, milk and salt.
- Heat on med. heat until cream cheese is melted and everything is well heated.
- Serve over spaghetti.
- Garnish with olives.

---

267. Salmon With White Wine Sauce Recipe

Serving: 4 | Prep: | Cook: 20mins | Ready in:

Ingredients

- 1 large salmon fillet cut into 4 pieces
- 1 cup chardonnay
- 1 cup water
- 2 tablespoons fresh chopped parsley
- 2 teaspoons dill
- 2/3 cup half and half
- 1 teaspoon dried tarragon
- 2/3 cup chardonnay
- 2 teaspoons fresh chopped parsley
- 1/2 teaspoon dill
- 1 teaspoon cornstarch
- 1 teaspoon salt
- 1 teaspoon pepper
- 2 egg yolks lightly beaten

Direction

- Place wine, water, parsley, dill and chardonnay in a large skillet over medium heat then add the salmon skin side down. Cover and simmer until fish flakes easily with fork about 10 minutes. Remove salmon to platter and keep warm. For the chardonnay sauce mix wine, half and half and herbs together in a sauce pan. Cook over medium heat stirring constantly just until hot. Take half of hot mixture and slowly add to beaten egg yolk. Add to the rest of the hot mixture into the saucepan. Whisk in cornstarch. Heat to boiling stirring constantly. Boil for 2 minutes until sauce thickens. Pour over salmon and serve.

268. Salmon And Cheese Pie Recipe

Serving: 6 | Prep: | Cook: 35mins | Ready in:

Ingredients

- potatoes
- 1 lb. potatoes, peeled
- 4 oz cream cheese
- 2 cloves garlic, minced
- 2 T. butter
- ¼ C. milk
- FILLING
- 2 carrots diced
- 1 med onion diced
- 2 stalks celery, diced
- 1 green bell pepper, diced
- ½ C. sliced mushrooms
- 1 lb cooked salmon
- cheese sauce
- 3 T. butter
- 3 T. flour
- 1 ¾ C. milk
- 2 C. grated cheese
- salt and pepper
- TOPPING
- ½ C. grated cheese

Direction

- Boil potatoes and mash with cream cheese, garlic, butter and milk.
- Put a little oil in skillet and sauté veggies till tender. Remove from heat, add salmon and flake.
- Melt 2 T. butter in saucepan on med heat, stir in flour to make a smooth paste. Sprinkle in salt and pepper and slowly pour in milk. Stir gently. Return to heat and stir until the sauce thickens. Add 2 C. grated cheese and stir through the sauce.
- Add salmon and veggies and stir until well mixed. Place in casserole dish and spread the mashed potatoes on top.
- Bake in a preheated 350°F oven until potatoes are golden, about 30 min.
- Sprinkle remaining grated cheese over the top and place back in oven until cheese melts.

269. Salmon And Dill In Puff Pastry Recipe

Serving: 4 | Prep: | Cook: 20mins | Ready in:

Ingredients

- 8 oz fresh salmon
- or
- 1 large can salmon
- 4 oz sour cream
- 1 oz fresh chopped or 1 Tbsp dried dill
- 8 oz roll puff pastry
- 1 egg, beaten with 2 tsp water

Direction

- Preheat oven to 350F.
- Grease cookie tray or line with parchment paper.
- Roll out puff pastry 1/4 inch thick on a lightly floured board.
- Cut into 4 equal rectangles or cut into 4 fish shapes.
- Make 4 small rectangles with raised edges .
- Place rectangles or 2 fish shapes on baking tray and bake for 5 minutes until pastry begins to become firm.
- Remove from oven and layer with salmon.
- Mix dill and sour cream, then spread over salmon.
- If you are using fish shapes, place the 2 remaining fish shapes on top of the salmon and sour cream.
- Brush pastry with beaten egg and water mixture.
- Place in oven and bake for 15 minutes or until pastry is golden brown.
- Serve topped with a sprig or two of fresh dill.
- If you are not artistic with puff pastry, you can roll out the puff pastry into 4 squares and

make a simple salmon wrap to bake. Be sure to seal the edges and brush with egg mixture.

270. Salmon And Leeks Recipe

Serving: 4 | Prep: | Cook: 20mins | Ready in:

Ingredients

- 1/2 cup butter
- 4 salmon fillets
- 2 leeks finely sliced
- 1/2 cup white wine
- 1/4 cup olive oil
- 2 tablespoons finely chopped chervil
- 1 tablespoon fresh lemon juice

Direction

- Preheat oven to 350 then smear 4 large circles of parchment paper with butter.
- Place a salmon fillet in center of each one and top with 1/4 of the leeks.
- Divide olive oil, wine and chervil among each and season well.
- Draw up edges of the paper and fold edges to make packets.
- Place on baking sheet and cook 20 minutes.
- Open packets carefully and keep juices and leeks with salmon as you serve it with lemon juice.

271. Salmon And Peas With Vegetable Spaghetti Squash Recipe

Serving: 3 | Prep: | Cook: 5mins | Ready in:

Ingredients

- 1 tbsp reduced sodium soy sauce
- 1 tbsp honey
- 2 tbsp water
- 1 tsp ground ginger
- 1 tsp cornstarch
- 2 slices of sweet onion diced
- 1 1/3 cups frozen peas
- 8oz salmon fillet cut in strips
- 2 cups cooked spaghetti squash
- salt and pepper to preference

Direction

- Whisk the soy sauce, honey, water, ginger and cornstarch.
- Set aside.
- Heat a skillet over medium setting.
- Warm the onion and add the frozen peas.
- Cook for a minute or two allowing the peas to defrost.
- Add the salmon and cook for 3-4 minutes only stirring about every minute.
- If you stir more, the salmon will break up too much.
- After the 4 minutes pour the soy sauce mixture over, stir in and cook for one minute.
- It will thicken and coat everything.
- Separate into two servings and scoop over warm spaghetti squash.

272. Salmon And Potato Fish Cakes Recipe

Serving: 4 | Prep: | Cook: 15mins | Ready in:

Ingredients

- 1 lb. cooked salmon
- 1 lb potatoes boiled and roughly mashed
- 2 tbsp. softened butter
- 1 tbsp fresh dill
- 1 tbsp fresh flat leaf parsley
- juice of 1/2 lemon
- salt and white pepper to taste
- plain white flour (for dredging)

- 1 beaten egg
- bread crumbs or panko crumbs (Japanese bread crumbs)
- 4 tbsp oil (or more for frying)

Direction

- Crush the cooked salmon with a fork, making sure that no bones or skin remain.
- Mix the salmon with the coarsely mashed potatoes in a large bowl.
- Add in the softened butter. Mix well, then add in the dill, parsley and lemon juice. Season with salt and pepper to taste.
- Divide the mixture into 8 parts, and with each, form into a ball and then flatten slightly into a disc.
- Coat each disc first in flour, then beaten egg, and finally in bread crumbs or panko crumbs.
- Warm the oil in a very hot frying pan.
- Fry the fishcakes until golden brown.
- Drain with absorbent paper, and serve hot. Served with a simple salad

273. Salmon And Spinach Stuffed Shells In Garlic Butter Recipe

Serving: 4 | Prep: | Cook: 45mins | Ready in:

Ingredients

- About 16 jumbo pasta shells
- 1 16-oz. container low-fat small curd cottage cheese
- 1/2 cup light sour cream
- 1 egg
- 1 7.5 ounce can salmon (boneless and skinless)
- 1 cup packed chopped fresh spinach
- 1/2 tsp. dried thyme
- 1/2 tsp. dried dillweed
- salt and pepper
- 1/4 cup butter
- 1 to 2 cloves garlic, minced

- 1/4 cup shredded mozzarella (or whatever cheese you like)
- 2 tbsp. grated parmesan cheese

Direction

- Parboil shells according to package directions until just al dente. Rinse in cold water and set aside.
- Preheat oven to 350*F. Place butter and garlic in a 9" x 9" (or similar sized) baking dish; place in oven while it is preheating, checking often to make sure garlic doesn't burn. When butter is melted and infused with garlic, remove from oven.
- In medium bowl, combine cottage cheese, sour cream, and egg; stir in salmon, spinach, thyme and dill, then season with salt and pepper.
- Fill shells with salmon mixture and place in baking dish.
- Sprinkle with mozzarella and parmesan.
- Cover with foil and bake 20 minutes. Remove foil and bake another 15 to 20 minutes or until cheese is bubbly.

274. Salmon And Tomato Mango Salsa Recipe

Serving: 4 | Prep: | Cook: 15mins | Ready in:

Ingredients

- 3 cups diced fully ripened tomatoes
- 2 cups diced fresh mango
- 1/4 sliced green onions
- 1 tbs minced jalapeno pepper, seeds removed (optional)
- 2 1/2 tsp. grated fresh ginger or one tsp ground ginger
- 1 tsp salt
- 1 1/2 tbs. lime juice
- 4 center cut salmon fillets

Direction

- Mix all salsa ingredients and let stand for at least 30 minutes.
- Grill the salmon fillets
- Serve the salsa on the side.

275. Salmon In Phyllo Pastry With Mango Curry Sauce Recipe

Serving: 4 | Prep: | Cook: 25mins | Ready in:

Ingredients

- 4 pieces of fresh salmon filet (about 1 lb)
- 16 pieces of phyllo pastry sheets
- 1 stick melted butter or margarine
- mango curry sauce:
- 1 large ripe mango, coarse chopped
- 1/2 cup mayonnaise, maybe a bit more if desired
- 2 tsp curry powder or to taste
- 1/2 cup toasted chopped walnuts (optional)

Direction

- Make the mango curry sauce by combining ingredients and chill well.
- To prepare salmon: salt and pepper pieces.
- Lay 2 sheets of phyllo on flat surface and brush with melted butter.
- Add 2 more sheets and brush with melted butter.
- Place 1/4 of mango mixture in middle of phyllo several inches up from bottom edge.
- Place on salmon. Fold (roll) phyllo over salmon and tuck under edges.
- Repeat for 3 more servings.
- Place salmon pastries into a buttered baking pan and brush tops of pastry with more melted butter.
- Bake 400F about 25 minutes or until pastry is golden.
- Makes 4 main dish servings or cut each in half for 8 appetizers servings

276. Salmon In Foil The French Way Recipe

Serving: 1 | Prep: | Cook: 30mins | Ready in:

Ingredients

- salmon fillet
- 1 courgette
- 1 carrot
- Half a lemon
- fresh basil leaves
- frozen peas
- 1 tomato
- 5 asparagus
- olive oil
- salt and black pepper

Direction

- Clean the salmon fillet and add salt and pepper on it.
- Cut a piece of foil into 20x26cm.
- Preheat the oven on 180C.
- Peel the vegetables and cut into slices (courgette, carrots, tomato, and lemon).
- Add the basil leaves on the foil, cover them with asparagus and some olive oil.
- After that add half the vegetables (carrots, courgettes, tomatoes, peas, and lemon), then the salmon fillet on top.
- Add the rest of the carrots, courgettes, and the peas around the salmon.
- On top of the salmon put basil leaves, lemon slices, and tomato slices, then on top add some olive oil.
- Close the foil and put it in the oven to cook for 30min.
- Served alone on a plate or with pasta or rice.

277.   Salmon Or Tuna Cakes Recipe

Serving: 3 | Prep: | Cook: 20mins | Ready in:

Ingredients

- 1/4 cup red peppers diced
- 1/4 cup onion diced
- 1/4 cup mayo
- 1 tblsp. lemon juice
- 1/4 tsp. season salt
- caynne pepper just a pinch (to your liking)
- 1 egg beaten
- 1 cup dried bread crumbs (ONLY ADD 4 tblsp. TO THE MIX reserve the rest)
- 2 - 12 oz. cans of salmon, or tuna
- SAUCE FOR ON TOP
- 3/4 cup mayo
- 1 tblsp. lemon juice
- 1 tblsp. horseradish
- a pinch of tyme
- 1 tsp. salt and pepper

Direction

- Mix tuna, or salmon, peppers, onions, mayo, lemon juice, season salt, cayenne pepper, egg and only 4 tbsp. of dried bread crumbs.
- Roll into 6 balls, and flatten into patties.
- Coat them with remaining bread crumbs.
- Fry on the stove top in 3 tbsp. butter until golden brown on each side.
- Should make about 6 patties.
- These patties are delicious just like this, however to make them even better just mix all the ingredients for sauce and pour over top of the patties.

278.   Salmon Served On Lentils With Bacon Recipe

Serving: 4 | Prep: | Cook: 30mins | Ready in:

Ingredients

- 1 cup lentils, rinsed
- 1 medium onion, minced (about 3/4 cup)
- 1 carrot, peeled and finely chopped
- 4 (2-inch long) orange peel strips (orange part only please, no white pith)
- 2 1/2 cups water
- 2 - 3 slices thick applewood bacon
- 4 (6-ounce) salmon steaks or filets (please use wild caught salmon; it's got better taste, better texture, it's good for YOU and it's good for the environment)
- 1/4 cup heavy cream
- 1/4 cup chopped fresh parsley
- 1/4 cup chopped chives or green onion tops (try the chives, they really are different than green onion tops)
- 2 tablespoons minced fresh tarragon or 2 teaspoons dried

Direction

- Combine the lentils, onion, carrot, orange peel and water in a heavy saucepan. Bring to a boil; reduce the heat and simmer until the lentils are tender, stirring occasionally, about 25 minutes. Drain, reserving 3/4 cup cooking liquid. Discard the orange peel. Return the lentils to the pan; season with salt and pepper. (Tip: Can be prepared 1 day ahead. Cover and chill the lentils and reserved cooking liquid separately.)
- While the lentils cook fry the bacon until crisp. Remove, drain and chop into pieces. (Hint: I like to have uniform pieces of bacon in my dish, so I slice the bacon first into uniform pieces and then fry them.)
- Place a frying pan over medium heat. Add a small amount of oil; heat until shimmering. Season the fish with salt and pepper and place in the frying pan. Cook until just opaque, turning once. (LindySez: Party Tip- to really impress...if using salmon steaks, cut out the center bone and separate each half. Starting at the thickest part; roll the salmon to form a circle; tie with kitchen string. After cooking,

remove the string and you have a nifty little salmon circle.)

- Meanwhile, add enough reserved cooking liquid to the lentils to moisten them; mix in the cream, parsley, chives and tarragon; bring to a simmer. Add the bacon. Spoon lentils onto warmed plates; top with the salmon and serve.

279.   Salmon To Die For Recipe

Serving: 3 | Prep: | Cook: 6mins | Ready in:

Ingredients

- 1 large fresh filet of salmon about eight inches long
- capers
- dash kosher salt
- fresh ground pepper
- 4 tbls white 'drinking wine' (serve with if so inclined)
- wax paper

Direction

- Gently wash fish and feel for any bones
- Pat dry
- Place skin down in middle of wax paper
- Add salt pepper and wine
- Fold paper till sides meet on top and fold over to close on top leaving air space between fish and 'roof' of paper
- Fold and enclose both ends
- Place in micro for 6 minutes

280.   Salmon With Avocado Recipe

Serving: 4 | Prep: | Cook: 20mins | Ready in:

Ingredients

- 1/2 cup chopped fresh cilantro leaves
- 2 jalapeno chilies seeded and minced
- 4 teaspoons grated fresh ginger
- 4 garlic cloves minced
- juice from 4 limes
- 1/3 cup soy sauce
- 1/4 teaspoon sugar
- 1 teaspoon salt
- 1 teaspoon freshly ground black pepper
- 1/4 cup plus 2 tablespoons extra virgin olive oil
- 4 blocks sushi grade salmon
- salt and pepper
- 2 ripe avocados halved pitted peeled and sliced

Direction

- Combine cilantro, jalapeno, ginger, garlic, juice, sauce, sugar, salt, pepper, and 1/4 cup olive oil.
- Place large skillet over medium high heat and coat with remaining 2 tablespoons olive oil.
- Sprinkle tuna pieces with salt and pepper then sear tuna for a minute on each side.
- Pour half of the cilantro mixture into the pan to coat the fish.
- Transfer seared tuna to plates and serve with sliced avocado and remaining cilantro sauce.

281.   Salmon With Cucumber Salad And Dill Sauce Recipe

Serving: 4 | Prep: | Cook: 15mins | Ready in:

Ingredients

- 6 tbl fat-free sour cream
- 2 Tbl plus 1 tsp finely chopped dill, divided
- 3 Tbl rice vinegar, divided
- 1 1/2 Tbl finely chopped shallots
- 1/4 tsp grated lemon rind
- 2 tsp fresh lemon juice
- 1 garlic clove, minced

- 4 (6 ounce) salmon fillets (about an inch thick)
- 1/4 tsp salt
- 1/4 tsp freshly ground black pepper
- olive oil
- 1/4 C dry white wine
- 1 english cucumber (about 1 lb)

Direction

- Combine sour cream, 2 tbsp dill, 2 tbsp rice vinegar, shallots, rind, juice and garlic in a bowl, stirring well; cover and chill.
- Sprinkle fish evenly with salt and pepper.
- Heat a large non-stick skillet over medium high and coat pan with a small amount of olive oil.
- Add fish to pan and cook for 5 minutes.
- Turn fish over and cook an additional 3 minutes.
- Remove from heat.
- Add wine; cover and let stand 3 minutes until fish flakes easily with a fork or it reaches preferred doneness.
- While fish is standing, use a vegetable peeler and shave cucumber lengthwise into ribbons to yield about 2 cups.
- Combine cucumber with remaining 1 tbsp rice vinegar and dill in a bowl; toss gently to coat.
- Place about 1/2 cup cucumber mixture on each of four plates; top with a fillet and 2 tbsp of sour cream mixture.

282.   Salmon With Cucumber Dill Cream Napoleons Recipe

Serving: 6 | Prep: | Cook: 15mins | Ready in:

Ingredients

- Thaw Time: 30 minutes
- ------------------------
- 1/2 pkg. pepperidge Farm® puff pastry sheets (1 sheet)
- 1 cup sour cream
- 1/2 cup chopped cucumber

- 3 tbsp. chopped fresh dill weed OR 1 tbsp. dried dill weed, crushed
- 1 can (14 oz.) Swanson® chicken broth (1 3/4 cups)
- 1/4 cup chablis or other dry white wine (optional)
- 1/4 tsp. ground black pepper
- 6 salmon fillets, 1" thick (about 1 1/2 lb.)

Direction

- THAW pastry sheet at room temperature 30 min. Preheat oven to 400°F.
- UNFOLD pastry on lightly floured surface. Cut into 3 strips along fold marks. Cut each strip into 2 rectangles. Place on baking sheet. Bake 15 min. or until golden. Let cool.

283.   Salmon With Garden Sauce Recipe

Serving: 4 | Prep: | Cook: 10mins | Ready in:

Ingredients

- 1 cup fresh parsley leaves
- 2 cups fresh spinach leaves, well washed
- 1/2 cup mayo
- 1/3 cup sour cream
- 1 Tbls fresh lemon juice
- 3/4 ts salt, divided
- 4 salmon steaks, 6 ounces each and about 3/4" thick

Direction

- Bring a medium sauce pan of water to a rapid boil over high heat
- Plunge spinach leaves into water just until wilted, approx. 10 secs.
- Rinse under cold running water and drain well.
- Transfer spinach and parsley to a blender or food processor.

- Add the mayo, sour cream, lemon juice and 1/4 tsp. salt to the mixture in the blender.
- Blend or process until smooth.
- Chill for at least 30 minutes up to 12 hours
- Preheat broiler.
- Sprinkle the salmon steaks with the remainder of salt.
- Place on broiler pan and broil 6" from heat, turning once just until cooked through, approx. 8 minutes.
- Transfer to serving plate and spoon the sauce over the salmon steaks or could serve the sauce on the side depending on preferences.

284. Salmon With Horseradish Cream Recipe

Serving: 2 | Prep: | Cook: 20mins | Ready in:

Ingredients

- 1/2 cup plain yogurt
- 4 teaspoons drained prepared horseradish
- 2 tablespoons chopped fresh chives
- 2 salmon steaks
- Whole fresh chives

Direction

- Preheat oven to 350 then lightly oil a glass pie plate
- Combine yogurt, horseradish and chives in small bowl then season with salt and pepper.
- Season salmon lightly with salt and pepper.
- Spread 1 tablespoon yogurt mixture over each salmon steak.
- Arrange salmon in prepared dish then bake salmon 18 minutes and transfer to plate.
- Garnish with chives and serve with remaining sauce.

285. Salmon With Jalepeno Lime Sauce Recipe

Serving: 4 | Prep: | Cook: 10mins | Ready in:

Ingredients

- 4 (5-ounce) salmon fillets, all bones removed
- 2 tablespoons fresh lime juice
- 1 teaspoon extra virgin olive oil
- salt and pepper, to taste
- Sauce
- 1 teaspoon extra virgin olive oil
- 1 teaspoon unsalted butter
- 3 large jalapeno peppers, seeded and cut into a julienne
- 1/2 cup sour cream (I use low-fat, but not non-fat)
- 2 teaspoons fresh lime juice
- Dash of salt and pepper
- Optional
- Fresh lime wedges
- Snipped fresh chives

Direction

- Preheat oven to 500 degrees F. Lightly oil a shallow baking dish. Place the salmon in the dish, skin side down. Combine the lime juice and olive oil; brush over the fish. Season with salt and pepper. Set aside for 15 minutes. Place the fish in the oven and bake until the fish is almost opaque, about 8 minutes for each inch of thickness. Remove the skin.
- While the fish cooks, prepare the sauce: Over a medium-low heat; heat the olive oil and butter together; add the jalapenos and sauté until tender, stirring occasionally, about 5 minutes. Add the sour cream and heat through, do not boil. Remove from heat; stir in the lime juice, salt and pepper.
- Transfer the fish to warm plates; spoon sauce over. Sprinkle with minced chives and serve with lime wedges, if desired.

286. Salmon With Maple Lemon Glaze Recipe

Serving: 4 | Prep: | Cook: 20mins | Ready in:

Ingredients

- 2 Tbs fresh lemon juice
- 2 Tbs maple syrup
- 1 Tbs cider vinegar
- 1 Tbs canola oil
- 4 (6oz) skinless salmon fillets
- 1/2 tsp salt
- 1/4 tsp fresh ground pepper
- cooking spray

Direction

- Preheat broiler. Combine first 4 ingredients in a large zip-top plastic bag. Add fish to bag; seal Refrigerate 10 mins, turning bag once.
- Remove fish from bag, reserving marinade. Place marinade in microwave-safe bowl. Microwave on high 1 min.
- Heat large oven-proof non-stick skillet over med-high heat. Sprinkle fish evenly with salt and pepper. Coat pan with cooking spray. Add fish to pan; cook 3 mins. Turn fish over. Brush marinade evenly over fish. Broil 3 mins or till fish flakes easily when tested with a fork or till desired degree of doneness.

287. Salmon With Sesame Ginger Glaze Recipe

Serving: 4 | Prep: | Cook: 10mins | Ready in:

Ingredients

- ¼ c packed brown sugar
- 2 Tbsp Dijon mustard
- 1 Tbsp grated fresh or 1 tsp ground ginger
- 1 Tbsp sesame seeds
- 4 6-oz wild Pacific salmon fillets, about 1" thick, skinned
- ½ tsp salt
- ½ tsp freshly ground black pepper

Direction

- 1. Coat rack of baking sheet with cooking spray. Preheat broiler.
- 2. In small bowl, combine sugar, mustard, sesame seeds and ginger. Season both sides of fillets with salt and pepper. Place salmon on broiler rack and brush glaze on top. Broil (6" from heat) 8 to 10 minutes or until fish is lightly browned.

288. Salmon With Three Melon Salsa Recipe

Serving: 6 | Prep: | Cook: 10mins | Ready in:

Ingredients

- 3/4 cup diced cantaloupe
- 3/4 cup diced watermelon
- 3/4 cup diced watermelon
- 1/4 cup chopped red onion
- 2 tablespoons fresh lime juice
- 2 tablespoons chopped cilantro
- 1 tablespoon chopped jalapeno pepper
- 1/4 teaspoon salt
- 1/2 teaspoon freshly ground black pepper
- 6 salmon steaks

Direction

- Combine all ingredients except salmon and let sit at room temperature for at least 2 hours.
- Season salmon with salt and pepper and grill over hot coals 4 minutes per side.
- Top with salsa and serve immediately.

289. Salmon With An Almond Crust Recipe

Serving: 12 | Prep: | Cook: 15mins | Ready in:

Ingredients

- 3 1/2 oz ground almonds
- 3 1/2 oz Fresh bread crumbs
- 1 oz Chopped parsley
- 2 eggs
- 4 oz butter, softened
- to taste --- salt & white pepper
- 4 lb salmon fillets
- 3 oz clarified butter
- 1 1/4 pt red wine butter Sauce for fish see recipe...
- =================================== ==============
- For sauce:
- 1 qt red wine
- 3 1/2 oz shallots, chopped fine
- 7 fl oz fish stock
- 1 lb Cold butter
- to taste: salt & white pepper

Direction

- Mix together the almonds, bread crumbs, and chopped parsley.
- Add the egg and mix gently.
- Add the soft butter and mix until incorporated.
- Season to taste with salt and white pepper.
- Cut the salmon fillets into 5-oz portions.
- Pan-fry the salmon in butter, starting with the flesh side down.
- Brown lightly.
- Turn over and continue cooking skin side down.
- Do not cook the fish completely, as it will continue cooking with the almond crust.
- It should still be somewhat rare inside.
- Spread a layer of the almond crust mixture over the salmon.
- Place under a salamander or broiler to brown the crust and finish cooking the salmon.
- Adjust the height of the broiler rack so the crust is not too browned before the salmon is cooked.
- Plate the salmon.
- Ladle the sauce around it, not over it.
- =================================== ================
- For the Sauce:
- Combine the red wine and shallots in a saucepan.
- Reduce until almost completely evaporated.
- Add the fish stock. Reduce by two-thirds.
- Cut the butter into small pieces.
- Add the butter to the hot reduction.
- Set the pan over moderately high heat and whip vigorously.
- When the butter is nearly all incorporated, remove from the heat and continue to whip until smooth.
- Season to taste.
- The shallots may be left in the sauce or strained out.
- Makes 1 pint --- this recipe may be doubled easily.

290. San Diego Style Blue Corn Salmon Tacos With Orange Habanero Hot Sauce Recipe

Serving: 12 | Prep: | Cook: 40mins | Ready in:

Ingredients

- 3 cold-smoked salmon fillets, 8 ounces each
- canola oil
- salt and freshly ground black pepper
- 1/4 head green cabbage, finely shredded
- 2 green onions, thinly sliced
- 1 cup best-quality mayonnaise or veg equivalent
- 1 tablespoon chipotle pepper puree
- 1 tablespoon fresh lime juice
- 1/4 cup finely chopped fresh cilantro

- 12 fried blue corn taco shells
- orange-Habanero Sauce, recipe follows
- Preheat grill or grill pan over high heat.

Direction

- Brush salmon with oil and season with salt and pepper. Grill on each side for 3 to 4 minutes.
- Let cool slightly and shred the meat with a fork. Place in a bowl with the cabbage and green onions.
- Combine the mayonnaise, chipotle and lime juice in a small bowl and season with salt. Add the mayonnaise and the cilantro to the salmon mixture and gently fold to combine. Season with salt to taste, if needed.
- Divide the salmon mixture among the taco shells and drizzle each with the Orange-Habanero Sauce.
- ********Orange-Habanero Hot Sauce:
- 6 cups fresh orange juice
- 1 habanero chili
- 1 tablespoon honey
- Salt
- Place juice and habanero in a medium nonreactive saucepan and cook over high heat until reduced to 1 cup, stirring occasionally.
- Remove the habanero, whisk in the honey and season with salt.
- Let cool to room temperature before serving.

---

291. Saumon Aux Lentilles Salmon With Lentils And Mustard Herb Butter Recipe

Serving: 4 | Prep: | Cook: 40mins | Ready in:

Ingredients

- For mustard-Herb Butter:
- 5 tablespoons unsalted butter, softened
- 1 tablespoon chopped chives
- 1 teaspoon chopped tarragon
- 2 teaspoons grainy mustard
- 2 teaspoons fresh lemon juice
- ~~~~
- For Lentils:
- 1 cup French green lentils
- 4 cups water
- 2 medium leeks (white and pale green parts only)
- 1 tablespoon unsalted butter
- 1/2 to 1 tablespoon fresh lemon juice
- ~~~~
- For Salmon:
- 4 (6-ounce) pieces skinless salmon fillet
- 2 tablespoons unsalted butter

Direction

- Make Mustard-Herb Butter:
- Stir together all ingredients with 1/4 teaspoon each of salt and pepper.
- ~~~~
- Cook Lentils:
- Bring lentils, water, and 3/4 teaspoon salt to a boil in a heavy medium saucepan, then reduce heat and simmer, uncovered, until lentils are just tender, 20 to 25 minutes.
- Remove from heat and let stand 5 minutes.
- Reserve 1/2 cup cooking liquid, then drain lentils.
- ~~~~
- While lentils cook, chop leeks, and then wash. Cook leeks in butter in a heavy medium skillet over medium-low heat, stirring occasionally, until softened, 6 to 8 minutes.
- Add lentils with reserved cooking liquid to leeks along with 3 tablespoons mustard-herb butter and cook, stirring, until lentils are heated through and butter is melted.
- Add lemon juice and salt and pepper to taste.
- Remove from heat and keep warm, covered.
- ~~~~
- Sauté Salmon While Leeks Cook:
- Pat salmon dry and sprinkle with 1/2 teaspoon salt and 1/4 teaspoon pepper (total).
- Heat butter in a large non-stick skillet over medium-high heat until foam subsides, then

sauté salmon, turning once, until golden and just cooked through, 6 to 8 minutes total.
- Serve salmon, topped with remaining mustard-herb butter, over lentils.
- ~~~~
- NOTES:
- ~ Mustard-herb butter can be made 1 day ahead and chilled, covered. Soften at room temperature before using (1 hour).
- ~ Lentils can be cooked (but not drained) 1 day ahead and chilled in cooking liquid, covered (once cool).

---

292.   Savory Salmon Loaf Recipe

Serving: 6 | Prep: | Cook: 45mins | Ready in:

Ingredients

- 7-3/4 ounce salmon drained with skin and bones removed
- 2 tablespoons butter
- 2 tablespoons white onion chopped
- 1 cup bread crumbs
- 2 eggs
- 3/4 cup milk
- 1/2 teaspoon salt
- 2 tablespoons parsley chopped
- 1/2 teaspoon worcestershire sauce
- 1 tablespoon lemon juice
- Sauce:
- 16 ounce can stewed tomatoes
- 1 tablespoon cornstarch
- 1/4 teaspoon thyme
- 1/4 teaspoon salt

Direction

- Heat oven to 350 then grease a loaf pan.
- Place lightly greased strip of aluminum foil down center of pan letting it extend over ends.
- Sauté onion in butter until tender then stir in bread crumbs and remove from heat.

- Beat eggs slightly then stir in milk, parsley, salt, Worcestershire and bread crumb mixture.
- Mix well then fold in salmon and lemon juice until well blended.
- Turn into loaf pan and bake 45 minutes.
- To make sauce drain 1/4 cup liquid from tomatoes into small saucepan.
- Stir in cornstarch until dissolved then stir in tomatoes, salt, thyme and remaining liquid.
- Bring to a boil stirring constantly then keep warm.
- Remove fish loaf from oven and allow to stand 3 minutes then loosen around edges with spatula.
- Holding foil gently lift onto platter so that brown crust is on top.
- Remove foil and serve with sauce.

---

293.   Savory Salmon Recipe

Serving: 4 | Prep: | Cook: 27mins | Ready in:

Ingredients

- 1 (2-pound) salmon fillet
- House seasoning, recipe follows
- 1 small red bell pepper, julienne
- 1 small green bell pepper, julienne
- 1 medium onion, sliced thin
- 1 medium orange, sectioned and seeded
- 1 pint strawberries, cleaned and sliced
- 1/2 cup water
- 1/2 cup honey
- 1/2 cup chopped fresh chervil or baby dill
- 4 cloves garlic, minced
- 2 tablespoons chopped green onion
- 2 lemons, juiced
- House Seasoning:
- 1 cup salt
- 1/4 cup black pepper
- 1/4 cup garlic powder
- Mix well. Store in shaker near stove for convenience.

Direction

- Preheat oven to 350 degrees F.
- Place salmon fillet on a foil-lined pan. Season with House Seasoning, then cover and surround fish with red and green bell pepper, onion, and sectioned orange slices. Mix strawberries, water, honey, chervil or dill, garlic and green onions together. Pour lemon juice over salmon. Ladle strawberry mixture evenly over salmon. Cover with foil and pierce foil, allowing steam to escape. Bake for 25 to 30 minutes. Serve with rice.

---

294. Seafood Sauce For Shrimp Lobster Crab Or Salmon Recipe

Serving: 4 | Prep: | Cook: 30mins | Ready in:

Ingredients

- seafood Newburg Sauce (Serve with shrimp, lobster, crab or salmon over hot rice)
- 2 tablespoons butter
- 2 teaspoons shallots, minced, or finely minced onion
- 2 tablespoons paprika
- dry sherry to taste
- 2 tablespoons tomato paste
- 2 teaspoons brandy or dry sherry
- 2 cups cream sauce or white sauce (See Below)
- 1/8 teaspoon dried thyme
- pinch cayenne pepper
- 2 cups to 2 lbs hot seafood
- 3 cups - hot rice

Direction

- Melt butter in sauté pan. Add the shallots or onion and sauté over medium-low heat for 2 to 3 minutes, until translucent. Add the paprika and sherry, and sauté for 2 minutes longer. Stir in the tomato paste.

- Add the brandy or sherry to the sauté pan and cook a few minutes longer. Add the cream sauce, thyme, and cayenne. Cook for 2 minutes more.
- Makes about 2 1/2 cups.
- Cream Sauce
- 1/4 cup butter
- 1/4 cup flour
- 2 cups light cream
- 2 onions, studded with 3 cloves
- 2 bay leaves
- Salt and pepper -- to taste
- Fresh nutmeg, grated -- to taste
- Melt the butter in a saucepan over low heat. Stir in the flour, and cook, stirring, for 3 to 4 minutes; do not brown.
- In another saucepan, bring the cream just to a boil. Stir the warm cream into the flour mixture, whisking until smooth.
- Add the onions and bay leaves, and simmer for 20 minutes on low heat. Season sauce with salt, pepper and nutmeg. Strain the sauce and serve. Makes 2 cups.

---

295. Seared Salmon With Cilantro Cucumber Salsa Recipe

Serving: 4 | Prep: | Cook: 20mins | Ready in:

Ingredients

- 1/2 cucumber, peeled, halved, lengthwise, seeded, halved lengthwise again, and thinly sliced crosswise
- 1 cup cherry tomatoes, quartered
- 1/2 yellow or orange bell pepper, seeded and cut into 1-inch julienne3
- 2 Tablespoons chopped shallot or red onion
- 1 Tablespoon chopped fresh cilantro (fresh coriander) plus sprigs for garnish
- 1 Tablespoon lime juice
- 1-1/2 teaspoons canola oil
- 1 teaspoon honey
- 1/2 teaspoon red pepper flakes

- 1 teaspoon salt
- 4 salmon fillets, each 5 oz., about 1 inch thick
- 1/4 teaspoon freshly ground black pepper
- lime wedges for garnish

Direction

- In a bowl, combine the cucumber, tomatoes, bell pepper, shallot, and chopped cilantro. Toss gently to mix.
- In a small bowl, whisk together the lime juice, 1 teaspoon of the canola oil, the honey, red pepper flakes, and 1/2 teaspoon of the salt. Pour the lime mixture over the cucumber mixture and toss gently to mix and coat evenly. Set aside.
- Sprinkle the salmon fillets on both sides with the remaining 1/2 teaspoon salt and the black pepper. In a large non-stick frying pan, heat the remaining ½ teaspoon canola oil over medium-high heat.
- Add the fish to the pan and cook, turning once, until opaque throughout when tested with the tip of a knife, 4-5 minutes on each side.
- Transfer the salmon fillets to warmed individual plates and top each with one-fourth of the salsa. Garnish the plates with the cilantro sprigs and lime wedges. Serve immediately.

---

296.   Seared Salmon With Quick Hollandaise Sauce Recipe

Serving: 4 | Prep: | Cook: 15mins | Ready in:

Ingredients

- Rub
- 1 Tbl each dried thyme, dried rosemary. dried oregano and mild paprika
- 1 tsp garlic powder
- 2 tsp cumin seeds
- 1 Tbl sea salt
- 4 salmon fillets
- 1 tbl oil
- scant 3 1/2 C baby spinach leaves
- Sauce
- 3 egg yolks
- 7 oz butter
- 1 Tbl lemon juice
- pepper

Direction

- Combine the dried herbs, paprika, garlic powder, cumin seeds and sea salt in a small grinder or grind by hand using a mortar and pestle....grind until smooth.
- Rub 1 tbsp of the mixture into the top of each fillet.
- Heat oil in a large skillet and cook salmon, herb side down, for 3 to 5 minutes or until golden.
- Turn over and cook to your liking, being careful not to overcook and dry out the salmon.
- To make the Hollandaise, place the egg yolks in a blender of processor.
- Melt the butter in a small pan until bubbling.
- With the motor running, gradually add the hot butter in a steady stream until the sauce is thick and creamy.
- Add the lemon juice and a little warm water, if the sauce is too thick, then season to taste with pepper.
- Remove from blender or processor and keep warm.
- Arrange baby spinach leaves on each of four plates.
- Top with salmon and Hollandaise, serve immediately.
- Note: Seal extra mixture in an airtight container for up to 2 months.
- Try it on chicken or steak for dinner.

297.   Seared Salmon With Balsamic Glaze Recipe

Serving: 4 | Prep: | Cook: 13mins | Ready in:

Ingredients

- 1/4 cup balsamic vinegar
- 1/4 cup orange juice
- 2 Tablespoons honey
- 1-5" sprig of rosemary
- 2 teaspoons vegetable oil
- 4 skin on salmon fillets (about 1 1/2 lbs.)
- 2 Tablespoons unsalted butter
- salt and pepper

Direction

- Whisk vinegar, honey and orange juice together in a small bowl, then add rosemary.
- Heat oil in large non-stick skillet over medium-high heat till smoking.
- Season salmon with salt and pepper and cook skin side up without moving till well browned about 4-5 minutes.
- Flip salmon skin side down and cook till all but the very center of it is opaque approx. 2-3 minutes.
- Transfer to platter and tent with foil.
- Wipe out pan with paper towels and lower heat to medium.
- Carefully pour balsamic mixture into pan. It will splatter.
- Simmer until thick and syrupy, about 5 minutes.
- Remove rosemary sprig.
- Whisk in butter, season with salt and pepper and pour over salmon.
- Serve.

298.   Seared Salmon With Strawberry Basil Relish

Serving: 0 | Prep: | Cook: | Ready in:

Ingredients

- 6 salmon fillets (4 ounces each)
- 1 tablespoon butter, melted
- 1/4 teaspoon salt
- 1/8 teaspoon freshly ground pepper
- RELISH:
- 1-1/4 cups finely chopped fresh strawberries
- 1 tablespoon minced fresh basil
- 1 tablespoon honey
- Dash freshly ground pepper

Direction

- Brush fillets with melted butter; sprinkle with salt and pepper. Heat a large skillet over medium-high heat. Add fillets, skin side up, in batches if necessary; cook 2-3 minutes on each side or until fish just begins to flake easily with a fork.
- In a small bowl, toss strawberries with basil, honey and pepper. Serve salmon with relish.
- Nutrition Facts
- 1 salmon fillet with 3 tablespoons relish: 215 calories, 12g fat (3g saturated fat), 62mg cholesterol, 169mg sodium, 6g carbohydrate (5g sugars, 1g fiber), 19g protein. Diabetic Exchanges: 3 lean meat, 1/2 starch, 1/2 fat.

299.   Sesame Salmon And Cream Sauce Recipe

Serving: 4 | Prep: | Cook: 5mins | Ready in:

Ingredients

- 1 1/2 poun salmon or trout fillets
- 2 tbsp light soy sauce
- 3 tbsp sesame seeds
- 3 tbsp sunflower oil
- 4 scallions, thinly sliced
- 2 large zucchini, diced
- grated rind of 1/2 lemon
- 1/2 tsp turmeric
- 1 tbsp lemon juice

- 6 tbsp fish stock or water
- 3 tbsp heavy cream
- salt and pepper

Direction

- Skin salmon and cut into strips about 1 1/2 x 1/4 inches. Pat dry on paper towels. Season lightly with salt and pepper, then brush with soy sauce and sprinkle all over with sesame seeds.
- Heat 2 tbsp oil in wok, swirling it around until really hot. Add salmon and stir fry 3-4 minutes until lightly brown all over. Remove fish, drain on paper towels and keep warm.
- Add remaining oil to wok. When hot add scallions and zucchini and stir fry 1-2 minutes. Add lemon, turmeric, stock and seasoning. Bring to a boil and boil for a minute or so.
- Stir in cream.
- Return salmon pieces to wok and toss gently in the sauce until they are really hot. Serve on warm plates.

300.   Simple Asian Flavored Salmon Recipe

Serving: 2 | Prep: | Cook: 20mins | Ready in:

Ingredients

- 2 4oz salmon steaks
- 2 TBS rice wine vinegar
- 4 TBS soy sauce (for those watching their sodium, use low sodium soy)
- 1 TBS hoisin sauce
- generous amount of chopped garlic
- dash or so of pepper (I used sansho pepper, which you should be able to find at any good Asian market)

Direction

- Heat oven to 400 F. Combine all ingredients except salmon together. Grease an ovenproof

dish, place salmon in it and cover with sauce. Cover dish with foil, or lid, if it has one and bake for 15 to 20 minutes.

301.   Slow Cooked Salmon With Leeks And Tomatoes Recipe

Serving: 2 | Prep: | Cook: 20mins | Ready in:

Ingredients

- 8-12 oz salmon, cut into two fillets
- 2 tsp olive oil
- 2 large leeks, halved vertically and thinkly sliced
- 1 large handful grape tomatoes, roughly chopped
- 1 tbs capers, or more to taste
- 1 tbs parsley or dill, or more/less to taste
- salt
- splash of red wine or apple cider vinegar

Direction

- Preheat the oven to 300.
- Line a shallow baking dish with foil and smear with 1 tsp. olive oil.
- Sprinkle the salmon with salt and place it, skin side up, on the foil.
- Bake for 12-15 minutes, until it's just starting to flake.
- While the salmon is baking, sauté the leeks in a bit of olive oil with a good pinch of salt. When they are melty and tender remove from the heat and set aside.
- Heap the tomatoes, capers and herbs onto a cutting board. Sprinkle with the other tsp. of olive oil and a splash of vinegar. Chop everything together roughly to meld the flavors.
- Divide the leeks between two plates. Remove the skin from the salmon and place a fillet over each serving of leeks. Top with the tomato

mixture and serve, accompanied by wedges of lemon, if you like.

---

302. Slow Baked Salmon With Tomato Orange Basil Sauce And Sauteed Greenbeans With Garlic Recipe

Serving: 4 | Prep: | Cook: 30mins | Ready in:

Ingredients

- 1 lb. salmon
- 1 tsp. olive oil
- salt & fresh ground black pepper, to taste
- 1-1/2 lbs. vine-ripened tomatoes (about 6 medium)
- 2 tsp. extra virgin olive oil
- 1 tsp. minced fresh garlic
- 1 medium orange
- 1/2 tsp. cornstarch
- 2 Tbs. finely sliced fresh basil leaves
- **
- Fresh greenbeans, uncut, tips removed
- garlic cloves, minced
- EVOO
- salt and pepper to taste
- (I gave no measurements because everyone is different with portion size. Me..........I have a problem!!! This salmon recipe serves 4, so if I had to guestimate, I would say......maybe.....a pound or so of green beans.......and.......maybe.......2 or 3 garlic cloves???!!!???)
- Ooooops................I think my eyes may have just swallowed my head!!
- ;-)

Direction

- For Salmon:
- Preheat oven to 300°F
- Place Salmon, skin side down on ungreased baking sheet

- Brush top with olive oil and season with salt and pepper
- Bake for 20 to 30 minutes (or until flesh in thickest part appears just set, Salmon will continue to cook while standing-separate flesh with tip of paring knife to check)
- For Sauce:
- While Salmon bakes, cut tomatoes in half crosswise
- Squeeze out seeds and discard
- Set box grater in medium bowl
- Holding hand flat, rub cut side of each tomato half over coarse side of grater until only skin remains; discard skins
- In large skillet, over medium heat, heat oil; add garlic and stir until fragrant and just beginning to color, about 30 seconds
- Add tomatoes and simmer until most of watery portion has evaporated, about 10 minutes, stirring occasionally
- Grate 1 tsp. orange rind and squeeze 3 Tbsp. juice from orange
- Combine orange rind and juice with cornstarch, stirring until cornstarch is dissolved
- Add mixture to tomato sauce along with basil, stir briefly until sauce has returned to simmer
- Use metal spatula to remove portions of Salmon, leaving skin behind
- **Serve with sauce spooned on top**
- **In a skillet, sauté green beans, over medium heat, in olive oil for a couple minutes, add minced garlic and season with salt. Sautee for another couple of minutes or until the green beans are crisp-tender. Remove from pan and season again lightly with salt and add fresh ground black pepper to taste**
- Mmmmmmmmmm!!

---

303. Smoked Salmon And Mozzarella Calzone Recipe

Serving: 4 | Prep: | Cook: 45mins | Ready in:

Ingredients

- Basic pizza dough
- 1/2 pound roma tomatoes, coarsely chopped (about 3 to 4 tomatoes)
- 1 teaspoon kosher salt
- 1 large egg
- 1 large egg yolk
- 1 teaspoon water
- 4 ounces cold-smoked salmon, thinly sliced
- 4 ounces fresh mozzarella, thinly sliced

Direction

- Prepare Basic Pizza Dough or you can buy premade. Keep at room temperature.
- Position rack in center of oven, and place a baking sheet on it. Heat oven to 400°F. Combine chopped tomatoes with salt, place in a colander or strainer set over a bowl, and let sit 20 minutes to drain.
- In a small bowl, whisk together egg, egg yolk, water, and a large pinch of salt until smooth; set aside.
- Divide pizza dough into 4 pieces. On a lightly floured surface, roll each piece into a paper-thin round, about 12 inches in diameter.
- Place 1/4 of the sliced salmon on the bottom left side of each dough round, about 1 inch from the edge. Top with 1/4 of the drained tomatoes, followed by 1/4 of the mozzarella. Brush the 1-inch-wide border of each dough round with egg mixture, then fold each dough round in half and then fold in half again (it will resemble a quarter-circle shape).
- Using a fork, crimp the edges of each calzone to seal in the filling, and trim any excess dough so the edges are even. Brush the top of each calzone and the edges with egg mixture, place on the heated baking sheet, and bake until golden brown and puffed around the edges, about 20 minutes. Serve immediately.

304.   Smoked Salmon Bagel Recipe

Serving: 4 | Prep: | Cook: | Ready in:

Ingredients

- 4 pumpernickel or plain bagels
- 8 tablespoons chive cream cheese
- 1 thinly sliced english cucumber
- 12 ounces thin-sliced smoked salmon
- 12 thin rings red onion
- 2 teaspoon2 drained capers

Direction

- Split bagels in half horizontally. Spread cut sides with cream cheese. Over cheese on 1 bagel half, layer cucumber, smoked salmon, red onion, and capers. Set remaining bagel half, cream cheese side down, over filling.
- Repeat with remaining bagels.
- Nutritional Information
- Calories: 680 (23% from fat)
- Protein: 34g
- Fat: 17g (sat 7.8)
- Carbohydrate: 100g
- Fiber: 7.1g
- Sodium: 2893mg
- Cholesterol: 50mg

305.   Smoked Salmon Cakes Recipe

Serving: 4 | Prep: | Cook: 10mins | Ready in:

Ingredients

- 3 tablespoons butter
- 1/2 cup minced onion
- 1 clove garlic, minced
- 3 cups diced potatoes
- 1/2 teaspoon salt
- 1/3 pound smoked salmon, flaked into pieces
- 1 egg, beaten

- 1 tablespoon lemon juice
- Dash of hot pepper sauce
- 3 tablespoons snipped chives
- lemon wedges
- 4 tablespoons vegetable oil

Direction

- Melt the butter in a small skillet. Add onions and garlic and cook, stirring frequently, until golden brown, about 5-6 minutes. Set aside.
- Place potatoes in a pan with the salt and cover with boiling water. Cook over medium heat until soft. Drain the potatoes and place in a mixing bowl.
- Add the smoked salmon to the potatoes and mash together with a potato masher. Beat in the sautéed onions and egg. Add the lemon juice, hot pepper sauce and chives. Mix well and form into patties.
- Heat oil in a large skillet. Brown cakes on both sides, about 2 1/2 minutes per side. Drain on paper towels. Serve with lemon wedges.

306.   Smoked Salmon Chowder Recipe

Serving: 6 | Prep: | Cook: 30mins | Ready in:

Ingredients

- 1/4 cup margarine
- 2 tablespoons bacon fat
- 1 small white onion diced
- 1/2 cup diced celery
- 3/4 pound red potatoes scrubbed and diced
- 1-1/2 teaspoons minced garlic
- 3/4 teaspoon dried thyme
- 1-1/2 teaspoons dried tarragon
- 3/4 teaspoon dried dill weed
- 1/2 cup all purpose flour
- 1-1/2 teaspoons paprika
- 7 cups fish stock
- 6 ounces smoked salmon diced
- 1 dried bay leaf

- 1 tablespoon lemon juice
- 1-1/2 teaspoons worcestershire sauce
- 1/8 teaspoon Tabasco sauce
- 3/4 teaspoon freshly ground black pepper
- 2 teaspoons salt
- 1/4 cup dry white wine
- 1 cup half-and-half
- 1/4 cup chopped fresh parsley

Direction

- In 4 quart pot melt margarine and bacon fat.
- Sauté onion, celery, potatoes, garlic, thyme, tarragon and dill over medium heat.
- When onions are translucent reduce heat and add flour and paprika blending well.
- Stir in stock then add salmon, bay leaf, juice, Worcestershire, Tabasco, salt, pepper and wine.
- Bring to a boil then reduce heat and simmer 20 minutes.
- Remove from heat and stir in half-and-half and parsley.
- Remove bay leaf before serving.

307.   Smoked Salmon Cream Pasta Sauce Recipe

Serving: 4 | Prep: | Cook: 20mins | Ready in:

Ingredients

- 8 ounces smoked salmon
- 8 ounces heavy cream
- 1 teaspoon freshly ground black pepper
- 1 tablespoon chopped fresh dill
- dill for garnishing
- 16 ounces uncooked angel hair pasta

Direction

- Cook pasta according to package directions.
- Slice salmon into thin strips.
- Heat cream over low heat until bubbly and thick.

- Combine with cooked pasta over medium heat then add salmon and chopped dill.
- Mix well and serve garnished with fresh dill sprigs.

308. Smoked Salmon Enchiladas Dated 1966 Recipe

Serving: 6 | Prep: | Cook: 30mins | Ready in:

Ingredients

- 1 tablespoon vegetable oil
- 32 ounces smoked salmon
- 1/4 teaspoon ground cumin
- 1/4 teaspoon chili powder
- 2 cups enchilada sauce (recipe below)
- 2 cups shredded iceberg lettuce
- 2 cups shredded colby cheese
- 12 ounce package corn tortillas
- 1 red onion chopped
- 1/2 cup sour cream
- Enchilada Sauce:
- 1/4 cup vegetable oil
- 1/3 cup finely minced white onion
- 2 cloves garlic finely minced
- 10 long red chilies
- 2 cups water
- 3 tablespoons flour
- 1/2 teaspoon salt
- 2 fresh tomatoes pureed

Direction

- Heat oil in a large skillet over medium heat.
- Add smoked salmon pieces and cook until light brown.
- Season with cumin and chili powder.
- Pour in enchilada sauce and simmer 15 minutes stirring occasionally.
- In a separate skillet over medium heat warm tortillas.
- To assemble enchiladas dip a tortilla in enchilada sauce and place on a serving plate.
- Spoon some salmon and sauce then add lettuce, cheese, onion and sour cream.
- Top with another tortilla that has been dipped in the sauce.
- Repeat layering as many times as you wish.
- To make sauce put chilies and water in saucepan and bring to a boil.
- Simmer 20 minutes.
- Remove chilies and cool under running water reserving cooking water.
- Cut off stem then cut chilies in half and remove seeds under running water.
- Cut in pieces and place in blender with 1 cup water then blend well to puree.
- In skillet brown flour a little then place oil in saucepan and sauté onion.
- When transparent add garlic and sauté one minute.
- Add flour to mixture and stir well for 1 minute.
- Add chili puree and cook stirring constantly for 2 minutes.
- Add reserved cooking water plus extra water to thin if necessary.
- Add salt and tomato or tomato sauce then simmer 10 minutes.

309. Smoked Salmon Enchiladas Recipe

Serving: 4 | Prep: | Cook: 12mins | Ready in:

Ingredients

- 1cup thin red onion slices
- ½ cup lime juice
- ¾ pound boned, skinned smoked salmon
- ½ cup cream cheese (4oz)
- 1can green enchilada sauce
- ½ cup chicken broth
- 8 corn tortillas (6")
- ¾ cup chopped green onions (including tops)
- ½ cup shredded jack cheese

Direction

- In a bowl mix red onion slices and lime juice. Cut cream cheese into 1/2 inch chunks. Mix enchilada sauce and chicken broth and pour 1 cup of the mixture into a shallow 3 quart (9X13 inch) casserole.
- Stack tortillas and put in a microwave safe plastic bag but do not seal. Heat in a microwave oven on full power just until hot, about 1 to 2 minutes.
- Dip tortillas, 1 at a time, in sauce in casserole and turn over to coat. Stack at 1 end of the casserole. Scatter 1/8 of the trout, cream cheese, and green onions across center of 1 tortilla. Roll to enclose filling and set, seam down, in sauce. Repeat to fill remaining tortillas, pushing unfilled ones to the end of the casserole as you work.
- Pour remaining enchilada sauce mixture over and around filled tortillas.
- Bake in a 400 F oven until sauce bubbles, 10 to 12 minutes. Sprinkle jack cheese over enchiladas and bake until melted, 2 to 3 minutes more.
- With a slotted spoon, lift the red onion slices from the bowl and scatter over the enchiladas. Serve with a wide spatula. Season to taste with lime juice from the bowl.

310. Smoked Salmon Fettuccine Recipe

Serving: 4 | Prep: | Cook: 20mins | Ready in:

Ingredients

- 1 (9-ounce) box frozen peas and onions
- 1 (4-ounce) package smoked salmon
- 8 ounces fettuccine (1/2 box)
- 1 tablespoon butter
- 3 cloves fresh garlic
- salt and pepper, to taste
- 1 tablespoon flour
- 1 cup whole milk

Direction

- Fill large saucepan 3/4 full of water. Cover and bring to a boil on high heat for pasta.
- Remove tray of peas and onions from carton. Peel back plastic film slightly to vent. Microwave on high 5 minutes.
- Preheat large sauté pan on medium-high for 2-3 minutes.
- Slice salmon into 1/4-inch strips. Set aside.
- Stir pasta into boiling water. Boil 8 minutes or until tender, stirring occasionally.
- Place butter in pan and swirl to coat.
- Using garlic press, crush one garlic clove at a time into sauté pan.
- Drain peas and onions if needed and add to garlic.
- Salt and pepper.
- Sauté 1 minute, stirring often.
- Stir in flour and milk.
- Reduce heat to low and simmer 4-5 minutes, or until sauce thickens, stirring occasionally.
- Stir in salmon, separating slices.
- Cook 2-3 minutes, stirring occasionally.
- Drain pasta and serve salmon mixture over pasta.

311. Smoked Salmon Lasagna Recipe

Serving: 12 | Prep: | Cook: 50mins | Ready in:

Ingredients

- 12 dried lasagna noodles
- 1/3 cup butter
- 1/3 cup all purpose flour
- 4 cups fat-free milk
- 1/2 teas. salt
- 1/2 teas black pepper
- 1/4 cup finely shredded parmesan cheese (1oz)
- 1/4 cup shredded swiss cheese

- 2 tablespoons dry sherry1 1/2 cups finely shredded Percorino romano cheese
- 1 cup shredded mozzarella cheese
- 1 cup shredded provolone cheese
- 1/2 cup shredded cheddar cheese
- 3 large roma tomatoes, peeled, seeded, drained and chopped
- 8 oz sliced mushrooms or 4 oz canned sliced mushrooms
- 8 oz smoked salmon, flaked

Direction

- Preheat oven to 375
- Lightly grease a 3 qt. rectangular baking dish
- Cook noodles according to package directions, drain, rinse with cold water and drain again
- For sauce:
- In a medium saucepan, heat butter over low heat
- Add flour and cook for 4 minutes stirring constantly (be careful not to let the flour brown)
- Gradually whisk in milk, salt and pepper
- Cook, and stir until slightly thickened and bubbly
- Reduce heat and stir in parmesan cheese, Swiss cheese and sherry
- Cook and stir until cheeses are melted
- In a medium bowl combine remaining cheeses
- To assemble:
- Spread one-fourth sauce in prepared baking dish
- Sprinkle with one-fourth of the cheese mixture
- Layer with one-third of the noodles, one-fourth of the sauce, half of the tomatoes, half of the mushrooms, half of the salmon and one-fourth of the cheese mixture
- Repeat layering noodles, sauce, tomatoes, mushrooms, salmon and cheese mixture
- Top with remaining noodles, remaining sauce and remaining cheese mixture
- Bake uncovered for 50-55 minutes or until edges are bubbly and top is slightly browned
- Let stand 15 minutes before serving

312. Smoked Salmon Sushi Recipe

Serving: 2 | Prep: | Cook: | Ready in:

Ingredients

- cucumber
- 1 avacado
- cream cheese block
- 1/4 pound smoked salmon
- 1 cup sushi rice
- 1 tbs rice vinegar (optional)
- 1 pckg seaweed wraps
- 1 1/4 cup water

Direction

- Rinse rice well in cold water until water runs clear.
- Boil rice in water, turn to simmer after boil, and cover for 15 minutes then remove from heat.
- Add vinegar to rice and mix well then let rice cool.
- Skin and slice cucumber into pencil-sized strips.
- Skin and slice avocado into pencil-sized strips.
- Cut cream cheese into pencil-sized strips (a wire cheese slicer works great, or use a hot, wet butcher knife).
- Flake salmon apart at natural segments.
- Spread handful of rice on seaweed wrap. Wet your fingers (rice is REALLY STICKY) to help when covering seaweed wrap in single layer of rice.
- Add cuke, avocado and cream cheese strips then lay in salmon at the front end of the rice covered wrap.
- Roll up the ingredients tightly by hand.
- Use a bamboo mat, if you have one, to tighten roll.
- Use sharp wet knife to slice off pieces from your roll.
- 8 pieces per roll is a good thickness.

- Serve with soy sauce and wasabi.

313. Smoked Salmon With Salsa Gluten Free Recipe

Serving: 4 | Prep: | Cook: 6mins | Ready in:

Ingredients

- smoked salmon
- 4 pieces of Atlantic salmon
- salt
- Chilli oil
- wood chips (fragrant)
- fresh herbs in season (for smoking)
- BBQ and rack
- salsa
- tomatoes, deseeded and roughly sliced
- cucumber, skinned and diced
- lime juice (to taste) plus extra for final dressing
- Chillies, combine 3 varieties, finely chopped
- coriander (cilantro) leaves to garnish, stalks finely chopped for the salsa
- spring onion (scallion), white parts only, minced
- salt
- avocado, diced
- olive oil (little bit)

Direction

- SALSA
- Combine all ingredients, including the oil
- Use extra lime juice to dress the combined ingredients
- Top with the reserved coriander (cilantro) leaves
- Refrigerate till needed
- SMOKED SALMON
- Rub the salmon fillets with salt and chilli oil
- Place fragrant wood chips in the base of the bbq
- Bring them up to temperature

- Place your selection of fresh herbs on the wood chips
- Place a rack over the wood chips and herbs and place the salmon fillets on this
- Cover and cook for 5-6 minutes
- TO SERVE
- Place a layer of salsa as a base
- Place the smoked salmon on top
- Finish with some more salsa
- SIDES
- A simple mixed green salad (different types of lettuce roughly torn and mixed)
- Some crusty bread
- A bottle of wine... enjoy!

314. Smoky Glazed Salmon Recipe

Serving: 4 | Prep: | Cook: 37mins | Ready in:

Ingredients

- 2lbs fresh salmon fillets(skin on is fine)
- 1/4 cup olive oil
- juice from 1 large, or two small lemons or 2 limes
- 1T dry dill weed
- 1/4-1t cayenne pepper or hot sauce
- 1-2T honey
- 2 cloves garlic, minced
- dash of worcestershire sauce
- 2T smoked paprika(sweet or hot...I used hot)
- 1t ground coriander
- kosher or sea salt and fresh ground black pepper

Direction

- Combine all ingredients except salmon and whisk to combine.
- Pour into bottom of baking dish with sides (I used cast iron and highly recommend it, if it's an option).

- Place salmon, skin side up into sauce in pan and let rest 15-30 mins at room temperature.
- Turn salmon pieces in the pan and roast them, skin side DOWN, in 425 oven for about 10-15 minutes or until salmon flakes. Do not overcook!

315. Southwest Salmon Salad Recipe

Serving: 0 | Prep: | Cook: 30mins | Ready in:

Ingredients

- 2lbs mixed greens
- 2 bell peppers, chopped
- 1-4 fresh jalapenos, chopped
- 3-4 green onions, chopped
- 2-3 meaty tomatoes, chopped
- 2-3 cups cooked black beans(drained if using canned)
- 2-3 cups frozen kernel corn off the cob, thawed but not cooked
- 1/4 cup sliced gourmet green olives
- Fried tortilla strips(if desired)
- 1 cup freshly shredded pepper jack cheese(if desired)
- Creamy avocado cilantro Dressing(avocado-cilantro-dressing.html">Creamy avocado cilantro Dressing)
- For Grilled Salmon
- 4-6oz salmon fillets
- Tajin, Latin, Cajun or creole seasoning, as desired
- fresh lime juice

Direction

- Grill salmon with the preferred seasoning and lime juice. Set aside.
- Arrange salad with the mixed greens, peppers, onion, tomato, beans and olives and lightly toss.

- Shred the salmon in large bite sized pieces and add that to the top of the salad with the tortilla strips, cheese and dressing.

316. Southwest Smoked Salmon Pitas With Chipotle Sauce Recipe

Serving: 4 | Prep: | Cook: 20mins | Ready in:

Ingredients

- 1 cup plain yogurt
- 4 tablespoons chopped green onions
- 2 chipotle peppers
- 4 tablespoons peanut butter
- 1/4 teaspoon salt
- 16 ounces smoked salmon cut into strips
- 1/2 teaspoon salt
- 1/2 teaspoon freshly ground black pepper
- 1/2 teaspoon chili powder
- 1/2 teaspoon garlic powder
- 1/2 teaspoon dried oregano
- 1/2 teaspoon ground cumin
- 3 tablespoons vegetable oil divided
- 1 medium white onion sliced
- 1 red bell pepper cut into julienne strips
- 4 pitas
- 1 cup shredded lettuce
- 1 cup shredded white cheddar cheese

Direction

- In blender combine yogurt, green onion, peppers, peanut butter and salt.
- Blend until smooth then place in a sealed container and refrigerate.
- Preheat oven to 350 then place smoked salmon in a large bowl.
- Mix 1/2 teaspoon salt, pepper, chili powder, oregano and cumin.
- Sprinkle over salmon then heat half the oil in skillet over medium heat.

- Sauté onions and red peppers until tender then transfer to a plate and set aside.
- Wrap pitas in foil and place in oven for 10 minutes.
- Heat remaining oil in skillet and sauté smoked salmon until slightly brown.
- Add onions and red peppers then cook 1 minute longer.
- Cut pitas in half and stuff with smoked salmon mixture.
- Serve with lettuce, cheese, and sauce.

317.   Special Salmon Cakes Recipe

Serving: 4 | Prep: | Cook: 20mins | Ready in:

Ingredients

- 1 14 oz can Alaskan salmon
- 1/2 c cornflake crumbs
- 2 wh green onions; chopped
- 1/4 c celery; finely chopped
- 1/4 c mayonnaise
- 2 ts dried thyme
- 1 ds worcestershire sauce
- 1 lg egg
- 2 tb butter (for cooking); (1/4 stick)
- pepper; to taste
- salt; to taste
- ---Sauce---
- 3/4 c mayonnaise
- 1 tb lemon juice
- 1 tb horseradish; prepared
- 1 ts dried thyme
- 1 ts dill weed
- 1 ts celery seed

Direction

- Combine salmon, cornflake crumbs, green onions, celery, 1/4 cup mayonnaise, 2 tsp. thyme, and Worcestershire sauce in medium bowl and stir gently to blend. Season with salt

and pepper. Mix in egg. Shape salmon mixture into 4 patties, about 3/4-inch-thick. Arrange on plate.
- Combine 3/4 cup mayonnaise, lemon juice, horseradish, and tsp. each of thyme, dill weed, and celery seed, in a small bowl. Season sauce with salt and pepper. (Salmon cakes and sauce can be prepared 1 day ahead. Wrap separately and refrigerate.)
- Melt butter in heavy large skillet over medium-low heat. Carefully add the salmon cakes and sauté until deep brown and crusty, cooked through. I usually have to press on the cakes to keep them together. About 5-10 minutes per side. Transfer to platter. Serve, covered with sauce.

318.   Speedy Salmon Patties Recipe

Serving: 3 | Prep: | Cook: 15mins | Ready in:

Ingredients

- 1 (14.75 ounce) can salmon, drained
- 1/3 cup finely chopped onion
- 1 egg
- 5 saltines, crushed
- 1/2 teaspoon worcestershire sauce
- 1/4 teaspoon salt
- 1/8 teaspoon pepper
- 2 teaspoons butter or margarine

Direction

- In a bowl, combine the first seven ingredients; mix well. Shape into six patties. In a skillet, fry patties in butter over medium heat for 3-4 minutes on each side or until heated through.

319.   Spicy Hoisin Salmon Recipe

Serving: 4 | Prep: | Cook: 15mins | Ready in:

Ingredients

- 1/4 c hoisin sauce
- 2Tbs soy sauce
- 2tsp rice vinegar
- 1/2tsp ground ginger
- 1/4tsp red pepper flakes
- 4 pieces salmon filet,about 6 ozs. each
- lemon wedges for garnish

Direction

- Heat oven to 450. Coat a baking dish with cooking spray.
- In a small dish, stir together the hoisin, soy sauce, vinegar, ginger and red pepper flakes. Place salmon in prepared dish and spread top of each filet with hoisin mixture.
- Roast at 450 for 10 mins. Spread remaining hoisin mixture over the salmon and top with the scallions. Roast an additional 5 mins.
- Serve with rice and broccoli and lemon wedges as garnish.

320.   Spicy Hot Baked Salmon Recipe

Serving: 4 | Prep: | Cook: 50mins | Ready in:

Ingredients

- 1.5 - 2 lbs whole salmon fillet (skin removed)
- 1/3 cup mayonnaise
- 2 Tbsp Masago (fish egg)
- 1 stick imitation crab meat, chopped
- 1 tsp dill or parsley (dried or fresh herb)
- 1 Tbsp Sriracha hot chili sauce (add more to make hotter)
- 1/2 onion, thinly sliced
- 1/2 lemon

- 1 Tbsp capers

Direction

- Preheat the oven at 360 F.
- Wash the fillet and pat dry.
- In a small bowl, add mayonnaise, Masago, chopped crab meat, dill or parsley, Sriracha sauce; mix well.
- Spray Pam on baking pan. Put the fillet,
- Spread mayonnaise mixture over the fillet; then onion slices and capers over the top. Sprinkle lemon juice over the top.
- Bake about 50 minutes until salmon flakes

321.   Spicy Pickled Salmon Dated 1972 Recipe

Serving: 6 | Prep: | Cook: | Ready in:

Ingredients

- 1 cup water
- 1 cup distilled white vinegar
- 3 tablespoons sugar
- 1/2 teaspoon salt
- 1 small white onion thinly sliced
- 1 lemon thinly sliced
- 1 tablespoon mustard seeds
- 1 teaspoon black peppercorns
- 2 bay leaves
- 3/4 cup firmly packed dill sprigs
- 2 pounds salmon fillet skinned rinsed dried and cut into small pieces

Direction

- Combine water, vinegar, salt, onion, lemon, mustard seeds, peppercorns and bay leaves.
- Bring to a boil over medium high heat stirring until sugar melts.
- Remove from heat and cool.
- Put fish and dill sprigs in glass container and pour cooled vinegar solution over top.

- Stir gently to coat all the pieces then cover and refrigerate at least 24 hours up to 5 days.
- To serve pour off liquid and arrange salmon with the pickled onion and lemon in a bowl.

---

322.   Spicy Salmon In A Tangerine Tomato Bisque Recipe

Serving: 6 | Prep: | Cook: 50mins | Ready in:

Ingredients

- 1 1/2 pounds salmon divided into 6
- 6 tangerines
- From Sas' tomato Bisque @ tomato-bisque.html">tomato Bisque
- 4 tablespoons unsalted butter
- 1 tablespoon minced bacon (about 1/2 ounce)
- 1 spanish onion, chopped
- 1 carrot, chopped
- 1 stalk celery, chopped
- 4 cloves garlic, minced
- 5 tablespoons all-purpose flour
- 4 cups chicken broth, homemade or low-sodium canned
- 1 (28-ounce) can whole, peeled tomatoes (with liquid), roughly chopped
- 2 tbs.cream sherry
- 2 cup heavy cream
- inspired by chef meow's five spice powder @ five spice powder
- In a tea ball or cheese cloth
- 1 teaspoon anise seed
- 1 teaspoon star anise
- 1/5 stick of cinnamon
- 1 2/5 teaspoon fennel seeds

Direction

- Begin preheating the oven to 500.
- Heat the butter in a large soup pot over medium-high heat. Add the bacon and cook, stirring, until crisp and most of the fat has rendered, about 1 minute. Using a slotted spoon, transfer the bacon to a paper towel-lined plate and set aside. Lower the heat to medium, add the onion, carrots, celery, and garlic and cook, covered, stirring occasionally, until soft and fragrant, about 8 minutes.
- Stir in the flour and cook, stirring, for 3 minutes. Pour in the broth, tangerines, and tomatoes and bring to a boil while whisking constantly. Hang the tea ball from the edge of the pot. Lower the heat and simmer for 40 minutes. Remove from heat and allow to cool.
- When the soup base is cool, remove and discard the herb bundle. Working in batches, transfer the mixture to a blender and puree until smooth. Using a sieve over a large bowl, strain the tomato puree. Return the puree to the pot add the sherry and reheat over medium heat.
- Whisk the heavy cream and salt into the soup and season with pepper to taste.
- Arrange salmon in a casserole dish, and pour bisque over top. Bake for 10 minutes at 500. Sever on a warm plate with rice or potatoes and enjoy.
- You could also use 1 small bread loaf pan per serving of salmon and save the bisque for re use.

---

323.   Spicy Sweet Savory Salmon Recipe

Serving: 68 | Prep: | Cook: 12mins | Ready in:

Ingredients

- 1 Tbsp orange juice (I squeeze it from an orange)
- 2 Tbsp honey
- 2 Tbsp Trader Joe's Chinese 5 spice (or Hoisin)
- 2 Tbsp honey dijon mustard
- 1 Tbsp ketchup
- 1 tsp lemon or lime juice
- 1/4 tsp salt & pepper

- 2 Tbsp sesame seeds (toasted)
- 6-8 4 or 6oz salmon fillets

Direction

- Pre-heat broiler
- Combine first 6 ingredients
- Spray broiler pan with cooking spray
- Brush salmon with mixture and place under broiler
- Brush mixture onto fish every 3-4 minutes
- Cook for 12 minutes
- Remove fish from oven and sprinkle with sesame seeds.
- Serve with your favorite side!

324. Spicy Wasabi Salmon Recipe

Serving: 4 | Prep: | Cook: 15mins | Ready in:

Ingredients

- 2 tbsp soy sauce (can substitute low sodium if desired)
- 1 tsp wasabi powder
- 1 tsp bottled fresh ginger (minced)
- 1/2 teaspoon dark sesame oil
- 4 (6-ounce) skinless salmon fillets (about 1 inch thick)

Direction

- Combine soy sauce, ginger, wasabi, and sesame oil in a dish and add salmon. Allow to marinade for 15 minutes.
- In a hot skillet (medium-high heat), cook salmon on one side for about 3 minutes.
- Turn the heat to medium and cook salmon on other side until cooked through (about 7-9 minutes).

325. Stuffed Salmon Recipe

Serving: 5 | Prep: | Cook: 40mins | Ready in:

Ingredients

- salmon
- 2-3 Garlic cloves- chopped
- 2 sleeves Ritz crackers
- 2 sticks butter
- I can whole artichokes - chopped
- 1/4-1/2 of red bell pepper -diced
- fresh crab meat
- White Wine- (I used Pinot Grigio)
- kosher salt pepper
- lemon
- Scallions- chopped (not in orginal recipe, my taste buds were missing the mild onion flavor of the scallions)

Direction

- Place Salmon is baking dish. Douse with lemon to get rid of fishy-ness. In a mixing bowl, combine chopped garlic, chopped artichokes, bell pepper, scallions, crushed Ritz crackers and melted butter, salt and pepper to taste. Mix until stuffing-like. Pat it on top of the fish. Pour white wine over top of stuffing and in baking dish (eyeball it). Bake at 400 degrees until done.

326. Stuffed Salmon With Shrimps And Crab Recipe

Serving: 4 | Prep: | Cook: 25mins | Ready in:

Ingredients

- 1 cup beurre blanc sauce (recipe below)
- 4 (5-ounce) halibut fillets (not steaks)
- 6 ounces Dungeness crab meat
- 6 ounces bay shrimp
- 6 ounces brie, cut into 1/2-inch cubes
- 3 tablespoons mayonnaise

- 1 tablespoon chopped fresh dill
- Pinch of salt
- Pinch of pepper
- Beurre Blanc Sauce
- Yield: 1 cup
- 6 ounces white wine
- 3 ounces white wine vinegar
- 3 whole black peppercorns
- 1 shallot, quartered
- 1 cup heavy cream
- 6 ounces cold, unsalted butter, cut into pieces
- 3 ounces cold butter, cut into pieces

Direction

- Preheat oven to 400°F. Prepare the beurre blanc sauce and set aside. Split the halibut fillets lengthwise to form a pocket for the stuffing. Combine the crab, shrimp, brie, dill, salt, and pepper. Gently blend in the mayonnaise to bind the mixture. Divide the stuffing mixture between the four pocketed fillets. When full, let the flaps cover the stuffing so that only a small amount is exposed. Bake in a lightly buttered baking dish for 10 to 12 minutes. Transfer to dinner plates and spoon the beurre blanc over the fish.
- Combine wine, vinegar, peppercorns, and shallot in a non-corrosive saucepan (stainless steel, Teflon, Calphalon). Reduce until the mixture is just 1 to 2 tablespoons and has the consistency of syrup. Add the cream and reduce again until the mixture is 3 to 4 tablespoons and very syrupy. Remove the pan from heat. Add the butter pieces, about 2 ounces at a time, stirring constantly and allowing each piece to melt in before adding more. (If the mixture cools too much, the butter will not melt completely and you will have to reheat it slightly.) Strain and hold warm on a stove-top trivet or in a double-boiler over very low heat until you are ready to use.
- Note: To make Lemon Butter Sauce, replace the white wine vinegar with 2 tablespoons of freshly squeezed lemon juice.

---

327. Super Simple Salmon Recipe

Serving: 4 | Prep: | Cook: 10mins | Ready in:

Ingredients

- fresh salmon, at least 1/4 lb. per person and 3/4" to 1" thick. (If you are grilling it's better to get salmon with the skin still on)
- Fresh lemon juice, about half a lemon per pound of salmon
- salt or seasoned salt
- dill (fresh or dried)
- Freshly ground pepper
- extra virgin olive oil

Direction

- Rinse the salmon in cold water and pat dry with paper towels.
- Squeeze lemon over one side of fish.
- Drizzle a bit of olive oil over same side.
- Season to your taste with salt, dill and pepper.
- Rub in and repeat on other side.
- Broil or grill 3 to 5 minutes on side one. You will be able to see how done the fish is on the side. Once it's cooked half way through, flip and grill an additional 3 to 5 minutes.
- I serve this with rice and asparagus. Simple, easy and good for you! And the fur kids too!

---

328. Supreme Salmon Recipe

Serving: 4 | Prep: | Cook: 30mins | Ready in:

Ingredients

- 4 salmon steaks
- salt and pepper
- 2 Tablespoons chopped onions
- 1 Cup cheddar cheese, Shredded
- 1 Cup sour cream

- 1 Tablespoon Chopped parsley
- paprika

Direction

- Place salmon in greased shallow baking dish.
- Sprinkle with salt, pepper and onions.
- Sprinkle with cheese.
- Spoon sour cream over salmon.
- Sprinkle with parsley and paprika.
- Bake 30 minutes in 350 degree oven or until salmon flakes easily.

---

329. Sushi 101 Recipe

Serving: 2 | Prep: | Cook: 30mins | Ready in:

Ingredients

- 1 bag roasted Seaweed paper (each bag holds 10 sheets)
- 1 1/2 cups white, short-grain rice
- 1/4 cup rice vinegar
- sea salt
- fish of your choice. You can use canned eel like we do, canned albacore, mackrel, even thin cuts of tuna or salmon steak. If you don't 100% trust your local fish market, it's okay to use frozen. Don't take chances with shady products and don't leave fish steaks out while preparing. Be smart!
- Little cup of room temperature water
- Optional: scallions, chopped avacado, spinach chiffonade, eel sauce or spicy mayo.
- Note: If you don't have a special bamboo rolling matt, use either plastic wrap or wax paper. You can even attempt to roll it with your bare hands but it's difficult to get it tight enough that way.

Direction

- Cook white rice well in boiling salted water until soft, use extra water and drain afterwards if you have to.
- Mix drained rice with vinegar.
- On the bamboo rolling matt, place a sheet of roasted seaweed paper, shiny side down.
- Using a spreading knife or a spoon, coat the nearest half of the paper to you with an even coating of rice. It's okay if the rice mixture is a bit liquidy.
- At the very bottom, put a thin line of your fish of choice, and any condiments/additions you want to put with it.
- Using the rolling mechanism, roll up the sushi as tightly as you can going from the bottom up, until you run out of rice. Now only the bare, dry seaweed paper should be showing. With either your fingers or a brush, use a little water you have put aside to moisten top edge of the paper. You may need to be liberal.
- Finish rolling and seal it closed with the moistened end. You know, like a blunt. [=)
- Leave it sitting there with the seam-side down to set for a few minutes before attempting to cut it.
- When you're ready, use a very sharp serrated knife to slice the roll into 6-7 pieces. Serve with premium or sashimi soy sauce.
- Yeah, it really is this easy. Try it!

---

330. Svizzere Di Salmone Aka Salmon Patties Recipe

Serving: 4 | Prep: | Cook: 30mins | Ready in:

Ingredients

- 1/3 loaf French of Italian-style bread
- scant 1 cup milk
- 1 lemon
- 14 ounces salmon fillet, chopped (two fillets)
- 5 tablespoons butter, softened at room temperature
- 1.5 cups panko or dry, unseasoned breadcrumbs
- 2 tablespoons oil + more as needed
- salt and pepper

Direction

- Tear the bread into pieces, place in a bowl, add milk to cover and let soak for 10 minutes, then drain and squeeze out, reserving milk.
- Grate the rind of half the lemon and peel the other half, removing all traces of pith from both halves, and slice thinly.
- Combine the salmon, soaked bread and butter in a bowl and season with salt and pepper.
- Divide the mixture into four, shape into balls, then flatten gently with your hand.
- Pour the remaining milk into a shallow dish and combine the bread crumbs and lemon rind in another shallow dish.
- Heat the oil on medium in a skillet.
- Dip the patties first in the milk, then in the bread crumb and lemon zest mixture and fry for 4 minutes on each side.
- Remove with a slotted spatula and drain on paper towels.
- Garnish with the lemon slices and serve immediately.

---

331. Sweet Black Pepper Salmon Recipe

Serving: 6 | Prep: | Cook: 10mins | Ready in:

Ingredients

- 6 4-5 oz. salmon fillets
- 3/4c real maple syrup
- 1/4c low sodium soy sauce
- 1Tbs olive oil
- 1Tbs black pepper

Direction

- Whisk together maple syrup, soy sauce, olive oil and black pepper. Place salmon in ziplock bag. Pour marinade in the bag and slosh it around to thoroughly coat the salmon. Refrigerate at least 4 hours. Preheat broiler or grill to med heat and cook salmon 4-5" from

the heat for about 4 mins a side or till desired degree of doneness.

---

332. Sweet Bourbon Salmon Recipe

Serving: 2 | Prep: | Cook: 10mins | Ready in:

Ingredients

- • 2 8 oz salmon fillets
- • 2 tsp chopped chives
- • 1 cup bourbon
- • 1/4 cup pineapple juice
- • 2 Tbls soy sauce
- • 2 Tbls brown sugar
- • 1/4 tsp salt
- • 1/4 tsp black pepper
- • 1/8 tsp garlic powder
- • 1/2 olive oil

Direction

- 1. Combine pineapple juice, brown sugar, bourbon, soy sauce, pepper and garlic powder in a bowl. Stir to dissolve sugar.
- 2. Add the oil.
- 3. Remove any skin on salmon fillets.
- 4. Put fillets in baking dish and pour marinade over and let sit in the fridge for one hour or longer. The longer it can sit the more the marinade seeps into the fillets.
- 5. Now you can put this on the grill or cook it on the stove top on medium heat. 5-7 minutes per side or until the fillet is cooked to your desire. Brush the marinade over the filets as they are cooking.
- 6. Arrange the fillets on a plate and sprinkle with the chopped chives.
- 7. Service with a brown rice and salad.

333.   Sweet Orange Salmon Recipe

Serving: 4 | Prep: | Cook: 8mins | Ready in:

Ingredients

- 2 Tablespoons brown sugar
- 1 Teaspoon chili powder
- 1/2 Teaspoon Grated orange rind
- 1/2 teaspoon ground cumin
- 1/2 teaspoon paprika
- 1/4 teaspoon salt
- 1/4 ground coriander
- 1/8 teaspoon black pepper
- 4 (6-ounce) salmon sillets

Direction

- Combine first 8 ingredients in a small bowl. Rub spice mixture over both sides of salmon fillets. Place salmon on a broiler pan coated with cooking spray. Broil for 8 minutes or until salmon flakes easily when tested with a fork

334.   Sweet Spiced Salmon Recipe

Serving: 4 | Prep: | Cook: 14mins | Ready in:

Ingredients

- 1/2 tsp. grated orange zest
- 1/4 cup fresh orange juice
- 2 Tbsp. fresh lemon juice
- 4 salmon fillets with skin
- 1-1/2 Tbsp. firmly packed brown sugar
- 1/2 tsp. paprika
- 1/2 tsp. ground curry
- 1/2 tsp. salt
- 1/4 tsp. cinnamon
- 1/8 tsp. cayenne
- 1 medium lemon quartered
- cooking spray

Direction

- Preheat the oven to 425*F.
- Set orange zest aside in a small bowl.
- In a large plastic zip top bag combine orange juice and lemon juice. Rinse salmon and pat dry with paper towels. Add juice mixture, seal bag. Turn several times to coat evenly.
- Refrigerate minutes, turning occasionally times.
- Meanwhile, stir brown sugar, paprika, curry powder, salt, cinnamon and cayenne into orange zest. Set aside.
- Remove salmon from marinade, discard the marinade.
- Arrange salmon with skin side down on baking sheet. Rub brown sugar mixture over the salmon.
- Line a baking sheet with foil. Lightly spray with cooking spray.
- Bake 14 minutes or until salmon flakes easily when tested with fork.
- To serve use a metal spatula to lift salmon flesh from skin. Place salmon on plates and serve with lemon wedges.

335.   Tandoori Style Salmon Recipe

Serving: 1 | Prep: | Cook: 20mins | Ready in:

Ingredients

- 1 salmon filet or steak per person
- Tandoori paste
- garam masala spices
- plain yogurt
- Sliced onions

Direction

- Coat the salmon with the paste and spread evenly with yogurt.

- If you can't find tandoori paste, season fish with the garam masala and then spread with yogurt.
- Cover with sliced onions.
- Wrap in foil or cook in a clay pot.
- Bake 425F about 20 to 25 minutes or until fish is done and tender.
- Remove fish with slotted spoon to plate.
- Serve with saffron rice.
- Note: Tandoori paste is a red seasoned paste most typically mixed with yogurt and usually used to coat chicken and imparts a deep red color to food.
- It is available at the gourmet section of most large supermarkets or gourmet grocers.

336. Tasty Salmon Filet Recipe

Serving: 2 | Prep: | Cook: 20mins | Ready in:

Ingredients

- 1 salmon fillet (half a salmon, skin on)
- dried tarragon
- dill weed
- granulated garlic (or powder)
- smoked paprika
- dried basil
- lemon peel
- salt
- butter (not necessary, but I did anyway)
- pepper

Direction

- This is what I do: Double some aluminum foil about 2 feet long
- Put on cookie sheet or other baking pan
- Place salmon skin side down on foil
- Sprinkle and rub all ingredients in equal portions on salmon (you choose amount)
- Dot with butter on top

- Seal foil around salmon pinching it closed, trying to keep above salmon, not touching it, just creating a tent so to speak
- Bake (or grill) in 375*F oven for approx. 20 min. depending on thickness of salmon (mine was perfect in 21 min - about 1" thick at biggest part) Do not overcook - it continues to cook a while when taken out of oven - if anything take out when you think it is almost done. It's better underdone than overdone.
- Usually comes off skin when lifted carefully with metal spatula or just scrape off on plate.

337. Tasty Salmon Pie With Dill Sauce Recipe

Serving: 6 | Prep: | Cook: 50mins | Ready in:

Ingredients

- Crust Ingredients:
- 1/4 cup butter
- 3/4 cup finely crushed dried crumbly-style herb seasoned stuffing
- ==========
- Filling Ingredients:
- 2 cups crushed dried crumbly-style herb seasoned stuffing
- 4 ounces (1 cup) cheddar cheese, shredded
- 1 cup water
- 1/2 cup milk
- 1 (16-ounce) can red salmon, drained, skin and bones removed, flaked*
- 2 eggs
- 2 tablespoons chopped fresh parsley
- 1 tablespoon finely chopped onion
- 1 teaspoon instant chicken bouillon granules
- 1/2 teaspoon dry mustard
- ==========
- Sauce Ingredients:
- 1/3 cup butter
- 2 tablespoons cornstarch
- 1 1/3 cups water
- 1 teaspoon dried dill weed

- 1/2 teaspoon salt
- 2 medium (2 cups) tomatoes, cubed 1/2-inch

Direction

- Heat oven to 350°F. Melt 1/4 cup butter in 3-quart saucepan; stir in 3/4 cup finely crushed stuffing. Press stuffing mixture on bottom and up sides of greased 9-inch pie pan; set aside.
- Stir together all filling ingredients in same saucepan; spoon into crust. Bake for 50 to 55 minutes or until heated through. Let stand 10 minutes.
- Meanwhile, melt 1/3 cup butter in 2-quart saucepan. Stir in cornstarch. Stir in all remaining sauce ingredients except tomatoes. Cook over medium heat, stirring occasionally, until mixture comes to a full boil (5 to 7 minutes). Add tomatoes; boil 1 minute.
- To serve, cut pie into 6 wedges; serve sauce over wedges.
- *Substitute 3 (6 1/8-ounce) cans tuna, drained, and flaked.

---

338. Ten Minutes To Make Salmon And Spinach Tarts Recipe

Serving: 4 | Prep: | Cook: 15mins | Ready in:

Ingredients

- 1 can pink or red salmon
- 4 frozen individual puff or pastry pie shells
- 1 egg
- 1/2 cup single cream
- 1 handful fresh spinach leaves
- Pinch of cayenne
- salt and pepper to taste

Direction

- Preheat oven to 400F.
- Divide salmon into 4 portions and place each portion in individual pie shell.

- In a mixing bowl, mix egg, spinach, cayenne, salt, pepper and cream with a hand blender until well blended.
- Pour into each pastry shell, covering salmon.
- Bake for 15 minutes or until golden.

---

339. Teriyaki Grilled Salmon Recipe

Serving: 4 | Prep: | Cook: 12mins | Ready in:

Ingredients

- 3 tablespoons oil
- 3 tablespoons soy sauce
- 1 1/2 tablespoons minced fresh garlic
- 1 1/2 tablespoons minced fresh ginger
- 4 4-ounce Alaska salmon steaks or fillets (4 to 6 ounces each)
- 1 sheet (12 × 18 inch) Reynolds wrap heavy duty aluminum foil

Direction

- In a shallow baking dish, combine brown sugar, oil, soy sauce, garlic and ginger.
- Place Alaska salmon steaks/fillets in a baking dish. Turn fish over several times to coat; refrigerate 30 to 45 minutes.
- Remove salmon from marinade.
- Cook on foil sheet on medium hot grill, turning once during cooking, about 6 to 12 minutes per inch of thickness.
- Do not overcook.
- ENJOY.....

---

340. Teriyaki Salmon Recipe

Serving: 4 | Prep: | Cook: 10mins | Ready in:

Ingredients

- 4 salmon steaks skinned

- 1-1/4 cup soy sauce
- 1/3 cup sake
- 6 tablespoons granulated sugar
- 3 garlic cloves minced
- 1 tablespoon minced ginger root
- 1/3 cup vegetable oil

Direction

- Combine all ingredients for the marinade in a small bowl and stir until sugar dissolves.
- To prepare salmon quickly rinse under cold running water and pat dry with paper towels.
- Divide each steak into 2 pieces by cutting along either side of the central bone.
- Discard bone the cut fillet into 8 equal pieces.
- Place salmon in a shallow glass or ceramic container and pour 1 cup marinade over the fish.
- Cover and refrigerate for 2 hours turning fish occasionaly.
- Let come to room temperature before cooking.
- Remove salmon from marinade reserving the marinade.
- Place fish on an oiled grill rack.
- Position fish 6 inches from heat source turning once.
- Bush several times with the reserved marinade and cook 5 minutes per side.
- Serve salmon immediately with reserved marinade as dipping sauce.

341.   Teriyaki Salmon And Green Onion Kabobs Recipe

Serving: 6 | Prep: | Cook: 10mins | Ready in:

Ingredients

- 3/4 cup teriyaki marinade
- 3 tablespoons minced fresh ginger
- 2 tablespoons minced garlic
- 1 tablespoon sugar
- 1/8 teaspoon hot chili flakes

- 2 pounds boned skinned salmon fillet rinsed patted dry and cut into cubes
- vegetable oil for grill
- 2 bunches green onions cut into 1" lengths

Direction

- In a medium bowl mix marinade, ginger, garlic, sugar and chili flakes. Add salmon and mix gently to coat. Cover and refrigerate 45 minutes. Prepare a gas grill for direct high heat. When hot brush grill with a generous coat of oil. While grill heats thread cubes of fish onto skewers alternating with pieces of green onion. Lay skewers on grill and cook about 4 minutes. Using two spatulas gently turn each skewer over and cook 4 minutes on other side.

342.   Tex Mex Salmon Recipe

Serving: 4 | Prep: | Cook: 11mins | Ready in:

Ingredients

- 4 6-oz. salmon steaks
- 2 fresh jalapeno Chiles, seeded, and finely chopped
- 2 Tbsp capers, drained
- 1/3 cup thinly-sliced pimento-stuffed green olives
- 3 Tbsp finely chopped fresh cilantro
- 2 Tbsp olive oil
- 1 large onion, chopped
- 2 cloves garlic, minced
- 4 tsp sugar
- 1 tsp salt
- 1/4 tsp ground cinnamon
- 1/4 tsp ground cloves
- 4 cups tomato puree
- 1 1/2 tsp lemon juice
- 1 1/2 tsp water
- 1 Tbsp cornstarch

Direction

- Heat the oil in a wide frying pan over medium heat.
- Add the onion and garlic and cook, stirring often, until the onion is soft. Stir in the sugar, salt, cinnamon, cloves, and puree.
- Cook over high heat until a thick sauce forms.
- Blend the lemon juice, water and cornstarch together, and stir into the tomato mixture.
- Cook until the mixture boils.
- Nestle the salmon steaks into the sauce, cover and cook over medium-high heat for about 4 minutes. Then turn the salmon steaks, cover and cook another 4-5 minutes, or until the salmon begins to flake at the touch of a fork.
- Add the chilies and capers, and cook another 2-3 minutes.
- To serve, place the steaks on individual plates, and surround and top the fish with the sauce.

343. Thai Chili Sauce Salmon Recipe

Serving: 4 | Prep: | Cook: 10mins | Ready in:

Ingredients

- 1/4 cup Asian sweet chili sauce
- 2 tsp soy sauce
- 1 tablespoon finely grated peeled fresh ginger
- 3 cloves garlic, minced
- 3 or 4 (or as needed) 6-ounce salmon fillets with skin

Direction

- Line rimmed baking sheet with foil. Coat with non-stick spray. Whisk chili sauce, soy sauce, garlic and ginger in small bowl. Place salmon fillets, skin side down, on prepared sheet. Spoon chili sauce marinade over and let stand at room temperature 30 minutes (Optional).
- Preheat broiler. Spoon any marinade remaining on baking sheet over salmon fillets. Broil salmon without turning until browned in

spots and almost opaque in center, 6 to 10 minutes, depending on thickness of fillet.

344. Thai Salmon With Shiitake Mushrooms Recipe

Serving: 4 | Prep: | Cook: 30mins | Ready in:

Ingredients

- 1 teaspoon peanut oil
- 1/2 teaspoon sesame oil
- 8 to 12 shiitake mushroom caps, cleaned and sliced
- 1/2 cup finely sliced leek
- 1 red bell pepper, seeded and cut in julienne strips
- 1 tablespoon fresh ginger
- 2 cloves garlic, minced
- 1 teaspoon (or to taste) Thai Kitchen red curry paste
- 1 cup coconut milk
- 1 pound Alaskan salmon, skin and bones removed and cut into 1-inch chunks
- 1 tablespoon lime juice
- 1 cup loosely packed spinach leaves, washed well
- 1/4 cup coarsely chopped fresh basil
- 1 tablespoon coarsely chopped fresh cilantro
- fish sauce to taste
- basil leaves for garnish
- jasmine rice

Direction

- Heat the oils in a wok or sauté pan. Add the mushrooms and leeks and cook for 3 minutes, or until softened. Add the red bell peppers, ginger and the garlic and stir-fry for 1 minute more. Stir in the curry paste and the coconut milk. Bring to a simmer and stir in the salmon. Cook for 3 minutes and gently fold in the lime juice, spinach, basil and cilantro. Season with fish sauce.

- Serve over steamed jasmine rice. Garnish with whole basil leaves.

---

345.   Thai Style Orange & Sweet Chili Salmon Recipe

Serving: 4 | Prep: | Cook: 30mins |Ready in:

Ingredients

- Salmon fillet (lets say, half a fish?)
- 1 yellow Onion in long strips
- Fresh Basil
- 1/2 bottle Mae Ploy (or whatever brand) Sweet-Chili sauce
- Juice of 3-4 Oranges
- Juice of 3 Limes
- minced Garlic (don't need that much)
- Fresh ginger, thinly sliced or grated
- 1-2 table spoons Sambal Olek/ Vietnamese red-chili hot sauce
- salt and pepper
- Serve with Jasmine rice.
- and a little fresh mint to garnish

Direction

- Set your rice!
- Sometimes I divide the fillet into equal portions. In either case, combine your salmon with the ingredients above mentioned into a proportional mixing bowl. Mix it up! You basically want enough sweet-chili and orange juice to cover the fish and onions, but you don't want it to be over saucy. Set aside and let marinade for 30-45 minutes.
- Pre-heat oven to 250. You'll want to move the Salmon and marinade onto a foil covered baking sheet, and bake for about 20 minutes. I forget it's been awhile. You want the salmon to be flaky and moist. This is a beloved dish.
- Serve with steamed rice and a vegetable. I usually combine this with a fried green-bean recipe I'll add next.

---

346.   Thyme And Citrus Baked Salmon Filets Recipe

Serving: 2 | Prep: | Cook: 18mins |Ready in:

Ingredients

- 1/2 teaspoon olive oil
- 2 fresh salmon filets
- 1 teaspoon minced fresh thyme
- 1/2 teaspoon minced fresh grated orange ring
- 1 teaspoon salt
- 1 teaspoon freshly ground black pepper

Direction

- Preheat oven to 400.
- Put oil on bottom of baking dish and rub salmon in oil.
- Combine thyme and orange rind then rub over fish.
- Season with salt and pepper.
- Bake 18 minutes.

---

347.   Tinks Chateau Libido Fettuccine In Salmon Basil Sauce Recipe

Serving: 4 | Prep: | Cook: 15mins |Ready in:

Ingredients

- 2-- Tablespoon butter.......................
- 8- ounces fresh salmon, boned and cut into 3/4" dice or you can use smoked salmon cut in to ribbon strips ....
- 1 -small onion, minced ....
- 1 - tomato, chopped ....
- 1/4- cup Sauternes or other dry white wine.....................
- 1 3/4 lb-. fettuccine........................
- 1- 2 -Tablespoon butter.......................
- 1/2 cup whipping cream ....

- 3 Tablespoon finely chopped fresh basil ....
- 1 -Tablespoon minced fresh parsley...........
- salt and freshly ground pepper to taste ....
- extra butter for sauteeing salmon

Direction

- Cook fettuccine according to package directions until al dente. Drain and move to warmed pasta bowl.
- Toss with butter.
- Sauté fresh salmon in a skillet with more butter or olive oil remove or if using smoked no need to heat unless you want to.
- Add cream and basil -wine and 1-2-tablespoons butter to frying pan.
- Bring heat to high and boil until sauce thickens slightly.
- Turn heat to low.
- Gently fold in sautéed salmon or smoked salmon, parsley, pepper, and salt.
- Pour sauce over pasta and toss gently; toss onions and tomatoes on top.
- Serve with crusty French bread and a bottle of your favorite wine

---

348. Tropical Salmon Three Ways Recipe

Serving: 6 | Prep: | Cook: 20mins | Ready in:

Ingredients

- 600 gm   Norway salmon
- 100 gm   Granulated sugar
- 100 gm   fine salt
- 40 gm   lemongrass
- 20 gm   fennel seed
- 20 gm   coriander Seed
- 10 gm   star anise
- 20 gm   cinnamon stick
- 50 gm   Shredded Dehydrated coconut
- 20 ml   vodka
- 10 ml   Malibu
- 1 pc   Lemon- In juice
- 1 pc   Lime- In juice
- 20 gm   ginger
- 3 pc   tomatoes
- 6 pc   Green asparagus
- 100 ml   extra virgin olive oil
- 500 ml   fish stock
- salt and Pepper- To Taste
- 100 ml   white wine
- 50 gm   spring onions
- Deco
- 10 gm   shallots
- 5 gm   garlic
- 12 pc   lime leaves
- Reduced balsamic vinegar
- Ginger- mango Coulis

Direction

- Cut the Salmon in 3/3, 2/3 and keep raw.
- 1. 1/3 for Marinate Salmon Tartar:
- Mix the granulated sugar, salt and the chopped lemongrass, the fennel, coriander seeds, star anise, cinnamon stick and shredded dehydrated coconut. Sprinkle a little salt on bottom, place salmon with skin down, cover upper part with rest of marinate mix, add Vodka and Malibu. Cover and keep refrigerated for 6 hrs.
- After, when ready. Wash salt away under clear running water and dry for other 12 hrs.
- 2. 2/3 for Salmon Carpaccio: with instead marinade
- Mix lemon and lime juice, add chopped ginger, shallots, garlic, salt and pepper, finish with extra virgin olive oil. Peel Tomatoes and cut into a small dice; blanch the asparagus and cut in slices.
- 3. 3/3 for Poached Salmon:
- Poaching Bouillon: mix flavorful fish stock, with white wine, add half cut lemongrass, few slices of ginger, shallots, spring onion;
- Poach slowly until the Salmon reaches 68 C° (or 154 F°)

349. Tuna Steak With Dungeness Crab Smoked Salmon And A Yellow Bell Pepper Coulis Recipe

Serving: 4 | Prep: | Cook: 15mins | Ready in:

Ingredients

- 20 oz. Fresh tuna
- 2 yellow bell peppers
- 6 Large Slices of smoked salmon
- 2 cups heavy cream
- 4 oz. crab Meat
- 4 oz. butter
- 24 Baby cabbage leaves
- 2 lemons
- salt, Pepper, paprika and nutmeg

Direction

- Cut the tuna in four equal portions (5 oz. each). They need to be as round as possible.
- Make a hole in the center of each of the portions, and keep cold.
- Sauté the fresh crab meat in a little bit of butter with the salt and pepper, lemon juice, paprika and nutmeg. Let cool down.
- Stuff the inside of the tuna with the crab, and wrap the outside with a smoked salmon strip.
- Put the cream and the yellow bell peppers in a saucepan. Then cook slowly until the peppers are fully cooked and blended adding 2 oz. of butter, salt and pepper. In a hot pan, sear the tuna steak on both sides, and cook to your liking.
- Presentation:
- Place six cabbage leaves in the center of each plate, then place the tuna on top. Next, add a julienne of smoked salmon on top. Sauce the plate with the yellow pepper coulis. Voilà!!!
- (Biltmore Cellar Club)

350. Tuscan Salmon Recipe

Serving: 4 | Prep: | Cook: 25mins | Ready in:

Ingredients

- ½ tsp kosher salt
- ¼ tsp lemon pepper
- 4 salmon fillets (5-6 oz.)
- 4 tsp olive oil
- 1 fennel bulb, chopped
- 2 garlic cloves, minced
- ¼ C sun-dried tomatoes, chopped
- 2 T chopped fresh dill
- 1/3 C lemon juice
- 2 T goat cheese

Direction

- 400 oven.
- Place fillets skin side down (or use skinned) in a lightly sprayed baking dish.
- Sprinkle with salt & lemon pepper; drizzle with 2 T olive oil. Set aside.
- Heat remaining oil in small pan over medium heat. Add fennel and garlic, sauté 5 mins or until tender.
- Remove from heat and stir in sun-dried tomatoes, dill and lemon juice, pour over salmon.
- Bake for 20 mins or until fish flakes with a fork.
- Sprinkle with cheese, bake 5 minutes more.

351. Vodka Martini Smoked Salmon Recipe

Serving: 8 | Prep: | Cook: 120mins | Ready in:

Ingredients

- 1 salmon, cleaned (about 3-4 pounds)
- 6 sprigs fresh dill
- 1/4 cup lemon juice
- 1/4 cup vodka

- 1/4 cup vermouth
- 3 tablespoons butter, melted
- 1 tablespoon horseradish
- 2 cloves garlic, minced
- 1 lemon, sliced
- 1/2 teaspoon hot sauce
- Preparation:
- Prepare charcoal grill for indirect cooking over hickory or alder wood chips.
- Wash salmon and pat dry. Fill with dill and lemon slices and set fish aside. Place remaining ingredients in small saucepan and bring to a boil. Remove from heat and set mixture aside.
- Lay salmon on a large piece of aluminum foil. Close three of the sides, pour in basting sauce, and fold over fourth edge. Place salmon on grill over a drip pan and allow to cook on low heat (about 225 degrees F.) for 1 hour. Open one side of the foil and let salmon cook for an additional hour.

Direction

- Prepare charcoal grill for indirect cooking over hickory or alder wood chips.
- Wash salmon and pat dry.
- Fill with dill and lemon slices and set fish aside.
- Place remaining ingredients in small saucepan and bring to a boil. Remove from heat and set mixture aside.
- Lay salmon on a large piece of aluminum foil.
- Close three of the sides, pour in basting sauce, and fold over fourth edge.
- Place salmon on grill over a drip pan and allow to cook on low heat (about 225 degrees F.) for 1 hour.
- Open one side of the foil and let salmon cook for an additional hour.

352. Walnut Ginger Salmon Recipe

Serving: 4 | Prep: | Cook: 9mins | Ready in:

Ingredients

- 1 Tbs brown sugar
- 1 Tbs Dijon mustard
- 1 Tbs soy sauce
- 1 tsp ground ginger
- 4 skinless salmon fillets(4 oz. ea)
- 1/4 c walnuts

Direction

- In large re-sealable plastic bag, combine brown sugar, mustard, soy sauce and ginger; add the salmon. Seal bag and turn to coat; refrigerate for 30 mins, turning occasionally.
- Drain and discard marinade. Place salmon on foil-lined baking sheet coated with cooking spray. Broil 4-6" from the heat or till fish flakes easily with a fork, sprinkling with walnuts during the last 2 mins of cooking time.

353. West Coast Garlic Salmon Recipe

Serving: 4 | Prep: | Cook: 8mins | Ready in:

Ingredients

- 4 large salmon steaks
- 3 tablespoons butter melted
- 3 tablespoons peanut oil
- 2 tablespoons fresh lemon juice
- 2 tablespoons fresh minced garlic
- 1 teaspoon fresh tarragon minced
- 1/4 teaspoon grated lemon peel
- 1/8 teaspoon red pepper flakes
- 1 teaspoon salt
- 2 teaspoons freshly ground black pepper
- lemon wedges

Direction

- Combine butter, oil, lemon juice, tarragon, lemon peel and pepper flakes to make a marinade.
- Place salmon and broiler and brush with half the marinade.
- Broil under pre-heated broiler 2 inches from heat for 4 minutes.
- Turn and brush with remaining marinade then broil until fish flakes about 4 more minutes.
- Season with salt and pepper.
- Serve immediately with lemon wedges.

---

354. White Wine Salmon Corn Cakes Dated 1966 Recipe

Serving: 8 | Prep: | Cook: 15mins | Ready in:

Ingredients

- 2 cups water
- 1 cup dry white wine
- 1 bay leaf
- 4 whole peppercorns
- 2 parsley sprigs
- 5 celery leaves
- 2 salmon steaks
- 1 cup fresh corn kernels cooked
- 1/2 cup finely chopped shallots
- 1/2 cup finely diced red bell pepper
- 1/2 cup finely diced celery
- 1/4 cup chopped fresh cilantro leaves
- 1/2 cup plain yogurt drained
- 1/2 cup mayonnaise
- 1/2 teaspoon spicy mustard
- 1/2 teaspoon Tabasco sauce
- 1/4 teaspoon granulated salt
- 1/2 teaspoon freshly ground black pepper
- 1 egg plus 1 egg white lightly beaten
- 1-1/2 cups cracker crumbs
- 4 tablespoons olive oil

Direction

- Combine water, wine, bay leaf, peppercorns, parsley and celery leaves in shallow pan.
- Slowly bring to a boil then reduce to a simmer and add salmon steaks.
- Simmer until salmon is just cooked through then remove with slotted spatula.
- Drain and cool slightly then flake salmon into a bowl.
- Add corn, shallots, red pepper, celery and cilantro then fold together gently with rubber spatula.
- Combine yogurt, mayonnaise, mustard and Tabasco then fold into salmon mixture.
- Season with salt and pepper then gently fold egg, whites and 1/4 cup crumbs into salmon mix.
- Form into 8 large patties then lay some crumbs on a plate and coat patties on both sides.
- Refrigerate covered for up to 1 hour then heat 2 tablespoons oil in skillet over medium heat.
- Cook salmon corncakes a few at a time until golden about 3 minutes per side.
- Add more oil to skillet as needed.

---

355. White Wine Salmon Corncakes Dated 1966 Recipe

Serving: 4 | Prep: | Cook: 10mins | Ready in:

Ingredients

- 2 cups water
- 1 cup dry white wine
- 1 bay leaf
- 4 whole peppercorns
- 2 parsley sprigs
- 5 celery leaves
- 2 salmon steaks
- 1 cup fresh corn kernels cooked
- 1/2 cup finely chopped shallots
- 1/2 cup finely diced red bell pepper
- 1/2 cup finely diced celery
- 1/4 cup chopped fresh cilantro leaves
- 1/2 cup plain yogurt drained

- 1/2 cup mayonnaise
- 1/2 teaspoon spicy mustard
- 1/2 teaspoon Tabasco sauce
- 1/4 teaspoon granulated salt
- 1/2 teaspoon freshly ground black pepper
- 1 egg plus 1 egg white lightly beaten
- 1-1/2 cups cracker crumbs
- 4 tablespoons olive oil

Direction

- Combine water, wine, bay leaf, peppercorns, parsley and celery leaves in shallow pan.
- Slowly bring to a boil then reduce to a simmer and add salmon steaks.
- Simmer until salmon is just cooked through then remove with slotted spatula.
- Drain and cool slightly then flake salmon into a bowl.
- Add corn, shallots, red pepper, celery and cilantro then fold together gently with rubber spatula.
- Combine yogurt, mayonnaise, mustard and Tabasco then fold into salmon mixture.
- Season with salt and pepper then gently fold egg, whites and 1/4 cup crumbs into salmon mix.
- Form into 8 large patties then lay some crumbs on a plate and coat patties on both sides.
- Refrigerate covered for up to 1 hour then heat 2 tablespoons oil in skillet over medium heat.
- Cook salmon corncakes a few at a time until golden about 3 minutes per side.
- Add more oil to skillet as needed.

356. Wild Pacific Salmon With Creamy Avocado Sauce Recipe

Serving: 6 | Prep: | Cook: 12mins | Ready in:

Ingredients

- 6 Wild Pacific salmon fillets (6 oz. each), about 1" thick

- 1/2 large avocado, peeled, pitted, and quartered
- 1/4 fat-free sour cream
- 1 Tbl. reduced-fat or light mayonnaise
- 1 tsp. lemon juice
- 1 clove garlic, minced
- 1/4 tsp. Hot-pepper sauce
- 1/4 tsp. salt
- 1/4 tsp. black pepper

Direction

- Place salmon fillets, skin side down, on foil-lined baking sheet. Coat fish with cooking spray (Olive Oil Spray) and season with salt and pepper.
- Preheat broiler. Cook salmon 10 to 12 minutes or until fish is opaque.
- While fish is cooking, combine avocado, sour cream, mayonnaise, lemon juice, garlic, hot-pepper sauce, Worcestershire sauce, salt, and pepper in a food processor. Process, scraping down bowl occasionally, until mixture is creamy and smooth.
- Serve dollop of sauce next to (or across the top of) salmon fillet.

357. Wine Poached Salmon With Black Truffles Recipe Recipe

Serving: 6 | Prep: | Cook: 25mins | Ready in:

Ingredients

- Sauce:
- 1 ½ cups dry white wine
- 1/2 cup shallots, chopped
- ¾ oz black truffles, finely chopped
- 1 1/3 cups heavy cream
- ½ teaspoon salt
- 1/8 teaspoon black pepper
- 2 tablespoons brandy
- 1 teaspoon arrowroot

- Poached salmon:
- 2 cups dry white wine
- ¼ teaspoon salt
- ¼ teaspoon dried dill
- 1 ½ lb salmon fillet

Direction

- To make sauce:
- Combine 1 ½ cups white wine with shallots and simmer until the mixture has reduced by about three-quarters volume – 12-15 minutes.
- Add truffles, cream, salt, and pepper and heat through.
- In a small bowl, mix arrowroot and brandy until smooth. Whisk brandy mixture into cream sauce, and heat over low heat, stirring, until it has thickened.
- To poach salmon:
- Place salmon in a large skillet with 2 cups white wine, cut for fitting if necessary, and sprinkle with salt and dill. Simmer ingredients for 10 minutes, until just done, and remove from poaching liquid.

---

358. Yellow Curry Thai Stylie Recipe

Serving: 8 | Prep: | Cook: 60mins | Ready in:

Ingredients

- For the Paste:
- 1 onion (i do one-half red and one-half white)
- 4+ cloves garlic (depending on personal taste)
- 1-2 chile peppers
- 2-3 jalapenos
- 3/4-1 tablespoon fresh grated ginger
- 2 teaspoons turmeric
- 1 2/3 teaspoon cumin
- 1 teaspoon coriander
- 2/3 teaspoon cayenne pepper
- 1/4 teaspoon cinnamon
- 1/5 teaspoon nutmeg
- 1/5 teaspoon allspice
- 1/4+ teaspoon black pepper
- 1/5 teaspoon white pepper
- olive oil
- For the Curry:
- 3 cans coconut milk (i personally dislike the lite version, but rock it if you feel it)
- 2 bay leaves
- 1 sweet potato or regular potato, cut into 1/2 inch squares
- 3 carrots, sliced into circles
- 1 zucchini, cut into squares
- 1 squash, cut into squares
- 1-2 red bell peppers, cut into 1 inch pieces
- green beans, cut into 1/2 or 1/3
- cabbage, sliced into 3 inches by 1/2 inch
- 1/2 package cherry tomatoes, cut in halves
- 8 oz fresh mushrooms, sliced
- (you can also add broccoli, cauliflower, peas, get creative with it!)
- **also, IF YOU'RE NOT A VEGETARIAN add 12oz+ meat such a chicken, salmon, tuna steaks, mahi mahi, etc-the fish oils work Wonders with the flavor of the curry**if you are, you can easily add tofu at the end, if so desired
- you can also add a tablespoon of fish oil if you're feelin frisky~~
- Serve With:
- couscous, rice, or acini de pepe pasta
- lime slices
- Greek yogurt or fat free cream cheese
- parsley, green onion, cilantro

Direction

- First, cut the onion, garlic, chilies into very small pieces. Grate the ginger.
- It works best if you prepare all the vegetables before starting to cook. Cut each as specified above.
- Next, add olive oil to a wok type pan or a medium-large cooking pot. Put on med-high heat and add onions, garlic, chilies. Allow to get sautéed and mildly mushy. Next, add ginger and all spices and constantly mix

together until paste-like. Keep stirring ingredients until consistent through-out.

- Next, add cans of coconut milk slowly. Add bay leaves now. Also add ingredients that will take the longest to soften, including sweet potato, carrot, and any meat that you are using. Allow coconut milk to begin boiling, the immediately turn it down to med-lo/med heat. Give the vegetable a good while to semi-soften. Check their status every so often, and also give the pot a good mix.

- This is a good time to taste test the curry flavor. I usually do eyeball method as to how much of each spice I use. That being said, the amounts listed above are GUESSES. So MAKE Sure to taste test and add more spices accordingly. I end up dashing things in throughout the whole process. If it's too spicy, I recommended adding more turmeric to cut down the bite.

- Then it is time to add the rest of the vegetables, including: zucchini, mushrooms, squash, red bell peppers, green beans, and cabbage. You have the option of adding the tomatoes now (if you like cooked tomatoes; otherwise, wait until right before you take the pot off the stove-top to add the tomatoes). Stir together and allow ingredients to cook. Keeping the lid on the pot is up to you, it tends to cook the ingredients faster.

- While it's cooking, make a side of rice, couscous, or acini de pepe pasta.

- Yay! It's done! I recommend pouring a generous amount of curry over the side you choose (stated above) and adding a fresh squeeze of lime juice and parsley/onion/cilantro garnish. If it's too spicy, cut the curry with some yogurt or fat free cream cheese. Both are delicious with the recipe.

359.   Zesty Salmon Burgers Recipe

Serving: 2 | Prep: | Cook: 15mins | Ready in:

Ingredients

- 1 egg
- 1/4c dry bread crumbs
- 2 Tbs fine chopped onion
- 2 Tbs mayonaisse
- 11/2 to 3 tsp prepared horseradish
- 11/2 tsp diced pimientos
- 1/8 tsp salt
- dash pepper
- 1 pouch (7.1 oz.) boneless skinless pink salmon,drained

Direction

- In a small bowl, combine first 8 ingredients. Add salmon, mix well.
- Shape into 2 patties. On grill, brushed with oil, grill burgers at med heat for 5 to 6 mins on each side or till browned.
- Serve on rolls with lettuce.

360.   Cinnamon Apricot Glazed Salmon Recipe

Serving: 4 | Prep: | Cook: 35mins | Ready in:

Ingredients

- 2 tablespoons low-sodium soy sauce
- 1 tablespoon minced peeled fresh ginger
- 2 (3-inch) cinnamon sticks
- 1 (12-ounce) can apricot nectar
- 4 (6-ounce) salmon fillets (about 1 inch thick)

Direction

- Combine the first 4 ingredients in a saucepan, and bring to a boil. Reduce heat, and simmer mixture until reduced to 3/4 cup (about 30 minutes). Strain the apricot mixture through a sieve over a bowl, and discard solids.

- Preheat broiler. Place salmon fillets on a broiler pan lined with foil; broil 5 minutes. Brush fish with 1/4 cup apricot mixture. Broil for 3 minutes or until lightly browned and fish flakes easily when tested with a fork. Serve the fish with the remaining apricot mixture.

361. Cold Salmon Salad Recipe

Serving: 2 | Prep: | Cook: | Ready in:

Ingredients

- 1/4 red onion, minced
- juice of 1/2 lemon
- zest of one lemon
- 2 tbsp capers
- 2 tbsp caper juice
- 2 tbsp greek yoghurt
- 1 can of salmon
- fresh cracked pepper to taste

Direction

- Mix all ingredients together in a bowl.
- Divide in two and serve over a bowl of whole wheat pasta or with whole wheat ryvita crackers. Try a sandwich on crispy whole grain bread.
- Elegant and easy.
- Healthy and delicious.
- Enjoy!

362. Fresh Salmon Stuffed Portobello Mushrooms Recipe

Serving: 4 | Prep: | Cook: 30mins | Ready in:

Ingredients

- 4 large portobello mushrooms clean insides
- 1/2 bunch fresh spinach steamed and drained
- 1 (8-oz) pkg cream cheese. low fat works fine too
- 1/4 cup sour cream, low fat works here also
- 1/2 tsp thyme
- 1 pound fresh salmon season with garlic
- sprinkle with mccmormick grill mate seasoning for steak or any other thing you want to season fish with.
- 1/4 cup parmesan cheese.
- drizzle olive oil in fry pan

Direction

- Fry salmon in olive oil.
- Shred with fork and set aside.
- Mix cream cheese, sour cream and thyme.
- Add salmon.
- Stuff mixture into mushrooms.
- Sprinkle with parmesan cheese.
- Place into 2-quart casserole and bake in a 350 deg. oven for 30 minutes.
- Mushrooms should produce enough juice, if not, add a little chicken broth to keep them moist in the last 15 mins of cooking.

363. Salmon Noodle Casserole Recipe

Serving: 6 | Prep: | Cook: 30mins | Ready in:

Ingredients

- 1 can (15 1/2 oz) slamon
- 3 tbsp butter
- 2 tbsp flour
- 1/2 tsp mustard
- 1 can evaporated milk
- 1 pkg frozen mixed veggies
- 3 cups noodles, cooked
- 1 1/2 cups shredded cheese

Direction

- Drain salmon and break into chunks.
- Melt butter in pan, stir in flour and mustard.
- Gradually stir in evaporated milk.
- Cook and stir over medium heat until slightly thickened.
- Stir in veggies, cooked noodles and 1 cup cheese.
- Gently fold in salmon.
- Pour into greased 2 quart baking dish.
- Bake, covered at 350 degrees for 25 minutes.
- Sprinkle with remaining cheese.
- Bake uncovered 5-7 minutes or until cheese melts.

364.   Sizzling Salmon Recipe

Serving: 2 | Prep: | Cook: 10mins | Ready in:

Ingredients

- 2 skinless and boneless fillets of salmon
- for the marinade:
- 1 and 1/2 tsp ginger paste
- 1 and 1/2 tsp garlic paste
- 1 tsp cumin powder
- 1 tsp corriander powder
- 1/2 tsp garam masala(optional)
- 1/2 tsp red chilli powder
- lemon juice(1 large lemon)
- salt to taste
- for pan frying:
- 1 tbsp cooking oil

Direction

- Mix all ingredients, except oil, in a bowl and marinade the salmon fillets in it for 15 mins.
- Take the oil in a non-stick frying pan.
- Heat the pan on medium flame.
- Pan-fry the marinated fillets from all sides for 10 mins or till the fillets change color.
- Serve hot on a bed of steamed rice or green salad.
- Goes well with a glass of white wine.

- Can be alternatively grilled in the oven (on medium for 5 mins on each side) or barbequed.

365.   Ziti With Honey Mustard Salmon Recipe

Serving: 4 | Prep: | Cook: 30mins | Ready in:

Ingredients

- 1 pound salmon fillet
- 1 tablespoon honey
- 1/2 teaspoon fresh-ground black pepper
- 1 tablespoon cooking oil
- 1 onion, chopped
- 1/3 cup dry white wine
- 1 teaspoon grainy or Dijon mustard
- 3/4 cup heavy cream
- 1 1/4 teaspoons salt
- 2 tablespoons chopped fresh parsley
- 3/4 pound ziti

Direction

- Heat the oven to 400°.
- Lightly oil a small roasting pan.
- Put the salmon in the pan, skin side down.
- Spread the honey over the salmon and then sprinkle with 1/4 teaspoon of the pepper.
- Roast the salmon until just barely done, about 12 minutes, depending upon the thickness of the fillet.
- Remove from the oven.
- In a medium saucepan, heat the oil over moderately low heat.
- Add the onion and cook, stirring occasionally, until translucent, about 5 minutes.
- Add the wine and simmer until about 1 tablespoon remains, about 2 minutes.
- Whisk in the mustard, cream, salt, and the remaining 1/4 teaspoon pepper.
- Turn off the heat.

- Flake the salmon and stir it and the parsley into the sauce.
- In a large pot of boiling, salted water, cook the ziti until just done, about 13 minutes.
- Drain the pasta and toss with the sauce.

Index

Conclusion

Thank you again for downloading this book!

I hope you enjoyed reading about my book!

If you enjoyed this book, please take the time to share your thoughts and post a review on Amazon. It'd be greatly appreciated!

Write me an honest review about the book – I truly value your opinion and thoughts and I will incorporate them into my next book, which is already underway.

Thank you!

If you have any questions, **feel free to contact at:** *author@cuminrecipes.com*

Kathi Hager

cuminrecipes.com

Printed in Great Britain
by Amazon

78353839R00108